THE WORD FOR ALL GOD'S FAMILY

Foreword

For both authors this book arises from two deeply held personal commitments: commitment to parish ministry and commitment to good quality educational theory and practice. We are grateful to those congregations with whom we have worked and worshipped for their part in shaping our thinking and practice.

This book represents collaboration not only between two individuals, but also between two Anglican Colleges, Trinity College in Carmarthen and the College of St. Mark and St. John in Plymouth. We are grateful to these institutions for fostering and encouraging our work.

Finally we wish to record our appreciation to Diane Drayson who helped to develop the work sheets and to edit the text; and to Anne Rees who shaped the manuscript.

LESLIE J FRANCIS
MARIAN CARTER

November 1996

Contents

Foreword — v

Introduction — ix

1. **Handicraft** 9th Sunday before Christmas — 2
2. **Barriers** 8th Sunday before Christmas — 8
3. **Bridges** 7th Sunday before Christmas — 14
4. **Rescue services** 6th Sunday before Christmas — 20
5. **Leftovers** 5th Sunday before Christmas — 26
6. **Christmas shopping** 1st Sunday in Advent — 32
7. **Christmas cards** 2nd Sunday in Advent — 38
8. **Christmas decorations** 3rd Sunday in Advent — 44
9. **Christmas crib** 4th Sunday in Advent — 50
10. **Christmas visitors** 1st Sunday after Christmas — 56
11. **Christmas presents** 2nd Sunday after Christmas — 62
12. **Coronation** 1st Sunday after the Epiphany — 68
13. **Friends** 2nd Sunday after the Epiphany — 74
14. **Wedding reception** 3rd Sunday after the Epiphany — 80
15. **Churches** 4th Sunday after the Epiphany — 86
16. **Hidden treasures** 5th Sunday after the Epiphany — 92
17. **Winter walk** 6th Sunday after the Epiphany — 98
18. **Signposts** 9th Sunday before Easter — 104
19. **Jigsaw puzzle** 8th Sunday before Easter — 110
20. **Rejects** 7th Sunday before Easter — 116
21. **Feeling hungry** 1st Sunday in Lent — 122
22. **Feeling sad** 2nd Sunday in Lent — 128
23. **Feeling hurt** 3rd Sunday in Lent — 134
24. **Feeling loved** 4th Sunday in Lent — 140
25. **Feeling free** 5th Sunday in Lent — 146
26. **Fan club** Palm Sunday — 152
27. **Spring** Easter Day — 158
28. **Butterflies** 1st Sunday after Easter — 164
29. **Bread** 2nd Sunday after Easter — 170
30. **Fish** 3rd Sunday after Easter — 176
31. **Mender** 4th Sunday after Easter — 182
32. **Sons and daughters** 5th Sunday after Easter — 188
33. **Kings and queens** Sunday after Ascension Day — 194
34. **Wind** Pentecost — 200
35. **Space travel** Trinity Sunday — 206
36. **Teams** 2nd Sunday after Pentecost — 212
37. **Baptism** 3rd Sunday after Pentecost — 218
38. **Growing up** 4th Sunday after Pentecost — 224
39. **Money** 5th Sunday after Pentecost — 230
40. **Railway turntables** 6th Sunday after Pentecost — 236
41. **Teddy bears** 7th Sunday after Pentecost — 242
42. **Fruit** 8th Sunday after Pentecost — 248
43. **Armour** 9th Sunday after Pentecost — 254

Contents *continued*

44	**Monks and nuns** 10th Sunday after Pentecost	**260**
45	**Cubs and brownies** 11th Sunday after Pentecost	**266**
46	**Adverts** 12th Sunday after Pentecost	**272**
47	**Heroes and heroines** 13th Sunday after Pentecost	**278**
48	**Family** 14th Sunday after Pentecost	**284**
49	**Police** 15th Sunday after Pentecost	**290**
50	**Neighbours** 16th Sunday after Pentecost	**296**
51	**Helping hands** 17th Sunday after Pentecost	**302**
52	**Fair shares** 18th Sunday after Pentecost	**308**
53	**Journeys** 19th Sunday after Pentecost	**314**
54	**Treasure trail** 20th Sunday after Pentecost	**320**
55	**Autumn days** 21st Sunday after Pentecost	**326**
56	**Crossroads** 22nd Sunday after Pentecost	**332**
57	**Light** last Sunday after Pentecost	**338**

Introduction

The Word for all God's Family is a project based programme of Christian education based on the Sunday readings. While it employs the themes of the Church of England's two year cycle of lections, it is sufficiently flexible to support a wide range of traditions. Its purpose is to develop understanding of biblical themes and to promote a positive attitude towards worship. This introduction contains three sections.

The first section **Why?** explains the principles on which the programme is based. It answers the question: What are the educational and theological ideas informing the book?

The second section **How?** describes the structure of the individual chapters. It answers the question: How can the book be used in the local situation?

The third section **Where?** gives particular attention to the different ways in which the work among children can be conducted. It answers the question: Where can children's work take place?

WHY?

Following the publication and debate of the General Synod report *Children in the Way* there is a growing awareness of the need for churches to offer good all-age worship and learning. At the same time, attendance at the Sunday service has come to play an increasingly important part in the Christian education and nurture of the young. Children are present for all or part of the main Sunday service in many churches.

When churches are using the thematic Sunday lectionary in the context of family communion or non-eucharistic family services, this means making the theme of the scripture readings accessible to people of all ages and of various levels of Christian maturity.

The Word for all God's Family has been designed to help clergy, lay ministers and children's work leaders reflect on the lectionary theme and to provide concrete examples of how this theme may be developed in church, Sunday school and other contexts of Christian nurture. The programme is committed to all age participation, concrete images and project learning.

ALL AGE PARTICIPATION
All age learning and worship recognises that all individuals, children and adults alike, come with different experiences, different needs and different ways of expressing themselves. All age learning and worship needs to take these differences seriously.

All age learning and worship also recognises that individual members of the church learn best from each other. Learning is a two-way process. Children learn from adults and adults learn from children. They are travelling together on a shared pilgrimage and are able to enrich and resource each other for the journey.

When children share the same theme as the adults are exploring they can enrich the learning with their fresh insight and enthusiasm. When adults share with children, the adults contribute their rich experience of life. Using a common image from *The Word for all God's Family* this sharing is fostered.

Because individuals differ so greatly there are times when their learning and worship can best take place in subgroups able to focus on specialist needs. Workshops or worship sessions for children may provide examples of such subgroups. Because individuals learn from others' differences there are other times when their learning and worship can best take place together.

CONCRETE IMAGES

The two year cycle of lections is thematically based. The readings for each Sunday have been chosen to reflect one specific bible theme. For example, the lectionary year begins with themes like the creation, the fall and the election of God's people.

We believe that it is possible to identify a simple and basic concrete image at the core of each Sunday's theme. *The Word for all God's Family* unwraps the bible themes of the lectionary to reveal the fundamental concrete images which underpin these themes. Then it suggests ways in which children and adults can explore the concrete image at their own level and, through such exploration, gain insight into the lectionary theme.

Religious language has its roots in concrete, everyday experiences, which are then qualified to enable us to speak about religious realities we are not able totally to grasp. By identifying the concrete image at the core of each Sunday's theme, it is possible to enable both adults and children to qualify and develop this image to a level consistent with their own religious maturity.

The concrete images underpinning religious language provide a crucial aid not only for children but for adults as well. After all, religious language is not meaningful until we have grasped the reality to which it points and from which it is derived.

PROJECT LEARNING

Language acquires its significance from being grounded in human experience. Project learning structures the opportunities for adults and children to experience the concrete images underpinning religious language. Adults and children are encouraged to explore these images at their own level and at their own pace. The fruits of such exploration are then to be shared.

In some cases the concrete image and the religious significance are already closely related in the languages of the scriptures themselves. For example, both Hebrew and Greek use the same word for 'wind' and 'Holy Spirit'. The wind is an essential concrete image underlying our understanding of God the Holy Spirit. The more we experience and think about the wind, the more we can understand and interpret our experience of the Holy Spirit.

In other cases, it is necessary to search further to find the most appropriate concrete image. For example, the lectionary begins with the theme of creation to establish the basis for God's relationship with the world and God's care for all forms of life. The creation story affirms that God loves the world and accepts responsibility for it precisely because in the beginning God made it. The concrete image to enable children and adults to grasp this point is the idea of 'handicrafts'. The more we experience and think about our creativity and the pride and care we have for the things we have made, the more we can interpret God's relationship with the world which God created.

LOCAL PRACTICE

Experience and research show that there is a wide diversity among local churches exploring and implementing good practice in Christian nurture and all age worship and learning. Churches vary greatly in available resources, commitment, and leadership, as well as in their educational philosophy and theological perspective. For example, some churches integrate children wholly within the main Sunday service, without making any separate provision. Some churches operate special children's groups throughout part of the service every week, throughout the whole service some weeks, or on a Saturday or weekday evening. Some churches operate all age project days. *The Word for all God's Family* has been designed as a flexible programme which can be used in a variety of ways. Local churches, therefore, will find themselves using this material in a variety of ways.

HOW?

The Word for all God's Family contains fifty-seven chapters, one for each Sunday in the church's lectionary year. Each chapter identifies a clear concrete image and relates this image to the bible theme.

Each chapter follows the same structure and is divided into five sections: preparation, exploring with children, exploring with adults, celebrating together, and worship resources. A sixth section, take-home sheets, is provided in the companion volume.

PREPARATION

The first section on preparation is there to help the leaders deepen their own understanding of the bible theme. There are three headings within this section.

Bible theme This introduction to the chapter demonstrates how the three bible passages hang together to illustrate the bible theme, and how the concrete image relates to the theme.

Aims The aims set out the intentions of the project programme. These aims include the rationale for the children's workshops, the all age project and the worship celebration together. At the end of each project and celebration the leaders should assess how far the aims have been realised.

Hearing the scriptures A short comment is made on each of the three bible passages in turn. Only aspects of the passages directly relevant to the bible theme are commented on.

EXPLORING WITH CHILDREN

The section on exploring with children provides seven headings. For each unit select ideas from these headings. You may choose to use an idea from each part;

you may choose to use an idea from only two or three parts. Select those that best suit the needs and interests of your participants.

Starting There are many different ways of initiating each project theme within children's workshops. While this section suggests one idea for each theme, experienced teachers may prefer to use their own ideas.

Making These activities suggest a range of things to make. Some of these activities are best suited for a single, relatively brief session. Other activities are best suited when the project theme is developed over a series of sessions or through a whole day workshop. Leaders may wish to select one or more of these activities for the whole group, or work on different activities with different groups and then share the results.

Doing These activities suggest a range of things to do. Some of these activities take little time and require comparatively little preparation. Other activities may be extended to occupy a half day or a whole day, like a group outing. Leaders may wish to select options according to the time and resources available.

Display headings The link between project learning and the bible theme is established by displaying the fruits of the children's workshops and all age projects in church. It is often helpful to leave this work on display after the service in which it has been celebrated. This section suggests a brief form of words to interpret the display for children and adults. Leaders may provide more extensive display headings of their own.

Using the bible As well as being introduced to the concrete image, it is important that the children experience how this image is related to the bible text. This section suggests ways in which the bible may be heard by the children.

Dance/drama Dance and drama are powerful ways for children to explore feelings and ideas which they can share creatively with the adult congregation. While suggestions are included for each theme, teachers and leaders may wish to use them only when time and space is available.

Games Each chapter includes one game which the children may enjoy and through which an aspect of the bible theme may be explored. Leaders and teachers will recognise when these games are appropriate for their groups.

EXPLORING WITH ADULTS

This section suggests a method for exploring the concrete image and the bible theme with adults. The method is ideally suited for use in weekday house groups to enable these groups to prepare for the Sunday service, or when the adults meet together on a Sunday before the worship service. The method involves five steps.

Introduction The first step grounds the theme in experience. A simple suggestion is made regarding how the concrete image underpinning the theme can be experienced by the group.

Experience The second step invites the group to discuss their own experience relevant to the theme.

Scripture The third step introduces the main reading from scripture and invites the group to discuss key ideas in this passage.

Integration The fourth step invites the group to integrate their experience with the passage from scripture.

Application The fifth step challenges the group to apply their understanding of the bible theme to their personal lives and to the life of their church, and then to ground their understanding in the worship service.

CELEBRATING TOGETHER

The section on celebrating together provides suggestions for the worship service. It contains three headings.

Welcoming children This section suggests ways in which the children's activities can be most effectively integrated within the worship service. Time needs to be given to help the children feel that they are contributing to the service and enhancing the quality of the teaching and worship.

All age activity The all age projects suggest ways in which the whole congregation, adults as well as children, can be involved in the same kind of project learning as promoted through the children's workshops. The fruits of the all age projects can, therefore, be placed alongside the fruits of the children's workshops to be discussed and interpreted in a similar fashion. Sometimes churches may decide to employ the ideas provided for the all age projects without operating the parallel activities within children's workshops.

Generally the all age projects benefit from forward planning so that regular worshippers can come to the service prepared with ideas and practical resources.

Teaching point The teaching point focuses the relationship between the bible theme and the concrete image.

WORSHIP RESOURCES

Three key worship resources are provided at the end of each chapter.

Prayer The collects accompanying the Sunday theme have been adapted from *The Alternative Service Book 1980* (Church of England) and *The Alternative Prayer Book 1984* (Church of Ireland) to embrace inclusive language.

Readings The three readings proposed by the lectionary are listed for easy reference.

Hymns and songs A few hymns and songs have been indicated as relevant to each project theme. It is important to recognise that hymns known best to children from school hymn books are unlikely to be known by many adult worshippers, while the church's traditional hymns are now relatively unknown to many children. Consequently, churches may need to introduce 'school' hymns to their adult congregation and 'church' hymns to their children. These hymns and songs are selected from *Come and Praise* (volumes 1 and 2) and *Hymns Ancient and Modern New Standard*.

TAKE-HOME SHEETS

For each unit two take-home sheets are provided, to support the work with children, in a form which can be easily photocopied. These can be found in the companion volume. The take-home sheets are for groups which wish to continue the learning activities at home, or to communicate to parents the content of the sessions. Each unit is complete without these sheets; their use is optional.

Two different types of sheets are included for each session. The **Worship resource** contains the prayer or collect used in the Sunday service and the key bible passage from the theme, together with a short explanation about the theme. This reinforces the children's learning and informs the parents of what the children are doing. In addition there is an activity for each unit that can be done at home with the family so that the learning extends to the home. The **Activity sheet** is a separate project to do at home, an activity to interest the children while it reinforces the theme of the unit.

Choose for yourself how to use these sheets, according to the needs of your group. Be prepared to change from unit to unit. For some units you may prefer to use neither sheet. For other units you may prefer just one or both sheets. It is your choice.

You can also choose when to use the sheets. The **Activity sheet** could be sent home before the unit in order to stimulate the children's thinking and to prepare them for the learning that will take place. Alternatively it could be sent home at the end of the unit in order to extend the children's learning. The **Worship resource** should be sent home at the end of the unit. Churches which spend several weeks on a specific unit may prefer to send the **Activity Sheet** home at the end of the first week, and then send the **Worship resource** home when the unit is completed.

WHERE?

Many factors influence how local churches organise their children's work, including patterns of Sunday services, numbers of children, willingness of teachers and leaders and availability of buildings. It is increasingly recognised that the key to effective work among children requires regular contact with the adult congregation. This can be achieved in a range of ways, including weekly withdrawal classes, a monthly pattern of Sunday school and family services, weekday evening sessions, project days and cooperation with church schools. *The Word for all God's Family* is appropriate for all these contexts but will be used differently in each setting.

WITHDRAWAL CLASSES
Some churches have children present for part of the main service each Sunday. Either they come to the first part of the service and are withdrawn before the sermon, or they begin their own classes separately and join the adults for the second half of the service. These withdrawal classes are likely to be relatively short and it is necessary to focus the lesson with care.

The Word for all God's Family can be used in two different ways when withdrawal classes are held. Some churches may decide to introduce a new project theme each week. They will select one or two key activities for the children to enjoy and then share these activities with the whole congregation later in the service. Other churches may decide to spend several weeks exploring one project theme before sharing it with the congregation. When the project is ready to share with the whole congregation it is an appropriate time to share the all age project as well.

SUNDAY SCHOOL AND FAMILY SERVICES
Some churches operate their children's work most Sunday mornings separately from the main service, but once a month integrate children and adults for a family service. This model has several advantages. Once a month it lets the

main service be more child-centred, while on the other Sundays it lets the adults tailor a service appropriate to their needs and allows more time for the children's work in their own classes.

If a monthly pattern is employed one theme can be developed more fully over three weeks. For the family service the children's project work can be displayed in the church during the previous week, the theme of the service can be developed around the project work, using the suggested collect and readings, and full use can be made of the ideas offered in the sections 'all age activity' and 'welcoming children'.

WEEKDAY EVENING SESSIONS

Some churches organise their children's work through weekday evening sessions. These churches either expect the children to be present at the main Sunday service each week, or arrange a special family service once a month.

Either a new project theme can be introduced each week or one theme can be developed over several sessions. If the church holds a monthly family service, the weekday evening sessions can prepare for these services, with dance, drama, music and display materials. Full use can be made in the monthly service of the ideas offered in the sections 'all age activity' and 'welcoming children'. If the church does not hold a monthly family service, display the children's work in church week by week and enable the children to contribute something from their project work most Sundays.

PROJECT DAYS

Some churches do all or part of their children's work through project days or project half days on a Saturday, during school holidays or at half-term. Project days permit a theme to be explored in depth and may include a wide range of craft, dance, drama and music, as well as special features like outings and field trips. Project days need to relate closely to the main service on the following Sunday, when the children's work can be integrated as they celebrate the climax of their project with the adult congregation.

CHURCH SCHOOLS

Some churches have a close link with a local church school. *The Word for all God's Family* is ideally suited for church schools which desire to link the general curriculum with the worship of the church. Teachers will identify many ways in which these projects can be promoted across the curriculum and how they can enable individual classes or the whole school to contribute constructively towards the Sunday service in church, as well as to school services.

Resources

1 Handicrafts

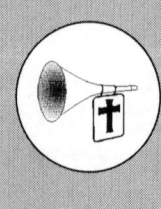

PREPARATION

Bible theme

The creation (9TH SUNDAY BEFORE CHRISTMAS)

The bible's teaching on creation emphasises God's relationship with the whole world, and with men and women in particular. God cares for the world because God made it. The Old Testament reading presents highlights from the creation story in Genesis when 'God saw all that God had made, and it was very good.' In the New Testament reading Christ is seen to share in the work of creation for 'all things were created through him and for him.' The Gospel reading from John's gospel makes the same point that 'all things were made through him.' We can begin to experience the significance of the bible's teaching on creation by exploring the special relationship we have with what we make. Human creativity, as expressed through handicrafts, gives insight into God's creativity.

Aims

- to build on our experiences of being creative;
- to develop our sense of involvement in and concern for what we have created;
- to see God as the creator who is involved in and concerned for all creation.

Hearing the scriptures

GENESIS 1, 1–3 and 24–31A

The opening chapter of Genesis does not set out to give a scientific account of how the world came into being, but a theological account of why it came into being. God took the initative; God cared about the consequences; and God saw 'all that God had made, and it was very good.'

COLOSSIANS 1, 15–20
This passage may have been an early Christian hymn which Paul adapts and quotes to combat the false view that Christ was part of the creation, rather than the creator. Here Paul emphasises that Christ shared in the work of creation, for 'all things were created through him and for him.'

JOHN 1, 1–14
John's gospel deliberately opens with the same words as the book of Genesis: 'In the beginning.' The Word who 'became flesh and dwelt among us' is the same Word through whom 'all things were made and without him was not anything made that was made.'

EXPLORING WITH CHILDREN

Starting
Make a display of handicrafts, for example a hand knitted jumper, a handmade wooden coffee table, homemade jams or cakes, works of a local artist, potter, basketmaker, a model made from matchsticks, a ship in a bottle, etc. Draw out ideas of:

- the materials from which the objects are made;
- the tools and equipment used to make them;
- the skills and concentration needed by the craftsman and craftswoman;
- the feelings experienced while working on these objects;
- the satisfaction when the objects are made;
- the pride, interest and care we give to the things we make.

Making
Give the children the opportunity to be creative, to make something and to experience the satisfaction of doing it well. Here are some suggestions.

- Bake a cake.
- Make a model from play dough.
- Make a cane work basket.
- Form a pot from clay.
- Draw a picture.
- Knit a set of patchwork squares.

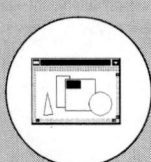

Doing
- Visit a pottery or craft workshop.
- Examine the stone or wood carving in church.
- Find out about the people who have made certain things, like Alexander Bell and the telephone, Edison and the electric light bulb, Constable and his paintings.
- Invite an artist or potter to demonstrate their skill.
- Invite a parent who is good at knitting or woodwork to display his or her skill.

Display headings
- Today's theme is the creation.
- God gives us skills to create things.
- Things we create are special for us.
- The whole world is special to God because God made it.
- Our project today is about handicraft.

Using the bible
The story of creation (GENESIS 1, 1 to 2, 4)

Help the listeners to hear this account as a rhythmic poem, with neat structure and balance. Such a poem is very different from the way in which an historical or scientific account is written. Different voices can present the seven ideas from different parts of the building.

> God said 'Let there be light,' and there was light: the first day.
> God said 'Let there be the heavens,' and it was so: the second day.
> God said 'Let there be dry land and plants,' and it was so: the third day.
> God said 'Let there be the sun and the moon,' and it was so: the fourth day.
> God said 'Let the seas be full of fish and the sky full of birds,' and it was so: the fifth day.
> God said 'Let there be animals on the earth,' and it was so.
> God said 'I will make men and women in my own image and give them authority over all the creatures,' and it was so: the sixth day.
> And on the seventh day God rested from all the work of creation.

Dance/drama
- Devise a dance of the rising sun on the fourth day of creation and its effects on the earth.
- Devise a dance to illustrate the birds, fish and animals, over which God gave men and women authority on the sixth day of creation.

Games
- In groups create a 'new' game, using just one piece of equipment, for example a ball, pencil, chair, etc. Invite each group to teach their game to the other groups.

EXPLORING WITH ADULTS

Introduction
Share with the group something which you have created yourself, for example, a cake which you have baked or a poem which you have written. Ask them what this says about you.

Experience
- In what ways are you creative?
- How do you feel when you are creative?
- How do you feel about sharing your 'creations' with others?

Scripture
Read GENESIS 1, 1-3 and 24-31A.
- What does this story of creation say about God?
- How do you interpret this story of creation today?
- What does this story say about God's relationship to the creation?

Integration
- What is the relationship between God's creativity and your creativity?
- What does it mean that you are created in God's image?
- As a created being how do you relate to your creator?

Application
- What is your relationship to the created world?
- What should be your Christian attitude to creation?
- What aspects of your creativity do you want to share in the service?

CELEBRATING TOGETHER

Welcoming children

Make space during the service for the display of the children's handicrafts to be viewed and discussed. Introduce the 'handicraft' produced during the children's activity session. Use an extended Offertory to present these handicrafts to God. If the children have prepared dance on the theme of creation, this could be presented during or after the Old Testament reading.

All age activity

Invite members of the congregation to bring some of their own handicrafts to the service. Display these handicrafts in the church. Some members of the congregation may be willing to talk about their handicrafts or to give a demonstration. The following ideas can be explored in buzz groups, discussion, or teaching:

- the things we have made ourselves;
- the things we have seen others make;
- the things we would like to make;
  God as creator;
- God's relationship with creation;
- our responsibility to share God's care for creation;
- implications for our attitude to the world.

Teaching point

The bible's teaching on creation emphasis God's responsibility, care and lordship for the whole world. God is ultimately in charge because God made it all. Through the skills God gives to each of us we are enabled to share in God's creativity.

WORSHIP RESOURCES
Prayer

Almighty God,
you created the heavens and the earth,
and made us in your own image:
Teach us to discern your hand in all your works,
and to serve you with reverence and thanksgiving;
through Jesus Christ our Lord.

Readings

Old Testament - GENESIS 1, 1-3 and 24-31A
New Testament - COLOSSIANS 1, 15-20
Gospel - JOHN 1, 1-14

Hymns and songs

Come and Praise
- 10 God who made the earth
- 12 Who put the colours in the rainbow?
- 13 Oh praise him!
- 76 God in his love

Hymns Ancient and Modern New Standard
- 101 O worship the king all glorious above
- 105 All creatures of our God and king
- 199 Immortal, invisible, God only wise
- 366 God of concrete, God of steel
- 411 O Lord of every shining constellation
- 468 God who spoke in the beginning
- 493 Lord of the boundless curves of space

2 Barriers

PREPARATION

Bible theme
The fall (8TH SUNDAY BEFORE CHRISTMAS)
The bible's teaching on creation emphasises that when God created the world, God 'saw all that had been made, and it was very good.' Then the early chapters of Genesis relate a series of narratives accounting for how God's good creation was spoilt by humankind's disobedience and sin. It is sin which quickly builds barriers between men and women and their creator. The Old Testament reading tells of the primordial conflict between Cain and Abel. The New Testament reading picks up this theme and draws a clear contrast between the love which characterises God's followers and the hatred which existed between Cain and Abel. In the Gospel reading Jesus reminds his followers how barriers are built by evil thoughts and ruthless greed as much as by murder. We can begin to experience the significance of the bible's teaching on the fall by exploring how barriers separate people and keep them apart.

Aims
- to build on our experiences of barriers;
- to help us understand how we build barriers to keep God out;
- to see how the barriers of sin spoil God's creation.

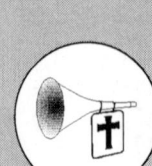

Hearing the scriptures
GENESIS 4, 1-10
According to Genesis, Cain and Abel are brothers. Abel, the shepherd, seems to find more favour with God than Cain, the farmer. Cain murders his brother Abel. The story goes on to show how God banishes Cain from his farm, just as Adam and Eve had been banished from the Garden of Eden for their sin. Cain's sin has erected a powerful barrier which affects the rest of his life.

1 JOHN 3, 9-18

The writer of 1 John argues that when the barrier between God and humankind is removed, the sort of anger and hatred which Cain felt for Abel must be replaced by mutual love.

MARK 7, 14–23

Jesus emphasises that the real barriers which we erect against God are not a consequence of breaking religious laws like dietary regulations. They are a consequence of our uncharitable thoughts and actions.

EXPLORING WITH CHILDREN

Starting

Display pictures of different sorts of barriers and discuss their purpose. Draw out ideas of:

- fences: surround playgrounds, gardens, to keep people out;
- hedges: mark territory limits, to keep animals in and to keep other animals out;
- electric fences: mark out pastures to stop sheep and cattle wandering;
- white lines on road: to divide the road for safety;
- road barriers: to stop vehicles from crossing carriageways in the event of accidents;
- rail crossing barriers: to separate rail and road traffic to avoid accidents;
- canal banks and sea walls: keep water in place;
- walls: divide people, like the Great Wall of China or the old Berlin Wall.

Making

Give the children the opportunity to make barriers and to explore how barriers work. Here are some suggestions.

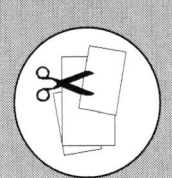

- Make a collage showing many different sorts of barriers, for example, fences, hedges, level crossings, sea walls, castles, fortresses, etc.
- Make a collage of newspaper headings showing the barriers we build between people, for example, muggings, violence, theft, murder, hijacking, etc.
- Build a model fort or castle, including the various barriers like walls, bailey tower, moat, drawbridge, etc.
- Collect pictures of barriers from magazines.

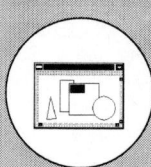

Doing

- Invite a farmer or gardener to talk about the importance of hedges and fences.
- Walk around your area and spot the barriers.
- Visit the seaside and look at the sea defences.
- Visit an old castle and discover how castles were built as barriers.
- Find out about the building of the Great Wall of China, Hadrian's Wall or the Berlin Wall.

Display headings

- Today's theme is the fall.
- Barriers are built to keep people out.
- Sin builds barriers to keep God out.
- Sin spoils God's world.
- Our project today is about barriers.

Using the bible

The story of Cain and Abel (GENESIS 4, 1-10)

Help the listeners to hear this story as a powerful drama of conflict and barriers between two brothers who follow very different lifestyles.

> Cain and Abel are brothers.
> Cain the elder was a farmer.
> Abel the younger was a shepherd.
> They both make a thank offering to God.
> Abel's offering is good and accepted by God.
> Cain's offering is not good and was not accepted.
> Cain becomes jealous of his brother and plans revenge.
> Cain tricks Abel to go alone to a secret place.
> Cain kills Abel.
> God banishes Cain from his farm.

Dance/drama

- Explore in mime or dance a sequence of situations which build barriers between people, for example, cheating in school, a deliberate foul in football, bullying, a quarrel over a shared toy.

Games

- Create an obstacle race in order to explore barriers, using, for example, chairs to climb, ropes to jump, netting to crawl under, etc.

EXPLORING WITH ADULTS

Introduction
Arrange the chairs back to back, forming a natural barrier in the room when members of the group come in to sit down. Ask them how they feel.

Experience
- What are the barriers that separate people today?
- How do you feel about these barriers?
- How do these barriers affect your life?

Scripture
Read GENESIS 4, 1-10
- What does this story say about the relationship between Cain and Abel?
- How do you interpret this story about Cain and Abel for today?
- What does this story say about God's relationship with men and women?

Integration
- What are the barriers that separate people from God today?
- How do you feel about these barriers?
- How do these barriers affect your life?

Application
- What can you do about barriers in your relationships with other people?
- What can you do about barriers in your relationship with God?
- How can the Confession help to break down these barriers?

CELEBRATING TOGETHER

Welcoming children

Make space during the service for the display of the children's work on barriers to be viewed and discussed. Use an extended confession to present these barriers to God. If the children have written poems or prepared dance about barriers, these can be shared after the Old Testament reading. As a special way of emphasising today's theme, the Confession can be placed after the three lectionary readings.

All age activity

Invite members of the congregation to bring a clipping from a recent newspaper to illustrate human sinfulness and the barriers created between human beings and God. Display these clippings in the church. The following ideas can be explored in buzz groups, discussion, or teaching:

- the examples chosen from the newspapers;
- what motivates people to do such things;
- who is to blame: the individual, society or God;
- the barriers we build to keep others out;
- what it feels like to have a barrier between you and another person;
- the barriers we build to keep God out;
- what it feels like to have a barrier between us and God.

Teaching point

The bible's teaching on creation emphasises that when God created the world, God 'saw all that had been made, and it was very good'. God's good creation was then spoilt by sin. Sin is a barrier which separates men and women from God.

WORSHIP RESOURCES

Prayer

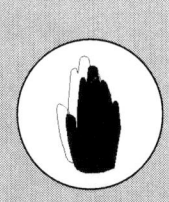

Almighty God,
your blessed Son was revealed
that he might destroy the works of the devil,
and make us the sons and daughters of God
and heirs of eternal life:
Grant that we, having this hope,
may purify ourselves even as he is pure;
that, when he shall appear in power and great glory,
we may be made like him
in his eternal and glorious kingdom;
where he lives and reigns with you and the Holy Spirit,
one God, now and for ever.

Readings

Old Testament - GENESIS 4, 1-10
New Testament - 1 JOHN 3, 9-18
Gospel - MARK 7, 14-23

Hymns and songs

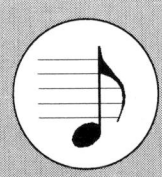

Come and Praise

39	O Lord, all the world belongs to you
44	He who would valiant be
47	One more step along the world I go
50	When a knight won his spurs in the stories of old
91	You can build a wall around you

Hymns Ancient and Modern New Standard

97	Father of heaven, whose love profound
117	Praise to the holiest in the height
246	Just as I am, without one plea
425	The God who rules this earth
432	What does the Lord require
522	We turn to you, O God of every nation

3

Bridges

PREPARATION

Bible theme

The election of God's people: Abraham (7th Sunday before Christmas)

The bible's teaching about the election of God's people opens with God's call of Abraham and Abraham's response to God's call. Abraham is celebrated in the bible for his faith in God and for the way in which he trusted God's promises. Abraham firmly believed that God would do all that God promises to do. In the Old Testament reading, Abraham is seen to set out from his home territory in response to God's call. He sets out into the unknown, trusting that God will lead him. In the New Testament reading Paul reflects on Abraham's faith and commends him as our example. In the Gospel reading Jesus is shown as one who is greater than Abraham. We can begin to experience the significance of Abraham's response of faith and trust by exploring the way we trust bridges to carry us safely to new places.

Aims

- to build on our experiences of bridges;
- to help us appreciate how we trust bridges;
- to help us see Abraham as a man who trusts God;
- to develop our own trust in God.

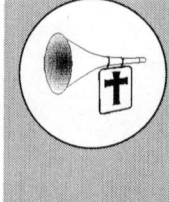

Hearing the scriptures

GENESIS 12, 1-9

The saga of Abraham occupies Genesis chapters 12-25. Here at the beginning of the saga, Abraham is seen to be responsive to God's call and to trust the promises which God has made to him.

ROMANS 4, 13-25

Paul argues that Abraham was blessed by God, not because he was obedient to the law (which had not yet been given to Moses), but because of his faith and his trust in God's promises. When God promised that Abraham would become the father of many nations 'even the thought that his body was past fatherhood … and Sarah too old to become a mother, did not shake his belief.'

JOHN 8, 51-59

In John's gospel Jesus demonstrates that his authority is greater than the authority of Abraham.

EXPLORING WITH CHILDREN

Starting

Display pictures of some famous bridges, for example, Tower Bridge, Humber Bridge, Forth Bridge, Severn Bridge, and well known local bridges. Ask the children to name the bridges and to talk about the bridges they have crossed on foot, bicycle, car, bus, train, etc. Draw out ideas of:

- the different kinds of bridges, for example, suspension, span, bailey, hump back;
- famous bridges;
- what bridges carry, for example, pedestrians, cars, trains and even canals;
- what bridges span, for example, rivers, railways, canals, motorways;
- how bridges are built and the skills involved;
- looking down over bridges and feeling suspended in mid air;
- trusting bridges to carry our weight and to bring us safe to the other side.

Making

Give the children the opportunity to build bridges and to explore how bridges inspire confidence and trust. Here are some suggestions.

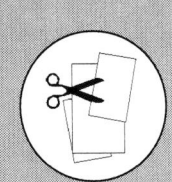

- Build bridges, using different materials, for example, lego, cardboard, stones and bricks, etc.
- Draw pictures or diagrams of different types of bridges.
- Make a collage of Abraham and his entourage crossing a bridge.
- Design a model railway layout using many different bridges.
- Make a huge mural of a bridge to stretch down the side of the church.

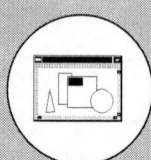

Doing
- Find out about famous bridge builders like Brunel.
- Invite an engineer or architect to show some plans of bridges.
- Visit a local bridge and discover all you can about it, including date, building materials, the builder, purpose, etc.
- Walk over the foot bridge at a railway station and look down on the track.
- Visit a bridge over a small stream and play Pooh sticks.
- Go for a car journey and list the bridges you see.

Display headings
- Today's theme is the election of God's people: Abraham.
- Bridges span deep rivers, busy roads and fast railways.
- We must trust the bridge before we use it.
- Abraham trusted God's promises.
- God's promises are to be trusted.
- Our project today is about bridges.

Using the bible
The story of Abraham's call (GENESIS 12, 1-9)
Help the listeners to hear this story as a powerful drama of human trust in God's promises.

> Abraham's family home is in Haran.
> God tells Abraham to leave his familiar home.
> God tells Abraham to set out for a place which 'I will show you'.
> God promises Abraham that he will become the father of a great nation.
> Abraham starts out for an unknown destination.
> Abraham spends a long time on that journey.
> Abraham trusts God's promises.

Dance/drama
- Do a television interview with Abraham, his wife and nephew Lot as they pack to leave Haran.
- Mime the different attitudes people have crossing a very tall and narrow bridge, ranging from fear to trust.

Games
- Explore some games that involve trust; for example, blindfold some of the children and allow others to lead them safely across an imaginary narrow bridge.

EXPLORING WITH ADULTS

Introduction
Use newspaper to mark out a pathway on the floor stretching from one corner to another corner. Tell the group that this is a high bridge. Ask for volunteers to be blindfolded and led across the bridge. Ask them how they felt about trusting their guide.

Experience
- What kind of people do you trust?
- Why do you feel that these people are trustworthy?
- What are your experiences of trusting others?

Scripture
Read GENESIS 12, 1-9
- What does this story say about Abraham's trust in God?
- How do you interpret this story about Abraham for today?
- What does this story say about God's relationship with men and women?

Integration
- How do people come to learn trust in God?
- How do you feel about trust in God?
- How should this trust affect your life?

Application
- How can your daily life reflect your trust in God?
- How can you help others to trust God?
- How can saying the Creed help to affirm your trust in God?

CELEBRATING TOGETHER

Welcoming children

Make space during the service for the display of the children's work on bridges to be viewed and discussed. Build a 'bridge' in a prominent part of the church and invite those children who wish to do so to walk across it during the presentation of their work. If the children have prepared a television interview with Abraham, this can be shared immediately after the Old Testament lesson.

All age activity

Invite the congregation to bring a picture of a bridge (say, a postcard) to the service and to make a display of these pictures around the church as they come to worship. The following ideas can be explored in buzz groups, discussion or teaching:

- the bridges we have crossed;
- the bridges we have seen in films and television;
- the views we have seen crossing bridges;
- the feelings we have experienced crossing bridges;
- the trust we place in bridges;
- the trust we place in God's promises.

Teaching point

We learn to trust that bridges will not let us down by using them regularly. Abraham learnt to trust God by setting out in obedience to God's call and by putting his faith in God's promises.

WORSHIP RESOURCES
Prayer
Almighty God,
your chosen servant Abraham faithfully obeyed your call,
and rejoiced in your promise
to bless all the families of the earth in him:
our faith, that in us your promise
may be fulfilled;
through Jesus Christ our Lord.

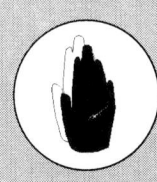

Readings
Old Testament - GENESIS 12, 1-9
New Testament - ROMANS 4, 13-25
Gospel - JOHN 8, 51-59

Hymns and songs
Come and Praise

19	He's got the whole world, in his hand
31	Can you be sure that the rain will fall?
47	One more step along the world I go
82	It's the springs up in the mountains

Hymns Ancient and Modern New Standard

214	Guide me, O thou great redeemer
216	O God of Bethel, by whose hand
223	Put thou thy trust in God
331	The God of Abraham praise
336	All my hope on God is founded
343	Be thou my vision, O Lord of my heart
372	Have faith in God, my heart

4

Rescue services

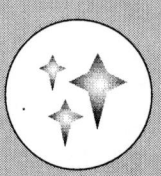

PREPARATION

Bible theme

The promise of redemption: MOSES (6TH SUNDAY BEFORE CHRISTMAS)
For the people of the Old Testament God's saving power was seen at work supremely through the exodus from Egypt. Here God redeemed the chosen people from slavery, rescued them from foreign rule and set them free to respond to God's call. God's chosen agent in leading this rescue from Egypt was Moses. The Old Testament reading tells of God commissioning Moses to rescue the people. For the people of the New Testament Jesus completes the work which Moses begun and fulfils the promise of redemption by rescuing God's people from the slavery imposed on them by their sins. In the New Testament and Gospel readings Jesus is explicitly compared with Moses. We can begin to experience the significance of the bible's teaching on the promise of redemption by exploring how rescue services work in today's world.

Aims

- to build on our experiences of rescue services;
- to develop our understanding of being rescued;
- to help us see how God rescues us.

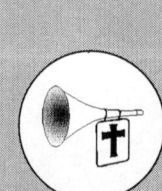

Hearing the scriptures

EXODUS 3, 7-15
While minding his father-in-law's sheep, Moses is attracted by the burning bush and God speaks with him out of the bush. Here Moses is commissioned to rescue 'my people, the sons of Israel, out of Egypt.'

HEBREWS 3, 1-6
The letter to the Hebrews interprets Jesus' work of redemption in imagery from the Old Testament. Here the author stresses that just as Moses was faithful as a servant, Jesus was faithful as a son.

JOHN 6, 25-35
According to the Old Testament, during the long journey from Egypt, God promised Moses that 'I will rain down bread from heaven for you,' and the people called this food manna. In John's gospel Jesus offers himself as the true bread from heaven which gives life to the world.

EXPLORING WITH CHILDREN

Starting
If the local congregation includes a fireman, ambulance driver, driver of a breakdown vehicle or representative of some other rescue service, invite them to introduce their work to the children and to bring some of their equipment with them. Or look at pictures of these services. Draw out ideas of:

- how the fire service is called;
- how quickly the fire service responds to a call;
- the equipment used by firemen;
- how firemen wear protective clothing;
- the dangers from which firemen rescue people.

Making
Give the children the opportunity to make a display about the rescue services. Here are some suggestions.

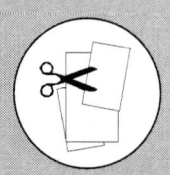

- Design a poster to recruit firemen.
- Make helmets for firemen.
- Make a cartoon book illustrating the firemen's job.
- Cut out and mount headlines of rescue services.
- Make a collage about Moses rescuing the people of God.

Doing
- Visit the local fire station.
- Collect information about life-boats.
- Watch a video about air or sea rescue services.
- Find out about the use of St Bernard dogs in rescue operations.
- Discuss people who have helped to set others free, like Martin Luther King, or Terry Waite.
- Visit a local car breakdown service.

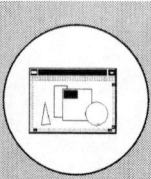

Display headings
- Today's theme is the promise of redemption: Moses.
- Rescue services set people free from danger.
- God chose Moses to rescue his people.
- Moses rescued the Hebrew people from slavery in Egypt.
- Our project today is about rescue services.

Using the bible
The story of Moses' call and the rescue from Egypt (EXODUS 3, 7-15)
Help the listeners to hear this story as a powerful drama of God's intervention to rescue the Hebrew people from slavery and oppression.

> The Hebrew people are slaves in Egypt.
> God hears their call for help.
> God chooses Moses to rescue the people.
> Moses is caring for his father-in-law's sheep.
> God speaks to Moses from the burning bush.
> God gives Moses the ability to fulfil the call.
> Moses rescues the Hebrew people from Egypt.

Dance/drama
- Learn the spiritual 'Let my people go' and work out some actions to illustrate it.
- Devise a dance about being rescued.

Games
- Play a game like freeze tag, in which the children can experience the liberation of being set free.

EXPLORING WITH ADULTS

Introduction
Set out in the front of the room a display of material from the AA and RAC, for example your membership badge and leaflets. Ask the group to describe their experiences of these rescue services.

Experience
- What are the rescue or caring services that people need today?
- What are your experiences of these services?
- How have these services helped you?

Scripture
Read EXODUS 3, 7-15
- What does this story say about God rescuing the Israelites?
- How do you interpret this story about Moses for today?
- What does this story say about God's commitment to men and women?

Integration
- From what do people need God to rescue them today?
- What are your experiences of being rescued by God?
- How do these experiences affect your life?

Application
- How can you be aware of God's rescuing power in your life today?
- How can you help others to be aware of God's rescuing power today?
- How can the Absolution help us be aware of God's rescuing power?

CELEBRATING TOGETHER

Welcoming children

Make space during the service for the display of the children's work on rescue services to be viewed and discussed. Invite some of the local rescue services to display their work in the church. Invite a local fireman, dressed for work, to read a lesson. If the children have prepared the spiritual 'Let my people go', this can be shared after the Old Testament reading. As a special way of emphasising today's theme, particular attention can be drawn to the Absolution.

All age activity

Invite members of the congregation to bring illustrations from papers and magazines of various rescue services. Particular attention may be drawn to organisations like the AA and RAC, as well as lifeboats, ambulance and fire services. Display this material in church. The following ideas can be explored in buzz groups, discussion or teaching:

- our experiences of rescue services in real life;
- the people we know who work for these services;
- our images of rescue services from films and television;
- the risks and dangers involved;
- the situations from which we may need to be rescued;
- God's promises to rescue us.

Teaching point

In the Old Testament God's power to rescue the people of God is seen at work supremely through the exodus from Egypt. God's chosen agent in leading this rescue is Moses.

WORSHIP RESOURCES

Prayer
Lord God, Redeemer of Israel,
you sent your servant Moses
to lead your people out of slavery and affliction:
Deliver us from the tyranny of sin and death
and bring us to the promised land,
where we may live in perfect union
with you and the Holy Spirit;
through Jesus Christ our Lord.

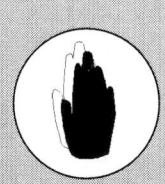

Readings
Old Testament - EXODUS 3, 7-15
New Testament - HEBREWS 3, 1-6
Gospel - JOHN 6, 25-35

Hymns and songs
Come and Praise
- 38 Now thank we all our God
- 39 O Lord, all the world belongs to you
- 65 When I needed a neighbour were you there, were you there?
- 88 I was lying in the roadway

Hymns Ancient and Modern New Standard
- 209 Through all the changing scenes
- 211 Through the night of doubt and sorrow
- 214 Guide me, O thou great redeemer
- 216 O God of Bethel, by whose hand
- 336 All my hope on God is founded
- 361 For the healing of the nations
- 419 Sing we a song of high revolt

5

Leftovers

PREPARATION

Bible theme

The remnant of Israel (5TH SUNDAY BEFORE CHRISTMAS)

The bible contains many examples of the unfaithfulness of God's people. Yet throughout history there has been a tiny minority who has remained faithful. It is through this tiny minority, this 'remnant', that God has renewed the people of God. The Gospel reading reminds us how Noah and his family were the remnants through whom God renewed the world after the great flood. In the Old Testament reading God promises Elijah that a remnant of 7,000 will be preserved in Israel. In the New Testament reading Paul uses the image of pruning and grafting to illustrate remnant and new growth. We can begin to experience the significance of the bible's teaching on the remnant by exploring how we can transform 'leftovers'.

Aims

- to build on our experiences of transforming leftovers;
- to help us understand the usefulness and potential of leftovers;
- to see how God has used the remnant to renew the people of God.

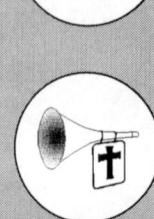

Hearing the scriptures

1 KINGS 19, 9-18

The prophet Elijah has fled to escape the vengeance of Jezebel, wife of King Ahab and supporter of the religion of Baal. It seemed to Elijah that he was the only person in the whole of Israel to remain loyal to God. God promises Elijah that a faithful remnant is left in Israel who has not turned to Baal.

Romans 11, 13-24

In Romans chapters 9, 10 and 11, Paul explores the relationship between God's chosen people Israel and the Christian church. He develops the image of Israel as an olive tree which God has pruned radically and the Gentiles as new branches grafted into the tree. Paul looks for the day when Israel is grafted back in also.

Matthew 24, 37-44

Jesus uses the story of Noah to illustrate the judgement which God brings. The promise is given that a faithful remnant will remain.

EXPLORING WITH CHILDREN

Starting

Have a 'useful' box filled with odds and ends: remnants of material, lace, ribbons, odd buttons, bits of wool, bolts, screws, string, etc. Encourage the children to look through the box and use its contents creatively. Draw out ideas of:

- the origins of the bits and pieces;
- the use of the word remnant;
- other uses of the word remnant: material shops, DIY shops;
- how leftovers have potential;
- how leftovers can be transformed.

Making

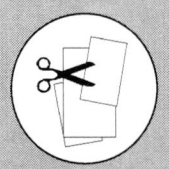

Give the children the opportunity to transform some leftovers into something interesting or useful. Here are some suggestions.

- Make a range of things from the remnants in the 'useful' box.
- Cook something interesting from leftovers, like bubble and squeak.
- Use remnants to make a collage showing Elijah looking for God in the wind, earth, fire.
- Design a poster or booklet giving ideas of interesting things to do with leftover food.
- Create a display of things made from remnants.
- Make a set of eucharistic vestments from remnants.

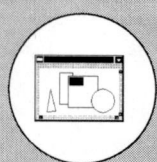

Doing

- Visit the remnant counter of a material shop or DIY shop.
- Find out how the remnants of endangered animals are being protected.
- Invite someone who is good at making things from remnants of material to display and talk about some of the things they have made.
- Invite someone who is skilled at making things from remnants of wood.
- Invite the children to bring a small quantity of leftover food from home which can be used in a picnic.
- Invite a cook to talk about the creative use of food leftovers.

Display headings

- Today's theme is the remnant of Israel.
- Remnants are leftovers.
- Leftovers can be transformed.
- Remnants can be made into beautiful and useful things.
- The remnant remained faithful to God.
- God uses the remnant to renew the people of God.
- Our project today is about leftovers.

Using the bible

The story of Elijah (1 KINGS 19, 9-18)

Help the listeners to hear in this story how God uses the few people who remain faithful to renew the people of God.

> The Jewish people are turning away from God to worship Baal.
> Queen Jezebel threatens to kill Elijah because he is against Baal.
> Elijah escapes to the cave.
> Elijah talks with God.
> Elijah says 'I am the only faithful one left'.
> God promises a remnant of 7,000 faithful people.
> God uses that remnant to renew the people of God.

Dance/drama

- Act out the Elijah story. Bring out Elijah's surprise and joy as he discovers that he is part of a much larger remnant.
- Devise a dance about the bits and pieces in the 'useful' box as they are transformed into something new.

Games

- Play a game like musical chairs. The group gets smaller and smaller until there is only a remnant of one. The one person left is given responsibility for organising the next game.

EXPLORING WITH ADULTS

Introduction
Display some remnants of fabric or wood at the front of the room. Ask the group how these remnants might be used.

Experience
- What remnants or leftovers are produced by your work?
- How do you use remnants or leftovers?
- What makes people feel like remnants?

Scripture
Read I KINGS 19, 9-18
- What does this story say about Elijah's experience as a remnant?
- How do you interpret this story about Elijah for today?
- What does this story say about God's attitude to the remnant?

Integration
- Should Christians feel like a remnant people today?
- How would you feel about being called a remnant people today?
- How does God transform a remnant people today?

Application
- How can you witness as part of a remnant people today?
- How can your church witness as a remnant people today?
- How can your worship help to renew the remnant people of God?

CELEBRATING TOGETHER

Welcoming children
Make space during the service for the display of the children's work on remnants to be viewed and discussed. If the children have made eucharistic vestments from remnants, these can be used by the president. If the children have prepared drama on the theme of Elijah, this could be presented after the Old Testament reading.

All age activity
Invite the members of the congregation to bring a remnant of something to the service with them. Make a display of these remnants during the service. At the end of the service ask those who wish to do so to take a remnant home with them and to transform it in time for next week's service. The transformed remnants could be sold for charity. The following ideas can be explored in buzz groups, discussion or teaching:

- our personal experiences of transforming leftovers;
- our knowledge of people who are good at transforming leftovers;
- the fate of leftovers if they are not transformed;
- God's promises to the remnant;
- God's remnant in today's world.

Teaching point
Throughout history there has been a remnant of people who have remained faithful to God. It is through this remnant that God renews the people of God.

WORSHIP RESOURCES

Prayer

Almighty God,
you have called your people to bear witness to you:
Give us grace to obey your commands
and keep us truly faithful,
that all nations may hear your voice,
return to you and glorify your name;
through Jesus Christ our Lord.

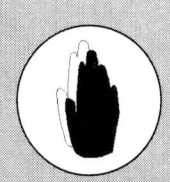

Readings

Old Testament - 1 KINGS 19, 9-18
New Testament - ROMANS 11, 13-24
Gospel - MATTHEW 24, 37-44

Hymns and songs

Come and Praise

    29 From the darkness came light
    31 Can you be sure that the rain will fall?
    57 Think of all the things we lose
    87 Give us hope, Lord

Hymns Ancient and Modern New Standard

    114 A safe stronghold our God is still
    162 Jesus, where'er thy people meet
    171 Thy hand, O God, has guided
    367 God of grace and God of glory
    372 Have faith in God, my heart
    397 Lord, save thy world; in bitter need
    416 Praise the Lord, rise up rejoicing

6 Christmas shopping

PREPARATION

Bible theme

The Advent hope (ADVENT SUNDAY)

The key idea which links all three readings on Advent Sunday is the theme of preparation, the call to get ready and to be prepared. It is this key note of preparation which defines the church's season of Advent. The word 'Advent' itself means 'coming'; the season of Advent prepares for the coming of God's Christ at Christmas and looks forward to Christ's second coming at the end of the ages. The Old Testament reading describes the herald who comes to bring the gospel, 'the good news'. Both the New Testament and the Gospel readings urge the church to be alert, awake and waiting for the coming of Christ. We can begin to experience the significance of the bible's teaching on the need for being ready and being prepared by exploring how Christmas shopping helps us to prepare for the secular side of Christmas.

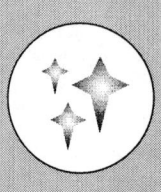

Aims

- to build on our experiences of Christmas shopping;
- to help us understand Christmas shopping as preparation for Christmas;
- to see how Advent prepares God's people for the coming of Christ at Christmas.

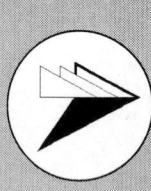

Hearing the scriptures

ISAIAH 52, 7-10

The Second Isaiah is speaking to his fellow exiles in Babylon before the armies of Cyrus, King of Persia, capture Babylon and allow the exiles to return home. Isaiah prepares them for the coming deliverance and announces that the Lord himself will set his people free. Later the church reapplied this prophecy to the coming of Christ.

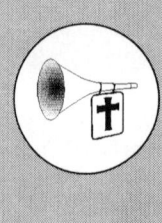

1 THESSALONIANS 5, 1-11

Paul is writing to the church in Thessalonica about the second coming of Christ. The church must be prepared because 'the day of the Lord comes like a thief in the night.' At the time of writing Paul was expecting the second coming within his own lifetime. Later Paul's views changed and he expected that he would probably die before the Lord came.

LUKE 21, 25-33

This is part of Luke's teaching about the last times. He urges the early church to read the signs of the times as clearly as they interpret the trees budding in spring.

EXPLORING WITH CHILDREN

Starting

Have a bag of wrapped shopping, including foods, particularly associated with the Christmas season: for example, nuts, tangerines, Christmas pudding, wrapping paper, candles, and perhaps several Christmas presents suitable for different age groups, like a teddy bear, tie, chocolates. Invite the children to feel the wrapped objects and to guess what is in each parcel. Draw out ideas of Christmas shopping:

- planning and drawing up a shopping list;
- excitement and anticipation;
- secrecy and surprise;
- hopes for Christmas gifts;
- the significance of some of the items, like the candles;
- the business of the local shops.

Making

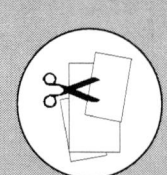

Give the children the opportunity to make a display concerned with Christmas shopping. Here are some suggestions.

- Design a collage of all the things bought at Christmas time.
- Draw a picture of the local shopping centre at Christmas.
- Make a display of Christmas shopping.
- Make a collage of advertisements promoting Christmas shopping.
- Make a Christmas shop window display.
- Make an Advent wreath, using metal coat hangers.

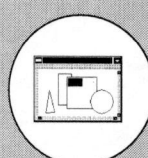

Doing
- Arrange a shopping trip.
- Go shopping for the ingredients of a Christmas cake.
- Visit the local town centre at night to see the lights.
- Look at pictures, postcards, videos of London's Oxford Street lights.
- Invite someone who works in a high street store to talk about their work at Christmas time.
- Invite a mother to tell about her Christmas shopping.

Display headings
- Today's theme is the Advent hope.
- Christmas shopping helps us to prepare for Christmas.
- During Advent we prepare for Christ's birth at Christmas.
- God wants us to be prepared and ready for Christmas.
- Our project today is about Christmas shopping.

Using the bible
The story of Isaiah's prophecy to the exiles (ISAIAH 52, 7-10)
Help the listeners to catch the feeling of excitement and preparation as the news that God is about to set free the people of God gets shouted from the herald to the watchmen and from the watchmen to the people in the city.

> The people of God are in exile.
> They are away from home, imprisoned.
> They are filled with fear for the future.
> They begin to despair.
> A herald comes shouting the news of freedom.
> The watchmen around the city walls repeat the message.
> The people inside the city shout the message as well.
> God comes to set free the people of God.

Dance/drama
- Act out a Christmas shopping scene.
- Develop a choral speech version of the Old Testament reading.

Games
- Fill a tray with Christmas objects. Show the tray for a limited period of time and ask the children how many items they can remember.

EXPLORING WITH ADULTS

Introduction
Bring in a bag of shopping, particularly associated with the Christmas season, for example, food stuffs such as tangerines, dates and mincepies and presents such as a toy and a tie. Ask the group how Christmas shopping helps us to prepare for Christmas.

Experience
- What do you include in a list of shopping to prepare for Christmas?
- How do you feel about Christmas shopping as a preparation for Christmas?
- What is important for you in preparing for Christmas?

Scripture
Read ISAIAH 52, 7-10
- What does this prophecy say about Isaiah's preparation of the people of God?
- How do you interpret this prophecy for today?
- What does this prophecy say about God's coming among men and women?

Integration
- Why does the church need the season of Advent?
- How does the church use Advent?
- How do individual Christians use Advent?

Application
- How can your church best use Advent to prepare for Christmas?
- How can you best use Advent to prepare for Christmas?
- How can the lighting of the Advent wreath help prepare the people of God?

CELEBRATING TOGETHER

Welcoming children
Make space during the service for the display of the children's work on Christmas shopping to be viewed and discussed. If the children have prepared a choral speech version of the Old Testament reading, this can be presented either after or in place of the Old Testament reading. As a special way of emphasising today's theme, make a ceremony of presenting the Advent wreath and of lighting the first candle as a symbol of the 'Advent hope' lit in the hearts of the people of God.

All age activity
Invite members of the congregation to bring advertisements promoting Christmas shopping. Display these advertisements in church in thematic groups, for example, toys, alcohol, tobacco products, foodstuffs, clothes, etc. The following issues can be explored in buzz groups, discussion or teaching:

- our personal experiences of Christmas shopping;
- stereotypes of Christmas shopping portrayed on film and television;
- the positive and negative aspects of the commercial Christmas;
- the need to prepare for Christmas presents and entertainment;
- the preparation which God requires of us for Christmas.

Teaching point
To celebrate Christmas properly we have to prepare for it well in advance. Christmas shopping helps us to prepare our homes. Advent helps us to prepare our hearts for the birth of Christ.

WORSHIP RESOURCES

Prayer

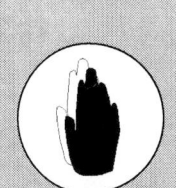

> Almighty God,
> give us grace to cast away the works of darkness,
> and put on the armour of light,
> now in the time of this mortal life
> in which your Son Jesus Christ
> came to visit us in great humility:
> So that, on the last day,
> when he shall come again in his glorious majesty
> to judge both the living and the dead,
> we may rise to the life immortal,
> through him who lives and reigns
> with you and the Holy Spirit,
> now and for ever.

Readings

> Old Testament - Isaiah 52, 7-10
> New Testament - 1 Thessalonians 5, 1-11
> Gospel - Luke 21, 25-33

Hymns and songs

Come and Praise

> 24 Go, tell it on the mountain
> 49 We are climbing Jesus' ladder
> 55 Colours of day dawn into the mind
> 127 Advent time is here

Hymns Ancient and Modern New Standard

> 24 Hark! a thrilling voice is sounding
> 32 Sleepers, wake! the watch-cry pealeth
> 301 How beauteous are their feet
> 342 Awake, awake: fling off the night!
> 367 God of grace and God of glory
> 397 Lord, save thy world; in bitter need
> 405 O day of God draw nigh

7 Christmas cards

PREPARATION

Bible theme
The word of God in the Old Testament (2ND SUNDAY IN ADVENT)
The theme for the second Sunday in Advent concerns the way in which the word of God in the Old Testament prepares for the coming of Christ. The point is made explicitly in the Gospel reading where Jesus says to the Jewish people, 'You study the scriptures believing that in them you have eternal life; now these same scriptures testify to me.' In the New Testament reading Timothy is exhorted to value the scriptures and in the Old Testament reading God promises that the word of God will be fruitful. We can begin to experience the significance of the church's teaching about the word of God in the Old Testament by exploring how even the simple messages in Christmas cards can point beyond themselves to a much greater message.

Aims
- to build on our experiences of Christmas cards;
- to help us understand the Christmas messages conveyed in Christmas cards;
- to see how certain passages in the Old Testament point to the message of Christmas.

Hearing the scriptures

ISAIAH 55, 1-11
The Second Isaiah is speaking to the people of God in exile in Babylon. God is promising his people a new start and a new hope. It is the prophet's task to make this word of God known. God's word has power to realise and to achieve all that it sets out to achieve.

2 Timothy 3, 14 to 4, 5

Timothy is portrayed as a young church leader being written to by the ageing Paul. Paul urges Timothy to stick to the basic truths of the faith and to ground those truths in scripture which 'is inspired by God and is useful for teaching the truth.'

John 5, 36-47

In John's gospel the Jewish people fail to recognise Jesus for who he is. Here Jesus accuses them of failing to grasp the true meaning of their scriptures: 'These same scriptures testify to me, and yet you refuse to come to me for life!' As a consequence of this, Jesus accuses the Jewish people of failing to take seriously the writing of Moses, whom they believe wrote the first five books of the Old Testament, 'since it was I that he was writing about.'

EXPLORING WITH CHILDREN

Starting

Look through a collection of old Christmas cards. Ask each of the children to choose a favourite one and to say why they have chosen it. Talk about the different themes used on Christmas cards and divide them into groups, for example, ye olde England, churches, nativity scenes, Christmas trees, teddy bears, robins and holly. Make a histogram showing how many cards fall into each group. Draw out ideas of:

- the variety of cards;
- reasons for sending cards;
- messages printed in and on cards;
- uses of scripture on cards;
- messages of hope and reassurance.

Making

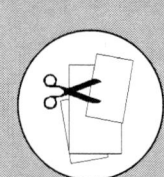

Give the children the opportunity to make a display about Christmas cards. Here are some suggestions.

- Make Christmas cards, using biblical passages.
- Create a collage of old Christmas cards.
- Make a Christmas postbox for the church.
- Make a display of Old Testament passages about Christmas.
- Design embroidery Christmas cards.

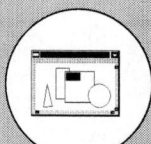

Doing

- Invite people to display their Christmas cards.
- Look at Christmas cards from another country or from an earlier age.
- Invite someone who makes their own Christmas cards to talk about this process.
- Visit a local card shop.
- Invite a postman to talk about the Christmas post.

Display headings

- Today's theme is the word of God in the Old Testament.
- Christmas cards send greetings and messages.
- The bible contains God's messages to the people.
- The Old Testament looks forward to the birth of Christ.
- The prophets prepare for the coming of Jesus.
- Our project today is about Christmas cards.

Using the bible

Give bibles to the children and invite them to find and copy out key Old Testament passages which point to Christmas. Use these passages in making Christmas cards. Here are some suggestions.

Isaiah 1, 3	The ass knows its master's crib.
Isaiah 7, 14	A young woman will bear a son.
Isaiah 9, 1	The people who walked in darkness.
Isaiah 9, 6	For a boy has been born for us.
Isaiah 11, 2	The Spirit of the Lord shall rest upon him.
Isaiah 40, 11	He will feed his flock.
Isaiah 42, 1	Here is my servant.
Isaiah 60, 3	Nations shall march towards your light.
Micah 5, 2	But you Bethlehem.
Zechariah 2, 11	Shout aloud and rejoice.
Psalm 72, 11	The Kings shall bring gifts.

Dance/drama

- Act out the postman or postwoman delivering Christmas cards, receiving and opening the cards and reading out the message inside.

Games

- In groups use old Christmas cards to make a picture alphabet for the Christmas season, for example Angels, Baby, Crib, Donkey, etc.

EXPLORING WITH ADULTS

Introduction
Look through a collection of Christmas cards. Ask the group to select a card which speaks to them about the meaning of Christmas.

Experience
- What messages do you prefer in the Christmas cards that you send?
- How do you feel about the messages in the Christmas cards that you receive?
- Which of these messages help you to prepare for Christmas?

Scripture
Read ISAIAH 55, 1-11
- What does this prophecy say about the word of God?
- How do you interpret this prophecy about the word of God for today?
- What does this prophecy say about the effectiveness of the word of God?

Integration
- How does the word of God come to people today?
- What does the word of God mean to you?
- How does the word of God affect your life?

Application
- What can your church do to hear and understand the word of God?
- What can you do to hear and understand the word of God?
- How can the Ministry of the Word affirm the bible as the word of God?

CELEBRATING TOGETHER

Welcoming children

Make space during the service for the display of the children's work on Christmas cards to be viewed and discussed. If the children have prepared drama on the Christmas post, this may be presented as part of the Ministry of the Word. Perhaps the postman could 'deliver' the text of the three readings to the readers. As a special way of emphasising today's theme, light the second of the candles on the Advent wreath, symbolising the word of God in the Old Testament.

All age activity

Invite members of the congregation to bring a specially chosen Christmas card addressed to their church. Arrange for a 'post box' to be placed by the door to receive these cards when people come into church. Open some of the cards and read their messages during the Ministry of the Word. Make sure that all the cards are displayed by the end of the service. The following issues can be explored in buzz groups, discussion or teaching:

- our personal experiences of sending and receiving Christmas cards;
- our likes and dislikes about Christmas cards;
- appropriate and inappropriate messages in Christmas cards;
- the messages which God wants us to hear in Christmas cards;
- how God's messages can be heard at Christmas.

Teaching point

Throughout the Old Testament God's plans are made known to the people of God. These plans prepare for the birth of Christ.

WORSHIP RESOURCES

Prayer

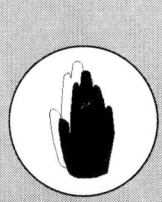

Blessed Lord,
who caused all holy Scriptures
to be written for our learning:
Help us so to hear them,
to read, mark, learn and inwardly digest them
that, through patience, and the comfort of your holy word,
we may embrace and for ever hold fast
the blessed hope of everlasting life,
which you have given us in our Saviour Jesus Christ.

Readings

Old Testament - ISAIAH 55, 1-11
New Testament - 2 TIMOTHY 3, 14 TO 4, 5
Gospel - JOHN 5, 36-47

Hymns and songs

Come and Praise

- 62   Heavenly father, may thy blessing
- 114 Flickering candles in the night

Hymns Ancient and Modern New Standard

- 30   Hark the glad sound! the saviour comes
- 166 Lord, thy word abideth
- 180 Thou, whose almighty word
- 379 Jesus, humble was your birth
- 417 Praise we now the word of grace
- 423 Thanks to God whose word was spoken
- 467 God, who hast caused to be written thy word for our learning
- 484 Long ago, prophets knew
- 509 Rise and hear! the Lord is speaking

8

Christmas decorations

PREPARATION

Bible theme

The forerunner (3RD SUNDAY IN ADVENT)

The theme for the third Sunday in Advent concerns the way in which the forerunner prepares for the coming of Christ. In the Gospel reading the forerunner is John the Baptist who prepares the way for Jesus' ministry in first century Palestine. John announces himself as 'a voice that cries in the wilderness: "make a straight way for the Lord."' John's announcement is a direct quotation from the Old Testament reading of Isaiah 40. In the New Testament reading Paul speaks of himself as a servant of Christ, one who continues to prepare the way for Christ's coming. We can begin to experience the significance of the theme of the forerunner by exploring how Christmas decorations help us to prepare the way for Christmas day.

Aims

- to build on our experiences of Christmas decorations;
- to help us understand Christmas decorations not as an end in themselves but as forerunners to the celebration of Christmas;
- to see how John the Baptist helps to prepare for the coming of Christ.

Hearing the scriptures

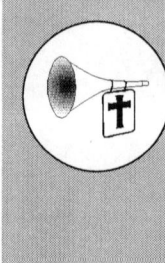

ISAIAH 40, 1-11

These verses open the book of the Second Isaiah who is speaking to the people of God in exile in Babylon. He announces a new exodus when the exiled people will be set free and enabled to return to their own land. A great highway will be prepared through the wilderness so that God can lead home the people of God.

1 Corinthians 4, 1-5

As John the Baptist pointed away from himself to the greater one who came after him, so Paul describes the apostle's work as leading others to Christ. Paul describes himself as a servant of Christ (someone who is at the Lord's beck and call) and as a steward of the mysteries of God (someone who draws attention to God's plan for the salvation of the world).

John 1, 19-28

In the fourth gospel John the Baptist emphasises very strongly that he is not the Messiah. John's job is to prepare the way and point others in the direction of the Messiah. John is the archetypal forerunner.

EXPLORING WITH CHILDREN

Starting

Invite the children to look at a Christmas tree which has not yet been decorated. Ideally this can be the tree which will later be used in church. Draw out ideas of:

- the significance of Christmas trees;
- what is needed to 'complete' the Christmas tree;
- electric lights and candles;
- tinsel and the star;
- decorations for the tree;
- other Christmas decorations, like holly, etc.;
- how decorations point to the celebration of Christmas.

Making

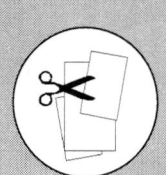

Give the children the opportunity to make Christmas decorations to use in church. Here are some suggestions.

- Make Christmas crackers.
- Print gift wrapping paper, using potato prints.
- Make Christmas candles.
- Make decorations for the Christmas tree in church.
- Make paper chains to hang in church.
- Make a collage of John the Baptist and incorporate Christmas decorations.

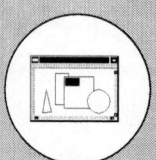

Doing
- Look at pictures of Christmas decorations.
- Visit a decorated Christmas tree (perhaps there is one in the town centre).
- Note the decorations in shop windows.
- Invite someone to demonstrate making Christmas decorations.
- Invite someone to demonstrate decorating a Christmas tree.

Display headings
- Today's theme is the forerunner.
- Christmas decorations help us to prepare for Christmas.
- John the Baptist is called the forerunner.
- John the Baptist prepared for the coming of Christ.
- Our project today is about Christmas decorations.

Using the bible
The story of John the Baptist (JOHN 1, 19-28)
Help the listeners to appreciate John the Baptist's ministry as concerned the whole time with preparing the way for Jesus and pointing people towards Jesus.

> John taught by the river Jordan.
> He wore a rough coat of camel's hair with a leather belt around his waist.
> He dressed in a strange way to draw attention to his message.
> He challenged people to turn to God.
> He baptised in the river.
> He prepared the way for Jesus.
> When Jesus came, John took a back seat.

Dance/drama
- Devise a dance to show the excitement of decorating the Christmas tree (children can be the tree).
- Learn the song from Godspell 'Prepare ye the way of the Lord'.
- Act out the story of John the Baptist.

Games
- See who can make the longest paper chain within a given time. Then join all chains together.

EXPLORING WITH ADULTS

Introduction
Place an undecorated Christmas tree at the centre of the room. Ask the group about the significance of decorating the tree as a preparation for Christmas.

Experience
- How do you decorate your Christmas tree?
- What is the significance for you of Christmas decorations?
- How are your decorations a preparation for Christmas?

Scripture
Read JOHN 1, 19-28
- What does this story say about John's ministry as a preparation for Jesus' coming?
- How do you interpret this story of John for today?
- What does this story say about preparation for Jesus' coming?

Integration
- What preparation do people make for Jesus at Christmas?
- How do you feel about this preparation?
- How do you prepare for Jesus' coming?

Application
- How can your church best respond to John the Baptist's call for repentance?
- How can you best respond to John the Baptist's call for repentance?
- How can your liturgy best call people to repentance?

CELEBRATING TOGETHER

Welcoming children

Make space during the service for the display of the children's Christmas decorations to be viewed and discussed. If the song from Godspell, 'Prepare ye the way of the Lord', has been practised, gradually involve the whole church in singing this short refrain after the Gospel reading. As a special way of emphasising today's theme, light the third of the candles on the Advent wreath, as a symbol of John the Baptist preparing the way for Christ.

All age activity

Invite members of the congregation to bring a decoration for the church's Christmas tree. During the service make an opportunity for some or all of these decorations to be hung on the tree. The following issues can be explored in buzz groups, discussion or teaching:

- our personal experiences of decorating for Christmas;
- images of Christmas decorations from films and television;
- ways of making Christmas decorations and their particular meaning or significance;
- how Christmas decorations prepare our homes;
- how we prepare ourselves for the birth of Christ.

Teaching point

In the gospels God calls John the Baptist to prepare for the coming of Jesus. Today we prepare for Jesus' coming by decorating our homes and churches and by inviting God to prepare our hearts.

WORSHIP RESOURCES

Prayer

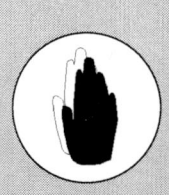

Almighty God,
you sent John the Baptist
to prepare the way for the coming of your Son:
Guide the ministers and stewards of your truth
to make our disobedient hearts obey the law of love;
that when Christ comes again in glory to judge the world
we may stand with confidence before him,
who lives and reigns with you and the Holy Spirit
now and for ever.

Readings

Old Testament - ISAIAH 40, 1-11
New Testament - 1 CORINTHIANS 4, 1-5
Gospel - JOHN 1, 19-28

Hymns and songs

Come and Praise
- 29 From the darkness came light
- 43 Give me oil in my lamp, keep me burning
- 118 When the winter day is dying

Hymns Ancient and Modern New Standard
- 24 Hark! a thrilling voice is sounding
- 26 O come, O come, Emmanuel
- 27 On Jordan's bank the Baptist's cry
- 364 God is light
- 384 Lo, in the wilderness a voice
- 431 We have a gospel to proclaim
- 483 Lift up your heads, you mighty gates
- 512 'The kingdom is upon you!'

9

Christmas crib

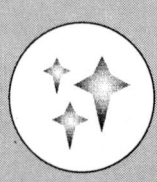

PREPARATION

Bible theme
The Annunciation (4TH SUNDAY IN ADVENT)
The fourth Sunday in Advent prepares for the birth of Christ by focusing on Mary and the story of the Annunciation. In the Gospel reading the angel Gabriel brings the news to Mary that she will have a son and name him Jesus. This passage stresses that Joseph is a direct descendant of King David. The Old Testament reading is a prophecy that the Messiah will be descended from David. The New Testament reading is chosen as a commentary on God's choice of Mary, an ordinary woman. We can begin to experience the significance of the church's teaching about the incarnation by exploring the imagery of the Christmas crib.

Aims

- to build on our experiences of the Christmas crib;
- to help us understand the significance of the Christmas crib;
- to prepare ourselves for celebrating Christ's birthday.

Hearing the scriptures
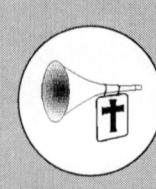

ISAIAH 11, 1-9
The first Isaiah sees the disaster that threatens Jerusalem from the Assyrians as God's judgement on Judah and her king. But then in this passage Isaiah expresses confidence that God will raise up a new King, a descendant of David (Jesse's son), who will restore the nation to its former glory and initiate a return to the peaceful existence of Eden. The church has interpreted this prophecy as pointing to Jesus, himself 'a shoot from the stock of Jesse.'

1 CORINTHIANS 1, 26-31

In this letter to Corinth Paul contrasts what the world values with what God values. He is making his point by inviting the Corinthian church to look at their own membership, for 'from the human point of view few of you are wise or powerful or of high social standing.' In Christian tradition Mary, too, is seen as God's choice of the lowly.

LUKE 1, 26-38A

In Luke's gospel, Jesus' family tree is of crucial significance. Mary is a relative of Elizabeth, who was descended from Aaron, the priestly family. Joseph is a descendant of David, the royal family. Jesus as Messiah combines the royal and priestly character.

EXPLORING WITH CHILDREN

Starting

Invite the children to look at a manger (an animal feeding trough) filled with straw, but as yet no baby. Ideally, produce something which looks as if it has just come straight from a farm and which can be used in the church's crib scene. Draw out ideas of:

- the normal use of the manger;
- the purpose of the straw;
- the emptiness;
- the normal preparations for the birth of a baby;
- why Mary was away from home;
- why Jesus was born in a stable;
- the lack of glamour and the poverty of Jesus' birth.

Making

Give the children the opportunity to become familiar with the Christmas crib and the expectations usually associated with the birth of a baby. Here are some suggestions.

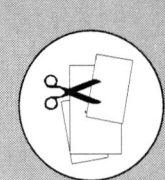

- Make a crib scene which can be used in church. At this stage concentrate on figures of Mary, Joseph, inn keeper and animals. The background can show the inn, stars, sky, etc. The scene can be further developed with shepherds and wise men on the two Sundays after Christmas.
- Make toys, clothes and gifts suitable for a newborn baby.
- Design a congratulations card to be sent to Mary and Joseph on the birth of their baby boy.

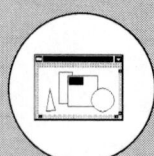

Doing
- Look at baby clothes, food, toys, etc.
- Invite a mother to talk about the preparation for the birth of her child and to show some of the baby clothes.
- Invite a midwife to talk about her work.
- Look at pictures of the nativity from different times and cultures.
- Look for nativity scenes in the local community.

Display headings
- Today's theme is the annunciation.
- The manger is an animal feeding trough.
- God chose an ordinary family to be Jesus' parents.
- Ordinary people are still chosen to do God's work.
- Gabriel prepared for the coming of Jesus.
- Our project today is about the Christmas crib.

Using the bible
The story of the Annunciation (LUKE 1, 26-38A)
Help the listeners to put themselves in Mary's shoes as she prepares for the birth of Jesus.

> Mary is a young woman from an ordinary background.
> Mary's family is distantly descended from Aaron, the priest.
> Mary is betrothed to Joseph, an ordinary man.
> Joseph's family is distantly descended from David, the king.
> Gabriel is God's messenger.
> Gabriel tells Mary that she will have a son.
> Mary is to call her son Jesus.
> Mary says 'I am the Lord's servant, let it happen as God has said.'

Dance/drama
- Devise a dance about the story of the Annunciation. Begin with Mary going about the normal household tasks, etc.
- Develop a nativity play.

Games
- Play animals, for example the children take turns in imitating an animal which may have come to the manger seeking food and have met there the infant Jesus.

EXPLORING WITH ADULTS

Introduction
Bring in a wooden box like those containing fruit at a green grocery. Ask the group about the use of this box as a make shift crib.

Experience
- What is your image of a manger (animal feeding trough) on a farm?
- What are the normal preparations for the birth of a baby?
- What does the use of the manger show about the birth of Jesus?

Scripture
Read LUKE 1, 26-38A
- What does this story show about Mary?
- How do you interpret this story about Mary for today?
- What does this story show about God's choice of men and women?

Integration
- How does God choose ordinary people to bring Christ to birth in today's world?
- How do you feel about God's choice of ordinary people?
- How does God's choice of ordinary people affect your life?

Application
- What can your church do to bring Christ to birth in today's world?
- What can you do to bring Christ to birth in today's world?
- How can your church best present the message of the Christmas crib?

CELEBRATING TOGETHER

Welcoming children

Make space during the service for the display of the children's crib to be viewed and discussed. Bless the crib scene in readiness for the Christmas services. If the children have prepared a dance about the story of the Annunciation, this can be presented after the Gospel reading. As a special way of emphasising today's theme, light the fourth of the candles on the Advent wreath, as a symbol of Gabriel preparing for the birth of Christ.

All age activity

Invite members of the congregation to bring a picture of a crib scene, perhaps on a Christmas card or a postcard of an old master. In small groups invite them to discuss the various images and then to group the different types of images around the church. The following issues can be explored in buzz groups, discussion or teaching:

- classical images of the Christmas crib;
- contemporary images of the Christmas crib;
- the different images of Mary;
- the different images of the Christ child;
- the reality behind the many images;
- the meaning behind the images.

Teaching point

The angel Gabriel was sent to prepare Mary for the birth of Jesus. Today we prepare for Jesus' coming by building his crib in church and by inviting him to be born in our hearts.

WORSHIP RESOURCES

Prayer

Almighty God,
you chose the Blessed Virgin Mary
to be the mother of the promised Saviour:
Fill us with your grace,
that in all things we may accept your holy will
and with her rejoice in your salvation;
through Jesus Christ our Lord.

Readings

Old Testament - Isaiah 11, 1-9
New Testament - 1 Corinthians 1, 26-31
Gospel - Luke 1, 26-38a

Hymns and songs

Come and Praise

    23 Jesus, good above all other
123 Mary had a baby

Hymns Ancient and Modern New Standard

  28 Lo, he comes with clouds descending
  31 Come, thou long-expected Jesus
309 The God whom earth and sea and sky
354 Every star shall sing a carol
360 For Mary, mother of our Lord
391 Lord Jesus Christ
400 No use knocking on the window
419 Sing we a song of high revolt
422 Tell out, my soul, the greatness of the Lord

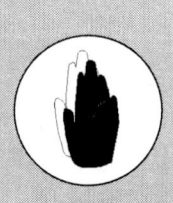

10

Christmas visitors

PREPARATION

Bible theme

The incarnation (1ST SUNDAY AFTER CHRISTMAS)

The word 'incarnation' means 'made flesh'. The theology of incarnation expresses the belief that God became human. The Gospel reading sums up this belief that 'the word became flesh and dwelt among us.' Through the incarnation God is made known in a form which we can recognise and to which we can respond. This is the God with whom we meet in the Christ child born at Christmas. According to the Old Testament reading this child called 'Emmanuel' is a sign given by God. According to the New Testament reading this sign guarantees our own acceptance by God. The incarnation demands a response from us just as the shepherds responded at that first Christmas by leaving their sheep and coming to Jesus. We can begin to experience the significance of the church's teaching on the incarnation by exploring how the first Christmas visitors came face to face with God in the Christ child.

Aims
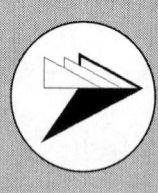

- to build on our experiences of Christmas visitors;
- to help us understand the visit of the shepherds;
- to shape our own response to the incarnation.

Hearing the scriptures
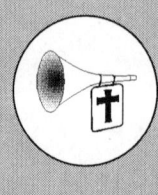

ISAIAH 7, 10-14

Names were important to the Hebrew people. The naming of the child in Isaiah's prophecy to King Ahaz is the assurance that God will return to be with the people. The name 'Emmanuel' means 'God is with us'. Matthew's gospel 1, 23 shows how this text was interpreted as a prophecy pointing to Jesus. In the person of Jesus God is with us.

Galatians 4, 1-7

Paul is expounding the significance of the incarnation from his personal experience. Once Paul had felt like a slave to the old Jewish law. After his conversion, Paul experienced a new freedom. Because of the incarnation of God's son, Paul too could experience what it is to be a child of God rather than a slave.

John 1, 14-18

At the beginning of his gospel John explores the idea of the incarnation: 'the word became flesh and dwelt among us.' In the Greek the idea translated 'dwelt' literally means 'pitched the tent'. Through the incarnation God is made known among people. What John expresses in philosophical language, Luke expresses pictorially by describing the visit and response of the shepherds.

EXPLORING WITH CHILDREN

Starting

Encourage the children to talk about their own Christmas. Give particular attention to the visits they made and to the visitors they received at home. Include mention of aunts, uncles, cousins, grandparents, neighbours, friends, perhaps even Father Christmas. Draw out ideas of:

- why people visit at Christmas;
- people we only see at Christmas;
- people we often see but in a special way at Christmas;
- how we welcome visitors at Christmas;
- special celebrations with visitors;
- special meals with visitors;
- exchanging presents with visitors.

Making

Give the children the opportunity to identify with the shepherds and, thereby, to make their own personal pilgrimage to the Christmas crib. Here are some suggestions.

- Extend the crib scene by adding sheep and shepherds, the angel messenger and the heavenly choir.
- Make a visitors' book for those who come to visit the crib in church.
- Make shepherds' crooks which can be given to the congregation.
- Make shepherds' head-dresses which can be given to the congregation.
- Make large cut out shapes of sheep which can be given to the congregation.
- Design a collage about the shepherds' visit.

Doing
- Invite someone to come as a surprise visitor.
- Invite parents with a newborn baby to visit the group.
- Arrange to go visiting, perhaps to housebound members of the congregation to sing carols with them.
- Invite an overseas visitor to talk of his or her Christmas traditions.
- Invite a health worker to talk about his or her job of visiting.
- Invite the clergy to talk about why they visit people.

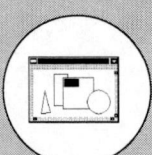

Display headings
- Today's theme is the incarnation.
- The shepherds were the first to hear about Jesus' birth.
- The shepherds responded to the good news by going to visit the baby Jesus.
- The incarnation means that God became human.
- Our project today is about Christmas visitors.

Using the bible
The story of the shepherds' visit to the baby Jesus (LUKE 2, 8-20)
Help the listeners to identify with the shepherds as they hear the good news of the birth of Christ, as they journey to Bethlehem and as they come face to face with God in the Christ child.

> The shepherds are on night duty caring for their sheep.
> They are surprised by the angel's visit.
> The angel's message says, 'I bring you good news'.
> The heavenly chorus sings, 'Glory to God'.
> The shepherds go immediately to Bethlehem.
> They find Mary, Joseph and the baby in the manger.
> The shepherds return to their fields glorifying God.

Dance/drama
- Devise a dance about visiting friends at Christmas time.
- Develop a play about the visit of the shepherds to see the baby Jesus.

Games
- Play 'who am I?' Invite the children to take turns in miming the activity of a Christmas visitor, for example carol singers, grandma, Father Christmas, the shepherds at Bethlehem, and for the other children to try to guess who it is.

EXPLORING WITH ADULTS

Introduction
Display a large poster listing all the Christmas services held in your church. Ask the group to talk about the many visitors who attended the services during the Christmas festival.

Experience
- Who were the visitors who came to your church this Christmas?
- How did your church make these visitors welcome?
- How did your church help these 'visitors' meet with Christ?

Scripture
Read LUKE 2, 8-20
- What does this story say about the shepherds coming face to face with Christ?
- How do you interpret the story of the shepherds for today?
- What does this story say about God's presence among men and women?

Integration
- How do men and women come face to face with Christ today?
- How do you come face to face with Christ today?
- How have you responded to Christ's presence?

Application
- How can your church help make Christ's presence known to visitors today?
- How can you help make Christ's presence known to visitors today?
- How can the eucharist help visitors to recognise the presence of Christ?

CELEBRATING TOGETHER

Welcoming children
Make space during the service for the display of the children's work on Christmas visitors to be viewed and discussed. If the children have devised a dance about visiting friends at Christmas, this can be presented at the Peace. If they have developed a play about the visit of the shepherds to see the baby Jesus, this can be presented during the Ministry of the Word.

All age activity
Invite members of the congregation to come to the service prepared to enter into the spirit of joining the shepherds on pilgrimage to Bethlehem. Some may wish to dress up for the occasion. When they come into church, invite as many of the congregation as wish to become shepherds. Give them a crook, a head dress, a cardboard sheep, or some other symbol made by the children. During the service place the model shepherds into the crib scene and invite all the shepherds in the congregation to make pilgrimage to the crib. Sing 'While shepherds watched.' The following ideas can be explored in buzz groups, discussion or teaching:

- our experiences of Christmas visitors;
- why people visit at Christmas time;
- the visits we would like to make at Christmas time;
- why the shepherds went visiting;
- the impact the visit made on the shepherds.

Teaching point
Ever since the first Christmas the birth of Christ has called out a response from men and women and changed their lives. The shepherds were the first to hear and they immediately left everything to go to visit the stable. This Christmas, we, too, are challenged to respond to the birth of Christ.

WORSHIP RESOURCES

Prayer

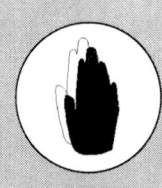

Almighty God
who wonderfully created us in your image,
and yet more wonderfully restored us
through your Son Jesus Christ:
Grant that as he came to share our humanity,
so we may share the life of his divinity;
who lives and reigns with you and the Holy Spirit,
one God, now and for ever.

Readings

Old Testament - ISAIAH 7, 10-14
New Testament - GALATIANS 4, 1-7
Gospel - JOHN 1, 14-18

Hymns and songs

Come and Praise

- 21 Come and praise the Lord our king, hallelujah
- 116 There's a star in the east

Hymns Ancient and Modern New Standard

- 325 Of the father's love begotten
- 34 O come, all ye faithful
- 35 Hark! the herald-angels sing
- 36 Christians, awake! salute the happy morn
- 37 While shepherds watched their flocks by night
- 39 Angels, from the realms of glory
- 413 O sing a song of Bethlehem
- 462 'Glory to God!' all heav'n with joy is ringing
- 527 Where is this stupendous stranger?

11

Christmas presents

PREPARATION

Bible theme

The Epiphany of our Lord (2ND SUNDAY AFTER CHRISTMAS/ EPIPHANY)

The word 'Epiphany' means 'showing'. The feast of the Epiphany celebrates the revelation (or showing) of Christ to the 'wise men', visitors from the east who symbolise the non-Jewish world or Gentile nations. The feast of the Epiphany, therefore, claims that Christ is born for the whole world. The Gospel reading is Matthew's account of these visitors and of the gifts which they bring. Both the Old Testament prophecy from Isaiah and the New Testament reading confirm that God's message is for the distant nations and for the Gentiles as well as for God's chosen people of old. We can begin to experience the significance of the church's teaching on the Epiphany of our Lord by exploring the response of the first Gentile visitors and the gifts they brought to the Christ child.

Aims
- to build on our experiences of Christmas presents;
- to help us understand the gifts brought by the wise men;
- to provide an opportunity for us to present our gifts to the infant Christ.

Hearing the scriptures

ISAIAH 49, 1-6

This passage is from the second of the four servant songs in Second Isaiah. The church has used this passage to illuminate the significance of the Epiphany where God makes the servant 'a light to the nations'.

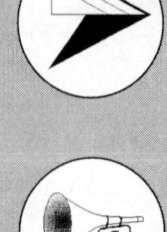

EPHESIANS 3, 1-12

Paul emphasises how God gave him the 'privilege of taking to the Gentiles the good news about the infinite riches of Christ.' In this work Paul is continuing the process begun when the infant Christ was made known to the wise men.

MATTHEW 2, 1-12

Mark's gospel says nothing about the birth and infancy of Jesus. Luke tells of the first Christmas night and the visit of the shepherds. Matthew tells of the wise men from the east and the gifts they bring. Matthew does not call them kings, nor does he number them. All this is left for later piety and legend. Matthew simply calls them 'magi'. Traditionally their gifts have been considered to symbolise wealth and kingship (gold), worship and priesthood (frankincense) and mortality and death (myrrh).

EXPLORING WITH CHILDREN

Starting

Bring some of the Christmas presents you received, wrapped up again as if it were Christmas morning. Choose things which are amusing rather than valuable and wrap them in several layers of paper. Perhaps include a box of sweets which can be later shared with the children. Unwrap the presents while the children watch. Draw out ideas of:

- why we give Christmas presents;
- how we choose Christmas presents;
- why we wrap them up;
- how we feel when we unwrap them;
- the presents they gave to others;
- the presents they received;
- their favourite presents.

Making

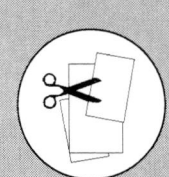

Give the children the opportunity to make a display concerned with Christmas presents and help them to identify with the wise men as they brought their presents to the infant Jesus. Here are some suggestions.

- Extend the crib scene by adding the wise men and their gifts.
- Make a display of Christmas presents.
- Make a display of Christmas wrapping paper.
- Design a collage of the wise men.
- Make a collection of gifts which can be given to a charity.

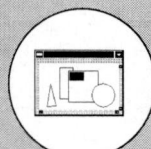

- Design gifts symbolic of gold, frankincense, myrrh.
- Make wise men's crowns for the congregation to wear.
- Make symbolic gifts for the congregation to carry.

Doing
- Invite the children to bring their favourite Christmas presents.
- Invite some people to talk about their Christmas presents.
- Discuss the twelve days of Christmas.
- Look at some gold.
- Burn some incense.
- Find out how Epiphany is celebrated in other parts of the world.

Display headings
- Today's theme is the Epiphany of our Lord.
- The wise men brought presents to the infant Jesus.
- Gold points to wealth and kingship.
- Frankincense points to worship and priesthood.
- Myrrh points to mortality and death.
- We bring our gifts to the infant Jesus.
- Our project today is about Christmas presents.

Using the bible
The story of the wise men (MATTHEW 2, 1-12)
Help the listeners to identify with the wise men as they see the Bethlehem star, set out on their long journey and present their gifts to the Christ child.

> The wise men came from the east.
> They had seen the Bethlehem star.
> They had travelled many miles.
> They ask King Herod for directions.
> They find Mary and Jesus and worship him.
> They offer him gifts: gold, frankincense and myrrh.

Dance/drama
- Devise a dance about giving and receiving Christmas presents.
- Develop a play about the visit of the wise men and the gifts they bring.

Games
- Wrap some small Christmas presents in many layers of wrapping paper and play 'pass the parcel.'

EXPLORING WITH ADULTS

Introduction
Bring some of the Christmas presents that the group has received. Share the significance of these gifts with one another.

Experience
- Why did you give Christmas presents?
- How did you feel about giving Christmas presents?
- How did you feel about receiving Christmas presents?

Scripture
Read MATTHEW 2, 1-12
- What is the significance of the magi's gifts in this story?
- How do you interpret the magi's gifts for today?
- What does this story say about offering gifts to God?

Integration
- What gifts can people offer to God today?
- How do you feel about offering these gifts to God?
- How can these gifts be used by God?

Application
- What gifts can your church offer to God?
- What gifts can you offer to God?
- How can the Offertory best symbolise offering our gifts to God?

CELEBRATING TOGETHER

Welcoming children

Make space during the service for the display of the children's work on Christmas presents to be viewed and discussed. If the children have devised a dance about giving and receiving Christmas presents, this can be presented at the Peace. If they have developed a play about the visit of the wise men and the gifts they bring, this can be presented during the Ministry of the Word.

All age activity

Invite members of the congregation to come to the service prepared to enter into the spirit of joining the wise men as they present gifts to the Christ child. Some may wish to dress up for the occasion. When they come into church, invite as many of the congregation as wish to become wise men or wise women. Give them a crown or a token gift. During the service place the model wise men into the crib scene and invite all the wise men or wise women in the congregation to make pilgrimage to the crib. Sing 'As with gladness men of old.' Perhaps incense can be used at the crib to highlight the gift of frankincense. Children and adults can be invited to bring a gift to the service which they can place by the crib and which can be used by a Christian charity. The following ideas can be explored in buzz groups, discussion or teaching:

- our experiences of giving and receiving presents at Christmas;
- the reasons for giving Christmas presents;
- why the wise men brought gifts to the Christ child;
- the impact the visit made on the wise men;
- the gifts we would like to present to the Christ child.

Teaching point

At Epiphany the wise men brought gifts of gold, frankincense and myrrh to the infant Jesus. We, too, are invited to bring our gifts to his cradle and to offer them to his service.

WORSHIP RESOURCES

Prayer

Eternal God,
by the shining of a star
you led the wise men to the worship of your Son:
Grant that all the nations of the earth,
may be guided by his light,
so the whole world may behold your glory;
through Jesus Christ our Lord.

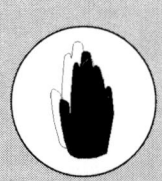

Readings

Old Testament - ISAIAH 49, 1-6
New Testament - EPHESIANS 3, 1-12
Gospel - MATTHEW 2, 1-12

Hymns and songs

Come and Praise

   26 There is singing in the desert
   59 I will bring to you the best gift I can offer
   64 The wise may bring their learning
115 Come in, my royal masters

Hymns Ancient and Modern New Standard

   48 Earth has many a noble city
   49 O worship the Lord in the beauty of holiness!
   51 As with gladness men of old
352 Dear Lord, to you again our gifts we bring
393 Lord of all good, our gifts we bring to thee
395 Lord of all power, I give you my will
495 Lord, to you we bring our treasure

12

Coronation

PREPARATION

Bible theme
The baptism of Jesus (1ST SUNDAY AFTER THE EPIPHANY)
The key reading is the Gospel: it describes Jesus' baptism as a form of anointing. In Hebrew thought kings are made by anointing. The Hebrew word 'Messiah' and the Greek word 'Christ' both mean 'the anointed one', 'the king'. The baptism of Jesus, thus, declares his kingship. The Old Testament reading is chosen to show Samuel anointing David as king. The New Testament reading also summarises the story of the baptism of Jesus. We can begin to experience the significance of the bible's teaching about the baptism and kingship of Jesus by exploring the coronation of kings and queens in history and in today's world.

Aims
- to build on our experiences of kings and queens;
- to help us understand the images of coronation;
- to see the baptism of Jesus as a proclamation of his kingship.

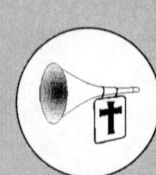

Hearing the scriptures
1 SAMUEL 16, 1-13A
Some years earlier Samuel had made Saul the first king of Israel, by anointing him with oil. Saul's kingship had not gone well and now the Lord tells Samuel to fill his horn with oil again, to go to Bethlehem and to anoint one of Jesse's sons as king in Saul's place. All of Jesse's sons are presented to Samuel, who eventually chooses the youngest, David, not the oldest. Samuel anoints David with the oil and 'then the Spirit of the Lord came upon David'.

ACTS 10, 34-38A
Peter is speaking to Cornelius, a Roman centurion. Peter summarises the gospel narrative of Jesus' ministry, death and resurrection. Like Mark's gospel, Peter starts his story, not by telling of Jesus' birth, but by telling of the baptism proclaimed by John and the way God anointed Jesus with the Holy Spirit.

MATTHEW 3, 13-17
Like Samuel in the Old Testament reading, John has an important and specific task to perform: he baptises Jesus with water. Just as Samuel's anointing was confirmed by God's spirit coming upon David, so John's baptism is confirmed by 'the Spirit of God descending like a dove' to alight on Jesus. The words 'This is my son' echo psalm 2, a psalm used to celebrate the anointing of a king.

EXPLORING WITH CHILDREN

Starting
Bring some pictures of the royal family, Buckingham Palace, Sandringham, the royal dogs. Encourage the children to talk about the royal family and develop any particularly topical events. Discuss what happens at a coronation. Draw out ideas of:

- the pomp and pageantry;
- the state coach and horses;
- the drive to the abbey;
- the crowds in the street;
- the procession in the Cathedral;
- the anointing;
- the crowning;
- the public parties and street celebrations;
- the flag waving.

Making
Give the children the opportunity to make a display associated with kings and queens, and coronations in particular. Here are some suggestions.

- Make crowns from card, with bright jewels.
- Make banners and flags to wave in the procession.
- Design a collage of the royal coach and procession; each child can add his or her own face to the crowd.
- Design a collage of the baptism of Jesus; again each child can add his or her own face to the crowd.

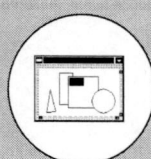

Doing

- Talk about street names, like Coronation Street, Jubilee Way, etc., and why they were so named.
- Produce photographs of the coronation, or of a local coronation party.
- Invite a member of the community to talk about their memories of a coronation.
- Display coronation souvenirs, like coronation mugs.
- Look at the king and queen from a chess set.

Display headings

- Today's theme is the baptism of Jesus.
- At his baptism Jesus was anointed with the Holy Spirit.
- Jesus is the Christ.
- Christ means 'the anointed one.'
- Kings and queens are anointed at their coronation.
- Jesus was anointed king.
- Our project today is about coronations.

Using the bible

The story of the baptism of Jesus (MATTHEW 3, 13-17)
Help the listeners to hear this account of the baptism of Jesus as his public anointing as the Christ.

> John the Baptist teaches at the river Jordan.
> Crowds of people come to be baptised.
> John meets with Jesus.
> Jesus is baptised in water.
> Jesus is anointed with the spirit, like a dove.
> The voice from heaven says 'This is my Son.'

Dance/drama

- Act out a coronation.
- Act out the baptism of Jesus.
- Devise a dance about crowning.

Games

- Adapt 'pass the parcel' to become 'pass the crown'. When the music stops the person left wearing the crown has to perform some 'royal task'; for example, launch a boat, feed the royal dogs, open a fête.

EXPLORING WITH ADULTS

Introduction
Take a jar of oil into the group. Ask the group to talk about the use of oil by the church at a service of coronation.

Experience
- What experiences have you of coronations, either in real life or on film?
- What public feelings are associated with coronations?
- How is the anointing given importance at coronations?

Scripture
Read MATTHEW 12, 13-17
- What does this story say about anointing with the Spirit at Jesus' baptism?
- How do you interpret the story of Jesus' baptism for today?
- What does this story say about the person of Jesus?

Integration
- What does Jesus' baptism say about his kingship?
- How is Jesus king in the life of God's people?
- How does Jesus' kingship affect your life?

Application
- How can your church best affirm the kingship of Jesus?
- How can you best affirm the kingship of Jesus?
- What hymns can help your church to celebrate Jesus as king?

CELEBRATING TOGETHER

Welcoming children
Make space during the service for the display of the children's work on coronations to be viewed and discussed. During the service let the children share their drama and dance. If they have made banners and flags for a coronation procession, let them process round the church while the congregation sings 'All hail the power of Jesus' name!' and enact the crowning during the last line of each verse.

All age activity
Invite members of the congregation to bring some memorabilia from past coronations, including pictures, photographs, souvenir mugs, etc. Display these pictures and artifacts in church. The following ideas can be explored in buzz groups, discussion or teaching:

- our experience of coronations in real life;
- our images of coronations from films and television;
- the ceremonies at the coronation service;
- the significance of anointing;
- the significance of John anointing Jesus with water.

Teaching point
We see today how at his baptism Jesus was declared to be the Messiah, the Christ, the king, the anointed one.

WORSHIP RESOURCES

Prayer

Almighty God,
who anointed Jesus at his baptism with the Holy Spirit
and revealed him as your beloved Son:
Inspire us, your children,
who are born of water and the Spirit,
to surrender our lives to your service,
that we may rejoice to be called sons and daughters of God;
through Jesus Christ our Lord.

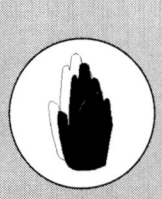

Readings

Old Testament - 1 SAMUEL 16, 1-13A
New Testament - ACTS 10, 34-38A
Gospel - MATTHEW 3, 13-17

Hymns and songs

Come and Praise

  54 The king of love my shepherd is
  58 At the name of Jesus
  63 Spirit of God, as strong as the wind
106 It's a new day

Hymns Ancient and Modern New Standard

  53 Songs of thankfulness and praise
139 Rejoice! the Lord is king!
140 All hail the power of Jesus' name!
142 Hail to the Lord's anointed
147 Crown him with many crowns
442 Christ, when for us you were baptised
526 When Jesus came to Jordan

13 Friends

PREPARATION

Bible theme

The first disciples (2ND SUNDAY AFTER THE EPIPHANY)

The key reading is the Gospel, which describes Jesus calling the first four disciples: Simon, Andrew, James and John. The disciples are Jesus' closest friends. They share his way of life, learn from his teaching and example, and help to extend his work. The Old Testament reading is chosen to show the call of Jeremiah, the prophet. The New Testament reading describes the way in which Paul was called to become an apostle. We can begin to experience the significance of the theme of the first disciples by exploring the idea of friends and friendship.

Aims

- to build on our experiences of friends;
- to develop our understanding of friendship;
- to see the disciples as Jesus' close friends.

Hearing the scriptures

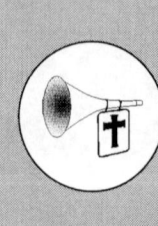

JEREMIAH 1, 4-10

These verses tell how Jeremiah experienced God's call to be a prophet, in the year 627 BC. God had chosen Jeremiah, even before he was born, and set him apart for a special responsibility. God says to Jeremiah, 'I appoint you a prophet to the nations.' Jeremiah is very conscious of his own inadequacy. God, however, promises to equip Jeremiah for the task to which he has been called.

Acts 26, 1 and 9-20

Paul is being tried before Agrippa and is given permission to speak in his own defence. Paul explains how his conversion came about, from being a chief persecutor of Christianity to becoming a Christian. He describes his meeting with Jesus on the Damascus road and how Jesus said, 'I have appeared to you for a purpose: to appoint you my servant and witness.'

Mark 1, 14-20

According to Mark's gospel Jesus begins his ministry not by teaching or by healing, but by choosing a group of disciples to be with him and to share his work. The first four to be chosen are Simon Peter and his brother Andrew, James and his brother John. A little later Mark describes the call of Levi. Eventually there are twelve chosen. Mark lists their names as Simon Peter, James and John, Andrew, Philip, Bartholomew, Matthew, Thomas, James son of Alphaeus, Thaddaeus, Simon the Zealot and Judas Iscariot.

EXPLORING WITH CHILDREN

Starting

Bring some pictures of children doing things with their friends, playing outdoors, walking, swimming, playing indoor games, and so on. Get the children talking about what they like doing with their friends. Draw out ideas of:

- the companionship of friends;
- competition and co-operation between friends;
- games friends play together;
- going places together;
- making things together;
- listening to music together;
- groups and organisations which friends attend together;
- schools where friendships are made.

Making

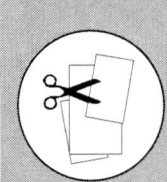

Give the children the opportunity to make a display about friends and friendship, and about disciples and discipleship. Here are some suggestions.

- Make a collage showing the things the children like doing with their friends.
- Create a set of life size pictures of the twelve disciples; the children can draw round each other to make the outline.
- Make a chain of friends, holding hands; fold paper into a concertina, draw a figure linking at both sides and cut out.

- Design a seaside scene of Andrew, Simon, James and John with their boats;
- Make some sort of insignia to show that we too are friends of Jesus; perhaps a simple label bearing the name 'Jesus', to be worn on a necklace or badge.

Doing
- Find pictures which illustrate friendship.
- Ask the children to bring their own pictures of their friends.
- Ask the children to talk about the kind of friend they would like.
- Invite a member of the community to talk about their friends.

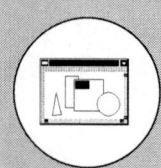

Display headings
- Today's theme is the first disciples.
- Jesus calls Simon and Andrew, James and John to become fishers of people.
- Jesus chooses twelve people to be his special friends or disciples.
- The disciples learn from Jesus and follow his example.
- Our project today is about friends.

Using the bible
Tell how Jesus chose a group of twelve people to be his close friends.
Help the listeners to appreciate the importance of the disciples in Jesus' life, and the great variety of people included among his closest friends.

> Simon Peter, Andrew, James and John had been fishermen.
> They had left their work and their home to be with Jesus.
> James and John he nicknamed 'Sons of Thunder' - they were a hot-headed pair (see LUKE 9, 54).
> Peter he nicknamed 'the Rock', a solid fellow (see MATTHEW 16, 18).
> The friends included Levi, who had worked for the Romans collecting taxes.
> The friends included Simon the Zealot, who belonged to the group who wanted to overthrow Roman rule.
> The friends included Judas Iscariot who turned traitor.

Dance/drama
- Act out the call of the first disciples.
- Devise a dance about Jesus calling Simon, Andrew, James and John away from their boats.

Games
- Explore some co-operative games, which can only be fulfilled with a friend; for example three legged race, wheelbarrow race, squeak piggy squeak, blind fold leading.

EXPLORING WITH ADULTS

Introduction
Show the group a gift that has been given by a friend. Ask the group to discover why the object is precious and what it represents to its owner.

Experience
- What are your experiences of friendship?
- What is important to you in friendships?
- What makes the relationship between friends special?

Scripture
Read MARK 1, 14-20
- What does this story say about Jesus' understanding of friends?
- How do you interpret this story about the first disciples for today?
- What does this story say about Jesus' friendship with men and women?

Integration
- How does Jesus call people to follow him today?
- How did you receive the call to follow Jesus?
- How does Jesus' call to follow him affect your life?

Application
- How can your church call people to follow Jesus today?
- How can you respond to Jesus' call to follow him today?
- How can the Offertory symbolise response to God's call to discipleship?

CELEBRATING TOGETHER

Welcoming children
Make space during the service for the display of the children's work on friends to be viewed and discussed. If they have prepared a dance about Jesus calling Simon, Andrew, James and John away from their boats, this can be presented after the Gospel reading. If they have made a set of necklaces or badges bearing the name 'Jesus', call them out one at a time and present the necklaces as a sign of their calling to be among Jesus' friends.

All age activity
Invite members of the congregation to bring something which reminds them of friendship, for example, a birthday card which has been sent to them, the special recipe used to cook a meal for friends, the golf clubs used to play with friends. Display these tokens of friendship in church. The following ideas can be explored in buzz groups, discussion or teaching:

- our experiences of deep friendship;
- our longest standing friends;
- what makes friends special;
- our images of the disciples;
- the part played by the disciples in Jesus' life.

Teaching point
We see today how Jesus began to choose a set of close friends to be his disciples, to learn from him, to follow his example and to share his work. We too are called to be Jesus' friends.

WORSHIP RESOURCES

Prayer
Almighty God,
by your grace alone we have been accepted,
and called to your service:
Strengthen and inspire us by your Holy Spirit,
and make us worthy of our calling;
through Jesus Christ our Lord.

Readings
Old Testament - JEREMIAH 1, 4-10
New Testament - ACTS 26, 1 AND 9-20
Gospel - MARK 1, 14-20

Hymns and songs
Come and Praise
- 25 When Jesus walked in Galilee
- 27 There's a child in the streets
- 57 Think of all the things we lose
- 69 I belong to a family, the biggest on earth
- 103 I am planting my feet in the footsteps

Hymns Ancient and Modern New Standard
- 115 Dear Lord and father of mankind
- 312 Jesus calls us! o'er the tumult
- 382 Jesus our Lord, our king and our God
- 391 Lord Jesus Christ
- 392 Lord Jesus, once you spoke to men
- 529 Who are we who stand and sing?

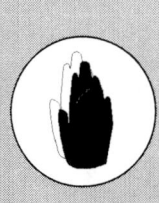

14

Wedding reception

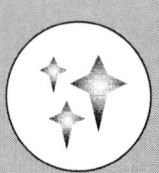

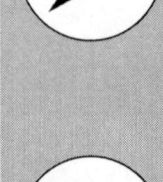

PREPARATION

Bible theme

Signs of glory (3RD SUNDAY AFTER THE EPIPHANY)

The key concept which draws these three readings together is the idea of glory. Glory means the visible signs by which God's presence is made known in the world. All three readings speak of ways in which God has been revealed and through which men and women have been enabled to see the glory of God. In the Old Testament reading Moses asks to see God's glory. In the New Testament reading John points to the way God's presence is known through Jesus. In the Gospel reading John points to the wedding at Cana-in-Galilee where Jesus' glory was revealed. We can begin to experience the significance of the gospel reading's teaching on glory by exploring the theme of wedding receptions.

Aims

- to build on our experiences of parties and celebrations;
- to help us understand the image of a wedding reception;
- to see the wedding at Cana-in-Galilee as the great celebration in God's kingdom, in which we share today through the eucharist.

Hearing the scriptures

EXODUS 33, 12-23

Moses has led the escape from Egypt. Now Moses seeks assurance that God will travel with the people on their journey. Moses asks God, 'Show me your glory, I beg you.' This was a bold request, for it was believed that men and women could not look on God and live. Moses' request was only partly granted; Moses is not allowed to see God's face, but only God's back.

1 JOHN 1, 1-7

The writer of the first letter of John argues that in Jesus we meet 'the word of life which has existed from the very beginning.' In Jesus God's presence is made known in the world.

JOHN 2, 1-11

John tells the story of the wedding at Cana-in-Galilee immediately after the call of the first disciples. When the wine runs out Jesus replenishes the supply, and water is turned into wine. It is verse 11 which explains why John starts with this story: it 'is the first of the signs by which Jesus revealed his glory and led his disciples to believe in him.' It is no accident that the first 'sign' takes place at a wedding feast. In Jewish thought the wedding feast is a way of speaking about God's kingdom, when the Messiah will preside at the banquet. By providing the new wine, Jesus is showing his claim to preside at the banquet and to be the Messiah.

EXPLORING WITH CHILDREN

Starting

Bring some pictures of weddings, the bride and groom at the church, the guests and the reception. Get the children talking about weddings which they have attended, or recent weddings at the local church, and concentrate particularly on the reception. Draw out ideas of:

- the clothes worn by the bride and groom;
- the bridesmaids;
- the wedding cars;
- the guests;
- the service in church;
- the photographer;
- the confetti;
- the reception;
- the food;
- the drink;
- the cake;
- the speeches.

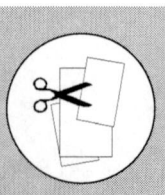

Making

Give the children the opportunity to make a display about weddings and wedding receptions. Here are some suggestions.

- Bake a special 'wedding cake'.
- Make wedding decorations, like hearts and bells from card covered with tin foil.
- Design wedding invitations and wedding cards.
- Design a collage of a wedding today; each child can add his or her own picture to the crowd.
- Decorate the church for a wedding.
- Design a collage of the wedding at Cana-in-Galilee; each child can add his or her own picture to the crowd.
- Design a collage of the communion service; each child can add his or her own picture to the congregation.
- Make a 'photograph album' of drawings showing various stages of the wedding service and reception.

Doing

- Ask the children to bring their own photographs of weddings.
- Invite a member of the community to talk about their own wedding.
- Look at pictures of wedding cakes, wedding dresses, etc.

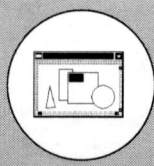

Display headings

- Today's theme is signs of glory.
- Glory means signs of God's activity in the world.
- Jesus attended a wedding at Cana-in-Galilee.
- Jesus turned water into wine.
- Jesus invites us to feast and drink with him.
- Our project today is about weddings and wedding receptions.

Using the bible

The story of the wedding at Cana-in-Galilee (JOHN 2, 1-11)

Help the listeners to identify with the drama of the story, to experience the excitement of the wedding and to feel the power of Jesus' presence.

> Jesus' mother and disciples are guests.
> The wine runs out.
> Jesus' mother tells him that the wine has run out.
> Jesus tells the servants to fill large stone jars with water.
> The water is turned to wine.
> The man in charge of the feast says the wine is even better than that which they had been drinking earlier.
> This is a sign by which Jesus makes himself known.

Dance/drama
- Act out a wedding and the reception.
- Act out the wedding in Cana-in-Galilee.
- Devise a dance about pouring wine.

Games
- Arrange some energetic dancing of celebration, like disco dancing or traditional country dancing, which might take place after the reception.

EXPLORING WITH ADULTS

Introduction
Look at some greeting cards read at a wedding reception. Read the messages. Ask the group to discuss the function of this part of the reception.

Experience
- What are your experiences of wedding receptions?
- What makes a good wedding reception?
- How do you feel about a wedding reception?

Scripture
Read JOHN 2, 1-11
- What does this story say about signs of God's glory?
- How do you interpret this story about the wedding at Cana for today?
- What does this story say about who Jesus is?

Integration
- How do people see God's glory revealed today?
- How do you see God's glory revealed today?
- What impact does experiencing God's glory have on lives?

Application
- How can the church make God's glory visible today?
- How can you make God's glory visible in your life?
- How can worship help people to experience the glory of God?

CELEBRATING TOGETHER

Welcoming children
Make space during the service for the display of the children's work on weddings and wedding receptions to be viewed and discussed. If the children have prepared drama on the wedding in Cana-in-Galilee, this can be presented after the Gospel reading. If they have devised a dance about pouring wine, this can be presented at the Offertory.

All age activity
Invite members of the congregation to bring a small contribution of food or drink which could be shared at a 'wedding reception' before the dismissal at the end of the service (or after the service). If the children have made a wedding cake, let them cut it into small pieces and share it with the whole congregation during the 'wedding reception'. The following ideas can be explored in buzz groups, discussion or teaching:

- our personal experiences of wedding receptions;
- images of wedding receptions generated by films or television;
- the special atmosphere of wedding receptions;
- the wedding at Cana-in-Galilee;
- the significance of Jesus' presidency at the wedding feast.

Teaching point
When Jesus turned the water into wine, he revealed his glory and began to lead his disciples to believe in him.

WORSHIP RESOURCES

Prayer

Almighty God,
whose Son revealed in signs and miracles
the wonder of your saving love:
Enrich your people with your heavenly grace,
and in all our weakness
sustain us by your mighty power;
through Jesus Christ our Lord.

Readings

Old Testament - EXODUS 33, 12-23
New Testament - 1 JOHN 1, 1-7
Gospel - JOHN 2, 1-11

Hymns and songs

Come and Praise

   5 Carpenter, carpenter, make me a tree
   9 Fill your hearts with joy and gladness
 32 Thank you, Lord, for this new day
 58 At the name of Jesus
 93 Morning sun, morning sun

Hymns Ancient and Modern New Standard

 53 Songs of thankfulness and praise
156 Come down, O love divine
262 Alleluia! sing to Jesus!
422 Tell out my soul
440 Christ is the world's light, he and none other
445 Christians, lift up your hearts

15

Churches

PREPARATION

Bible theme

The new temple (4TH SUNDAY AFTER THE EPIPHANY)

All three readings develop the significance of the 'temple' in Christian thinking. The Old Testament reading emphasises that the temple is not a place where God lives; rather the temple stands as a symbol for God's presence among the people. Where the temple is, there God's presence is demonstrated. The Gospel reading is saying that Jesus, like the temple of old, demonstrates God's presence. The New Testament reading is saying that Christian men and women continue the function of God's temple in today's world. We can begin to experience the significance of the bible's teaching on the temple by exploring how churches function in today's world.

Aims

- to build on our experiences of church buildings;
- to help us understand churches as symbols of God's presence in the world;
- to see how God's people use church buildings to witness to God's presence in the world.

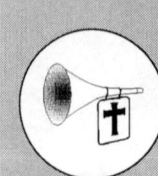

Hearing the scriptures

1 KINGS 8, 22-30

King David planned to build a temple in Jerusalem; his son Solomon completed it. Here Solomon is offering his prayer for the dedication of the temple. The prayer begins by calling to mind the promises God made with David. Then the prayer emphasises that God cannot be limited to a building. God does not live in the temple, but chooses to let God's 'name' be there. The idea of God's name indicates God's abiding presence among the people.

1 CORINTHIANS 3, 10-17
Paul describes God's people in Corinth as a temple, 'where the Spirit of God dwells.'

JOHN 2, 13-22
In Matthew, Mark and Luke this story of Jesus cleansing the temple is placed just before the crucifixion. In John's gospel it is placed as the first public act of Jesus' ministry, directly after the more private act of turning water into wine at the wedding feast. The passage indicates both the inadequacy of the old temple as a sign of God's presence and points forward to Jesus' resurrection body as the new temple or the new sign of God's presence among the people.

EXPLORING WITH CHILDREN

Starting

Explore the local church building, inside and outside. Get the children talking about the different parts of the church, the furnishings and what happens there. Draw out ideas of:

- the tower;
- the nave;
- the chancel;
- the sanctuary;
- the porch;
- the altar;
- the pulpit;
- the lectern;
- the font;
- the churchyard.

Making

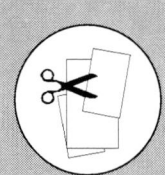

Give the children the opportunity to make a display about churches. Here are some suggestions.

- Make models of key features of the local church, for example, font, altar, pulpit.
- Draw a plan of the local church, filling in names, like nave, pulpit, etc.
- Do rubbings of different surfaces in the church.
- Design a collage of all the different services which happen in church, for example, weddings, harvest festivals, etc.
- Make a picture of Jesus cleansing the temple.

Doing

- Visit other churches and chapels.
- Make a trip to see the cathedral.
- Bring in pictures and guidebooks of churches and cathedrals.
- Invite some members of the church to talk about how the local church is used, for example for special services and special occasions.
- Look at pictures of the temple in Jerusalem.

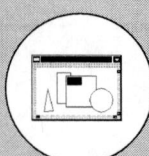

Display headings

- Today's theme is the New Temple.
- The temple is a sign of God's presence among the people.
- Churches are a sign of God's presence among the people.
- Today we are the church.
- Like the temple, we are signs of God's presence in the world.
- Our project today is about the church.

Using the bible

The story of the cleansing of the temple (JOHN 2, 13-22)

Help the listeners to hear in this story how Jesus asserts his presence within the temple and how Jesus reshapes the temple to show a new understanding of God's presence.

> The temple is in Jerusalem.
> Jesus goes to the temple at Passover time.
> Inside the temple Jesus sees the market stalls.
> There are cattle, sheep and pigeons for sacrifice.
> There are money changers to change coins for the temple tax.
> Jesus drives out the traders.

Dance/drama

- Devise a play about Jesus cleansing the temple.
- Choose some key parts of the church (for example, the font and water, the tower and bells) and devise a series of short dances to express what happens there.

Games

- Play 'I Spy' in the church building as a way of helping the children to be alert to the church furnishings and decorations.

EXPLORING WITH ADULTS

Introduction
Display as many different church guide books as you can. Ask the group to look at the books and the pictures of church buildings. Ask them to describe how church buildings can act as symbols of God.

Experience
- What is your church building like?
- How do you feel about your church building?
- How does your church building symbolise the presence of God?

Scripture
Read JOHN 2, 13-22
- What does this story show about Jesus' attitude to the temple?
- How do you interpret this story about the temple for today?
- In what sense is Jesus the new temple?

Integration
- How is God's presence known today?
- How do Christians make God's presence real today?
- How do you make God's presence real today?

Application
- How can your church witness to God's presence today?
- How can you witness to God's presence today?
- How can movement to different parts of the church witness to God's presence?

CELEBRATING TOGETHER

Welcoming children
Make space during the service for the display of the children's work on churches to be viewed and discussed. If the children have prepared drama on the cleansing of the temple, this can be presented after the Gospel reading. If they have prepared dance about what happens at different parts of the church, these dances can take place in the appropriate parts of the church and at different stages of the service.

All age activity
Invite members of the congregation to bring favourite pictures of churches, chapels and cathedrals, choosing both interior and exterior views. These can be grouped to display the different perspectives and significance of church buildings. The following ideas can be explored in buzz groups, discussion or teaching:

- our personal experiences of church buildings;
- the significance of the outward appearance of churches for the wider community;
- the significance of the design and atmosphere inside churches;
- Jesus' expectations of the temple in Jerusalem;
- Jesus' expectations of our own church.

Teaching point
We see today how Jesus begins to replace the old temple with his new church, and we are that church today.

WORSHIP RESOURCES

Prayer

Almighty God,
in Christ you make all things new:
Transform the poverty of our nature
by the riches of your grace,
and in the renewal of our lives
make known your heavenly glory;
through Jesus Christ our Lord.

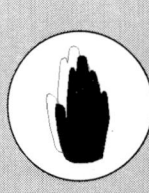

Readings

Old Testament - 1 KINGS 8, 22-30
New Testament - 1 CORINTHIANS 3, 10-17
Gospel - JOHN 2, 13-22

Hymns and songs

Come and Praise

    30 Join with us to sing God's praises
    47 One more step along the world I go
    69 I belong to a family, the biggest on earth
    95 Rejoice in the Lord always

Hymns Ancient and Modern New Standard

    131 Love divine, all loves excelling
    160 We love the place, O God
    161 Christ is our corner-stone
    170 The church's one foundation
    332 Christ is made the sure foundation
    336 All my hope on God is founded
    519 We are your people

16 Hidden treasure

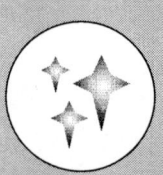

PREPARATION

Bible theme
The wisdom of God (5TH SUNDAY AFTER THE EPIPHANY)
The three readings are linked by the idea of wisdom. In the Old Testament the 'wisdom literature' brings together books like Job, Proverbs and Ecclesiastes. Today's Old Testament reading sets out very clearly what the wisdom literature is all about: wisdom is as precious as silver and buried treasure. The most famous teacher of wisdom in the Old Testament is King Solomon. Today's Gospel reading compares Jesus with Solomon and describes him as 'greater than Solomon'. In the New Testament Jesus is sometimes referred to as 'the wisdom of God'. Today's New Testament reading contrasts what this world calls wisdom with God's wisdom. We can begin to experience the significance of the bible's teaching on wisdom by exploring the image of hidden treasure.

Aims
- to build on our experiences of hidden treasure;
- to help us understand wisdom as hidden treasure;
- to see the wisdom of God as treasure worth digging for.

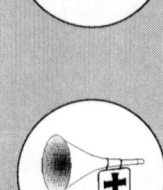

Hearing the scriptures
PROVERBS 2, 1-9
The author of Proverbs argues that the pursuit of wisdom leads to the knowledge of God and to a moral life. The teacher of wisdom in the Old Testament exhorts his pupils to 'seek her out like silver and to dig for her like buried treasure.'

1 Corinthians 3, 18-23
Paul argues that those who consider themselves wise by the world's standards need to 'become a fool to gain true wisdom in God's sight.'

Matthew 12, 38-42
The Queen of Sheba came to visit King Solomon because she had been impressed by his wisdom. Although Jesus is 'greater than Solomon', the leaders of his own day refused to acknowledge him.

EXPLORING WITH CHILDREN

Starting

Before the lesson prepare a large map of a treasure island and a sealed envelope containing information about where the treasure is hidden. Each child with a marked pin attempts to find the treasure. Draw out ideas of:

- why treasure is hidden;
- what the child considers to be 'treasure';
- why they look in certain places for the treasure;
- their reason for hunting for the treasure;
- the hard work of a treasure hunt;
- the excitement of a discovery;
- the value of discovering treasure.

Making
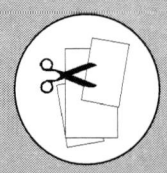
Give the children the opportunity to make a display about hidden treasure. Here are some suggestions.

- Make a map or model of a treasure island.
- Organise a display of things the children regard as their treasures.
- Design banners which illustrate some of the texts from the book of Proverbs.
- Transform a corner of the church into a 'treasure island'; make a big cask for the treasure.

Doing

- Look at pictures of discovered treasure, for example, the raised wreck of the Mary Rose, or Sutton Hoo.
- Visit an archaeological site where some of the things found are on show, or a similar display in a museum.
- Watch a film about discovering treasure or a treasure island.
- Try out a metal detector.
- Invite someone who uses metal detectors, or an amateur archaeologist to talk about their interest.

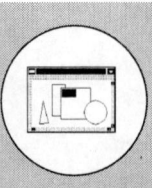

Display headings
- Today's theme is the wisdom of God.
- Wisdom is like hidden treasure.
- The book of Proverbs is a treasure trove of wisdom.
- God's wisdom is made known in Jesus.
- Our project today is about hidden treasure.

Using the bible
Give bibles to the children and invite them to conduct a treasure hunt in the book of PROVERBS. Ask them to find and copy out certain 'treasure' verses:

6, 6	the ant;
10, 4	idle hands;
11, 3	the gossip;
15, 1	sharp words;
15, 13	smiling face;
15, 17	a vegetable stew;
16, 28	telling tales;
25, 16	too much honey;
25, 21	love your enemies.

When they have found the proverbs, discuss what they mean. Are the treasures worth finding?

Dance/drama
- Develop a play about treasure seekers.
- Devise a dance about finding hidden treasure on a desert island.

Games
- Play hunt the silver thimble.

EXPLORING WITH ADULTS

Introduction
Borrow and display a metal detector. Talk about how it works. Ask the group about their experiences of such machines and about finding hidden treasure.

Experience
- What is your experience of finding a hidden treasure (an object or a new idea)?
- How did you feel about your discovery?
- How did this discovery affect your life?

Scripture
Read PROVERBS 2, 1-9
- What does the writer of Proverbs say about finding wisdom?
- How do you interpret this teaching about wisdom for today?
- Where can the wisdom of God be found?

Integration
- What is the evidence of God's wisdom in a person's life?
- How is God's wisdom like hidden treasure?
- How does God's wisdom affect your life?

Application
- How can the church continue to discover the wisdom of God?
- How can you continue to discover the wisdom of God?
- How can wisdom from Proverbs inspire and challenge us in worship?

CELEBRATING TOGETHER

Welcoming children

Make some space during the service for the display of the children's work on hidden treasure to be viewed and discussed. If the children have prepared dance about finding hidden treasure on a desert island, this can be presented after the Old Testament reading. After the dance, the children can read out the proverbs they have discovered in their treasure hunt through the book of Proverbs.

All age activity

Invite members of the congregation to select a favourite text from the book of Proverbs and to write it carefully on a postcard. During the peace invite the congregation to read each other's cards. Ask those who have chosen the same or similar texts to form groups. Display the cards around the church. The following ideas can be explored in buzz groups, discussion or teaching:

- our experiences of 'hidden treasure';
- images of hidden treasure from films and television;
- the kinds of 'treasure' we would find valuable;
- the hidden wisdom of the Old Testament;
- the memorable sayings from the book of Proverbs.

Teaching point

The wisdom writers of the Old Testament likened the pursuit of wisdom to the discovery of hidden treasure. True wisdom involves the knowledge of God and the moral life.

WORSHIP RESOURCES

Prayer

Give us, Lord, we pray
the spirit to think and do always
those things that are right;
that we, who can do no good thing without you,
may have power to live
according to your holy will;
through Jesus Christ our Lord.

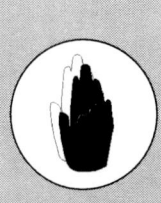

Readings

Old Testament - PROVERBS 2, 1-9
New Testament - 1 CORINTHIANS 3, 18-23
Gospel - MATTHEW 12, 38-42

Hymns and songs

Come and Praise

    12 Who put the colours in the rainbow?
    31 Can you be sure that the rain will fall?
    64 The wise may bring their learning
    96 A still small voice

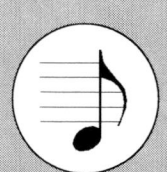

Hymns Ancient and Modern New Standard

    112 God moves in a mysterious way
    117 Praise to the holiest in the height
    199 Immortal, invisible, God only wise
    343 Be thou my vision, O Lord of my heart
    438 Can man by searching find out God
    469 God, you have giv'n us power to sound
    495 Lord, to you we bring our treasure

17

Winter walk

PREPARATION

Bible theme

Parables (6TH SUNDAY AFTER THE EPIPHANY)

In the synoptic gospels Jesus is portrayed as someone who had a very keen eye for all that was going on around him. He often observed and described the natural processes in nature and in the relationships between people. His audience easily identified with what he was describing because they lived in the same world themselves. But then comes the twist in the tale, as Jesus applies the knowledge they already have to a new situation and opens their eyes to new insights. The Gospel reading is one of Jesus' parables. The Old Testament reading portrays the prophet Nathan also as a master of parables. In the New Testament reading Paul argues that God has placed signs of his presence in the natural world all around us. We can begin to experience how the parables of the bible work by exploring the messages of the natural world glimpsed during a winter walk.

Aims

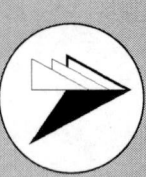

- to take a walk in the local park or countryside and to be alert to all that is going on;
- to encourage us to look around for signs of God's presence and activity;
- to see how Jesus made use of everyday experiences in his parables.

Hearing the scriptures

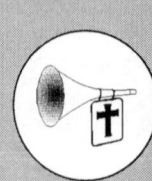

2 SAMUEL 12, 1-10

King David had deliberately arranged for Uriah to be killed in battle so that he could claim his wife, Bathsheba. Nathan the prophet confronts David by telling him a simple tale about a rich man and a poor man: the rich man took the poor man's lamb. David gets caught up in the tale and makes judgement against the rich man. Nathan turns the tale on David and David sees that the judgement he has made really applies to himself.

Romans 1, 18-25
Paul argues that since the beginning of the world God has been disclosed 'in the things God has made.' Knowledge of God is available to those who will reflect on the created universe around them.

Matthew 13, 24-30
In chapter 13 Matthew collects seven of Jesus' parables: (1) seed which falls on to different types of soil, (2) weeds and corn, (3) mustard seed, (4) yeast, (5) buried treasure, (6) fine pearl, (7) catch of fish. By drawing on these everyday images and experiences Jesus teaches about the kingdom of God.

EXPLORING WITH CHILDREN

Starting
Go for a walk in the local area, if possible including a park or countryside. Ask the children to be totally alert to all the things that are going on around them. Draw out ideas of:

- the landscape;
- the natural environment: trees, plants, grass, animals, birds, etc.;
- the manufactured environment: houses, walls, gates, etc.;
- signs of the winter season in the sky, earth, etc.;
- footprints of animals, birds, etc.;
- any first signs of spring;
- things we generally do not notice or generally ignore.

Making
Give the children the opportunity to make a display about a winter walk. Here are some suggestions.

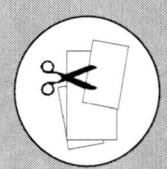

- Design a collage of a winter walk, using magazine cut outs.
- Make a collection of things brought back from the walk.
- Draw a map of the walk showing what has been found in different places.
- Illustrate a 'Winters Trail': a short guide to help visitors to the area, telling them where to walk and what to see at this time of year.
- Design a collage illustrating some of Jesus' parables of nature.

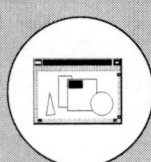

Doing

- Look at pictures of winter.
- Invite someone who has a special interest in the environment, for example a birdwatcher, a conservationist, etc., to talk about their interest.
- Look for photographs in local papers which show the winter landscape of the area.
- Visit a nature trail.
- Watch a video about the countryside in winter.

Display headings

- Today's theme is parables.
- On our winter walk we looked very closely at everything around us.
- Jesus looked very closely at everything going on around him.
- Jesus uses everyday things to illustrate his teaching.
- Parables help us to learn about God from the world around us.
- Our project today is about a winter walk.

Using the bible

The parables of Jesus (MATTHEW 13)

Help the listeners to appreciate Jesus' keen eye for all that was going on around him and how he uses what he sees to shape his teaching. Look at some of the ideas in Matthew 13.

> The seed has different chances of growth depending on the type of soil.
> The weeds and corn grow together.
> The mustard seed starts small but produces a big tree.
> The yeast changes the whole dough.
> The buried treasure is worth finding.
> The fine pearl is worth all the others.
> The catch of fish includes good and bad.

Dance/drama

- Devise a dance portraying two different ways of taking a winter walk: with eyes closed ignoring the environment and with eyes open and being alert to all that is around.

Games

- Arrange an outdoor treasure hunt, making full use of the natural and manufactured environment in structuring the clues. Let the 'treasure' be something that can be used at the service in church and shared with the whole congregation.

EXPLORING WITH ADULTS

Introduction
Display in the centre of the room a vase of twigs collected on a winter walk. Ask the group what they noticed when walking to the session.

Experience
- What is your experience of a winter walk?
- How does what you see and hear tell you of God's activity?
- How does the experience of a winter walk affect you?

Scripture
Read MATTHEW 13, 24-30
- What do these parables say about God's kingdom?
- How do you interpret these parables of Jesus for today?
- What do the these parables say about God's presence and activity?

Integration
- What subjects would Jesus choose today for parables?
- What have you learnt about God's kingdom from a winter walk?
- How has this understanding affected your life?

Application
- What stories can your church tell to proclaim God's presence and activity?
- What stories can you tell to proclaim God's presence and activity?
- How can parables be presented in the Ministry of the Word?

CELEBRATING TOGETHER

Welcoming children

Make space during the service for the display of the children's work on the winter walk to be viewed and discussed. If the children have prepared dance about taking a winter walk, this can be presented after the Gospel reading. If a 'winter's trail' has been written up, make enough copies to give one to each member of the congregation; encourage the congregation to follow these trails. If a 'treasure hunt' was arranged, share the treasure with the members of the congregation.

All age activity

Invite members of the congregation to take a winter walk, to write down the things they particularly noticed and to bring this list to the service. Invite the congregation to share their lists during the Peace, noting similarities and dissimilarities. A comprehensive list can be generated at the front of the church. The following ideas can be explored in buzz groups, discussion or teaching:

- our experiences of winter walks;
- what particularly caught our attention;
- what we saw on this walk that we may not have noticed so clearly before;
- how what we saw speaks to us of God;
- the parables we found in the winter walk.

Teaching point

In the synoptic gospels Jesus is shown as having a very keen eye for all that was going on around him. He used his observations of everyday things to teach about the Kingdom of God.

WORSHIP RESOURCES

Prayer

Almighty God,
your Son taught us in parables:
Enable your church to speak
to the minds of people of every generation
constantly renewing us through the Holy Spirit
that we may fully proclaim the everlasting Gospel;
through Jesus Christ our Lord.

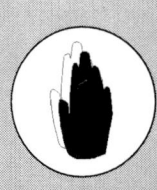

Readings

Old Testament - 2 SAMUEL 12, 1-10
New Testament - ROMANS 1, 18-25
Gospel - MATTHEW 13, 24-30

Hymns and songs

Come and Praise

    3 All things bright and beautiful
    9 Fill your hearts with joy and gladness
  10 God who made the earth
  12 Who put the colours in the rainbow?
  93 Morning sun, morning sun

Hymns Ancient and Modern New Standard

101 O worship the king all glorious above
104 For the beauty of the earth
240 Teach me, my God and king
390 Lord God, we see thy power displayed
468 God who spoke in the beginning
531 With wonder, Lord, we see your works

18
Signposts

PREPARATION

Bible theme
Christ the teacher (9TH SUNDAY BEFORE EASTER)

All three readings develop ideas about the role of the teacher in the community of God's people. The teacher offers signposts to God and to life in God's kingdom. The key reading is the Gospel which illustrates Jesus the teacher offering clear signposts in the opening words of Matthew's sermon on the mount. In the Old Testament reading, Isaiah says that God will provide teachers to guide the people. In the New Testament reading Paul describes the life and status of a Christian teacher. We can begin to experience the significance of the gospel theme of Christ the teacher by exploring how signposts work.

Aims
- to build on our experiences of signposts;
- to help us understand the signposts which God gives to us;
- to see the sermon on the mount as offering signposts for the Christian life.

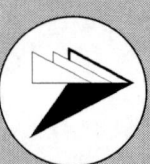

Hearing the scriptures
ISAIAH 30, 18-21

In this passage Isaiah's message changes from warning about impending disaster to the promise that God will act on behalf of the people. Isaiah now encourages the people to wait expectantly for God to act: 'Happy are all who wait for God.' A key part of the promise is that the people will be instructed in God's law. God's appointed teachers will give clear signposts: 'This is my way; walk in it.'

1 CORINTHIANS 14, 8-13

Paul's correspondence shows that he assumed an important role as teacher in the early church. In this letter Paul is taking the Corinthian church to task and uses irony to make his point. Paul accuses the Corinthians of behaving as if their various gifts were due to their own efforts. He contrasts their situation with his own. The life of the apostle reflects the sermon on the mount.

MATTHEW 5, 1-12

The synoptic gospels portray Jesus as a great teacher. Jesus' usual teaching style is through stories, parables or by doing things. Matthew's sermon on the mount stands out as something quite different. The book of Exodus tells how Moses went up the mountain to receive the old law. Here Matthew portrays Jesus going up the mountain to proclaim the new law. The old law was a list of commandments, things to avoid doing; the new law is a list of beatitudes, blessings based on the new way of life. The beatitudes are signposts in God's kingdom.

EXPLORING WITH CHILDREN

Starting

Prepare a quiz on signs of the Highway Code. Select examples from the range of Highway Code signs: instructions, warnings and commands. Draw out ideas of:

- the significance of the different shapes of the signs;
- the significance of the different colours;
- the purpose of signs;
- the universal language of 'picture' signs;
- other examples of picture signs, for example, pubs, shops, toilets.

Making

Give the children the opportunity to make a display about signs and signposts. Here are some suggestions.

- Make a range of road signs, large enough to be used in church.
- Design new signs to position at different places in church as appropriate for the font, the organ, the exit, etc.
- Design signs to illustrate some of the beatitudes.
- Draw a picture of Jesus teaching on the mount.
- Prepare a set of instructions to help a visitor to find your church. Make use of all the available signposts.
- Make a set of playing cards using road signs, with several copies of the same card, to play the game of snap.

Doing

- Go and look at the signposts in the local community.
- Invite someone who has recently been abroad, or who used to live abroad, to talk about signposts in other countries.
- Go for a coach or car ride and note all the signposts on the journey.
- Look to see other examples of picture signs in the local community.

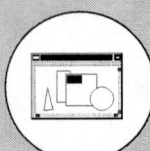

Display headings

- Today's theme is Christ the teacher.
- Road signs warn us of danger.
- Road signs set us going in the right direction.
- Road signs help us get there safely.
- Jesus the teacher gives us signposts to God.
- The beatitudes are signposts in the Kingdom of God.
- Our project today is about signs and signposts.

Using the bible

The introduction to the sermon on the mount (MATTHEW 5, 1-12)

Help the listeners to hear the beautiful rhythm of the famous beatitudes which open the sermon on the mount in the gospel of Matthew.

> God blesses those who know their need of God.
> God blesses those who are sorry for their sins.
> God blesses those who are of a gentle spirit.
> God blesses those who strive to see right prevail.
> God blesses those who show mercy.
> God blesses those who are pure in heart.
> God blesses those who are the peacemakers.
> God blesses those who are persecuted for doing what God requires.

Dance/drama

- Develop a mime to portray car drivers responding to a range of road signs, for example, steep hill, bends, uneven road surface, water splash, hump back bridge, etc.
- Arrange for the beatitudes to be read in choral speech and for the idea of blessing to be expressed through dance.

Games

- Use a set of road sign playing cards to play snap.

EXPLORING WITH ADULTS

Introduction
Display copies of the Highway Code. Look at the section on road signs. Ask the group which signs are the most helpful to motorists.

Experience
- What is your experience of local signposts?
- How do you feel about the effectiveness of these signposts?
- How have you been influenced by signposts?

Scripture
Read MATTHEW 5, 1-12
- What does this teaching say about Jesus and the new law?
- How do you interpret this teaching of Jesus for today?
- What does this teaching say about God's kingdom?

Integration
- What signposts point people to God's kingdom today?
- How do you feel about these signposts?
- How do these signposts affect your life?

Application
- How can the church be an effective signpost of God's kingdom?
- How can you be an effective signpost of God's kingdom?
- How can the Beatitudes be presented in worship?

CELEBRATING TOGETHER

Welcoming children
Make space during the service for the display of the children's work on signs and signposts to be viewed and discussed. Set road signs up at appropriate places in the church, for example, a speed limit on the organ, a water splash by the font, etc. During the service arrange for the children to involve the adults of the congregation in a quiz about road signs. If the children have prepared dance and choral speech based on the beatitudes, this can be presented after or in place of the Gospel reading.

All age activity
Invite members of the congregation to bring an example of a sign, including pictures of road signs, trade signs from boxes or tins. Display these signs in the church. The following ideas can be explored in buzz groups, discussion or teaching:

- our personal experience of signs;
- signs which fascinate, amaze or puzzle us;
- how signs work;
- the signposts which Jesus gives pointing to God;
- how the church may signpost its message more effectively.

Teaching point
In the sermon on the mount, Jesus the teacher offers signposts to God and to life in God's kingdom.
Worship Resources

WORSHIP RESOURCES

Prayer

Eternal God,
whose Son Jesus Christ is for all people
the way, the truth, and the life:
Grant that we may walk in his way,
rejoice in his truth and share his risen life;
who lives and reigns
with you and the Holy Spirit,
one God, now and for ever.

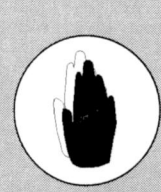

Readings

Old Testament - Isaiah 30, 18-21
New Testament - 1 Corinthians 14, 8-13
Gospel - Matthew 5, 1-12

Hymns and songs

Come and Praise
    25 When Jesus walked in Galilee
    27 There's a child in the streets
    45 The journey of life
    92 When night arrives

Hymns Ancient and Modern New Standard
    128 Thou art the way: by thee alone
    166 Lord, thy word abideth
    238 Blest are the pure in heart
    240 Teach me, my God and king
    392 Lord Jesus, once you spoke to men
    512 'The kingdom is upon you!'
    513 The prophets spoke in days of old

19 Jigsaw puzzle

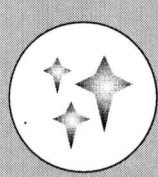

PREPARATION

Bible theme
Christ the healer (8TH SUNDAY BEFORE EASTER)
The three readings are linked by the idea of 'wholeness of life,' an idea emphasised in the collect. The key reading is the Gospel account of the paralysed man who was let down through the roof by his four friends. The wholeness which Jesus offers to this man is both physical and spiritual. In other words, his paralysis is healed and his sins are forgiven. The New Testament reading also links sickness and sin as two qualities which detract from wholeness. In the Old Testament reading Zephaniah promises true wholeness for God's people, when God himself 'is in your midst.' We can begin to experience the significance of the bible's teaching on wholeness by exploring how jigsaw puzzles can be either fragmented or integrated.

Aims
to build on our experience of jigsaw puzzles;
to help us understand the wholeness when the puzzle is completed;
to see the healing which Jesus offers as a form of wholeness.

Hearing the scriptures
ZEPHANIAH 3, 14-20
In the first two and a half chapters Zephaniah has threatened God's punishment on the unfaithfulness of the chosen people. In the closing verses of his book Zephaniah promises God's forgiveness and restoration. God will bring wholeness to the people by dwelling among them. The wholeness which God brings will include recalling the exiled and saving the lame.

JAMES 5, 13-16A

James gives some insights into how an early Christian church cared for the troubled, the sick and the sinful. The early church emphasises the central place of prayer in restoration to wholeness of body as well as spirit: 'Pray for one another, that you may be healed.'

MARK 2, 1-12

Mark portrays Jesus as restoring people to wholeness of life. It is this gift of wholeness which is a sure sign of the kingdom which Jesus comes to proclaim. Wholeness for the Christian occurs when the barriers between God and humankind are removed, or in other words when sins are forgiven. For some this wholeness will involve physical restoration (as in the present story) while others, in spite of physical sickness, discover a wholeness which not even death can destroy.

EXPLORING WITH CHILDREN

Starting

Share the pieces of a jigsaw puzzle among the children, but keep several pieces hidden away. Do not let the children see the picture on the box. Make the jigsaw, letting each child take a turn. Draw out ideas of:

- whether the children can guess what the picture is from the few pieces in their hand;
- which is the easiest way to start;
- matching to complete a colour or shape;
- the gradual emergence of a picture;
- the missing pieces which spoil the whole;
- completing the picture;
- wholeness when all the pieces are in place.

Making

Give the children the opportunity to make a display about jigsaw puzzles, and how the assembled pieces lead to wholeness. Here are some suggestions.

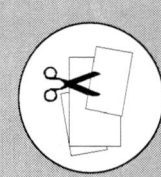

- Assemble a pile of lego pieces and make them into an object.
- Do a large jigsaw so it can be displayed.
- Stick pictures on cardboard and cut out your own jigsaw.
- Make a display of many different sorts of jigsaw puzzles.
- Draw a picture of the paralysed man being lowered through the roof.

Doing
- Look at some jigsaws and discover how they are made.
- Invite someone who likes doing large jigsaws to bring one along and to talk about it.
- Invite someone who is disabled to talk about the wholeness they experience through faith in Jesus.
- Visit someone who makes jigsaws with a fret-saw.

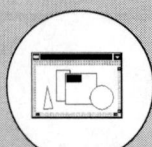

Display headings
- Today's theme is Christ the healer.
- Jigsaws are incomplete until made up.
- When the jigsaw is made it is whole.
- Lives can be in pieces.
- Jesus restores broken lives to wholeness.
- Our project today is about jigsaw puzzles.

Using the bible
The story of the man let down through the roof (MARK 2, 1-12)
Help the listeners to hear this story as a powerful drama of restoration to wholeness when sins are forgiven and paralysis is healed.

> The man is paralysed and helpless.
> He is brought to Jesus by four friends.
> The friends cannot reach Jesus because of the crowd.
> They break open the roof.
> The man is let down through the roof.
> Jesus makes the man whole.
> His sins are forgiven and his paralysis is healed.

Dance/drama
- Act out the story of the paralysed man.
- Devise a dance about being the fragmented pieces of a jigsaw puzzle which are gradually assembled into a picture.

Games
- Invite the children to work in groups of equal size. Give each group a jigsaw puzzle and see which group completes the picture first.

EXPLORING WITH ADULTS

Introduction
Arrange the chairs so that the room looks disturbed. Allow the group to comment as they enter the room. When everyone is present invite them to arrange the chairs and bring order. Ask the group to describe their experience.

Experience
- What experiences disturb and break people's lives?
- How far reaching can such experiences be?
- How are the broken pieces put together?

Scripture
Read MARK 2, 1-12
- What does this story say about Jesus healing broken lives?
- How do you interpret this story about Jesus' healing power for today?
- How does Jesus bring wholeness to the broken?

Integration
- When do lives become broken?
- How has your life been broken?
- How has God given you wholeness?

Application
- How can your church be a place of wholeness and healing?
- How can you be an agent of God's wholeness and healing?
- How can the Absolution proclaim God's wholeness and healing?

CELEBRATING TOGETHER

Welcoming children
Make space during the service for the display of the children's work on jigsaw puzzles to be viewed and discussed. If the children have prepared drama on the story of the paralysed man, this can be presented after the Gospel reading. If they have devised a dance about the jigsaw puzzle this can be presented at an appropriate point in the service.

All age activity
Invite members of the congregation to bring a jigsaw puzzle with them if they have one at home. These can be displayed around the church to illustrate the many different kinds of jigsaw puzzles. Have prepared enough large-piece jigsaw puzzles for each member of the congregation to have a piece. Write a large letter A on the back of all the pieces from the first puzzle and so on, so that the sets remain distinct. Give the pieces out to members of the congregation when they come into church. At the Peace ask them to go into groups according to the letter on the back of their piece and then to make the picture. The following ideas can be explored in buzz groups, discussion or teaching:

- our experiences of jigsaw puzzles;
- the kinds of jigsaw puzzles we like most and like least;
- the feeling of satisfaction when the pieces fall into place;
- the idea of wholeness in the Christian life;
- how Jesus brings wholeness to the people of God.

Teaching point
The jigsaw illustrates the principle of wholeness. It is incomplete until all the individual parts are put together. So our broken lives need completing and making whole by Jesus.

WORSHIPRESOURCES

Prayer

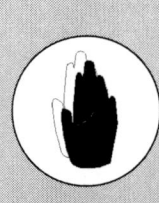

Almighty and everlasting God,
whose Son Jesus Christ healed the sick
and restored them to wholeness of life:
Look with compassion on the anguish of the world
and heal the afflictions of all your people;
through our Lord and Saviour Jesus Christ,
who lives and reigns with you and the Holy Spirit,
one God, now and for ever.

Readings

Old Testament - ZEPHANIAH 3, 14-20
New Testament - JAMES 5, 13-16A
Gospel - MARK 2, 1-12

Hymns and songs

Come and Praise

    24 Go tell it on the mountain
    26 There is singing in the desert
    65 When I needed a neighbour were you there, were you there?
    91 You can build a wall around you

Hymns Ancient and Modern New Standard

    115 Dear Lord and father of mankind
    122 How sweet the name of Jesus sounds
    285 Thine arm, O Lord, in days of old
    286 From thee all skill and science flow
    361 For the healing of the nations
    406 O God, by whose almighty plan
    408 O God, whose will is life and good

20

Rejects

PREPARATION

Bible theme

Christ the friend of sinners (7TH SUNDAY BEFORE EASTER)

The idea which links these reading is God's acceptance of and love for those who appear deliberately to put themselves outside his love. The key reading is the Gospel in which Jesus is portrayed associating with 'many bad characters' and making a special point of counting one of them, Levi, among his closest companions. In the Old Testament reading Hosea shows that God is willing to rehabilitate Israel in spite of the fact that the peoples' iniquity was the cause of their downfall. In the New Testament reading Paul pleads for the restoration of Onesimus who had been a runaway and renegade slave before his conversion to Christ. We can begin to experience the significance of the bible's teaching on God's acceptance of sinners by exploring our personal acceptance and trans-formation of rejects.

Aims

- to build on our experiences of rejects;
- to help us understand the acceptance and transformation of rejects;
- to see God's love for and acceptance of all people, however much we may be rejects.

Hearing the scriptures

HOSEA 14, 1-7

Hosea's marriage to an unfaithful wife teaches him about God's patience and forgiveness. In this passage Hosea portrays God continuing to love the people and inviting them to return to God in spite of their iniquity. God says 'I will heal their disloyalty, I will love them with all my heart.'

Philemon 1, 1-16

Philemon seems to have owed his conversion to Christianity to Paul. His slave Onesimus had run away, perhaps with stolen goods. The punishment for such a crime was execution. Now Onesimus had met Paul in prison and had been converted. Paul writes to Philemon asking him to take Onesimus back, forgiven, as a fellow Christian. The slave's name means 'useful': Paul argues that 'at one time he was of no use to you, but now he is useful both to you and to me.'

Mark 2, 13-17

Levi, son of Alphaeus, was a Jew, found here working for the occupying Roman authorities as a tax-collector. Tax-collectors in the Roman Empire made their living by inflating what was demanded and creaming off their own profit. They were hated as traitors and extortionists. Jesus calls Levi to be a disciple and shows his complete acceptance of Levi by table fellowship, a sign and pledge of intimacy in the ancient world.

EXPLORING WITH CHILDREN

Starting

Begin by bringing in and sharing a packet of 'misshaped' sweets or biscuits. Draw out ideas of:

- what the sweets look like (less good than the perfect ones);
- what they taste like (just as good);
- reasons for misshaped sweets being rejected;
- why misshaped sweets are sold more cheaply;
- other examples of rejects.

Making

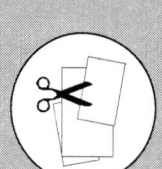

Give the children the opportunity to make a display about rejects. Here are some suggestions.

- Make some recycled paper out of waste paper.
- Design a collage of the call of Levi, made from reject material.
- Make a collection and display of rejects.
- Draw a picture of a reject shop.
- Display examples of models made from reject material.

Doing

- Visit a junk shop and look round it; discover uses for objects which other people have rejected.
- Collect a pile of jumble; invite each child to pick out something they could use and talk about it.
- Invite a scrap merchant to talk about how he or she recycles what others reject.
- Invite someone to talk about the work of a local charity shop, for example, Oxfam.
- Visit a reject shop or a factory where they package rejects.

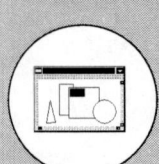

Display headings

- Today's theme is Christ the friend of sinners.
- Rejects are discarded or sold cheaply.
- People can be treated like rejects.
- Levi was treated like a reject.
- Jesus accepts rejects.
- Our project today is about rejects.

Using the bible

The story of the call of Levi (MARK 2, 13-17)

Help the listeners to hear this story as a powerful account of how Jesus accepts people whom others may reject as worthless.

> Levi was working for the occupying Roman army, collecting taxes.
> His fellow countrymen rejected Levi as a traitor.
> Tax gatherers made a living by charging more taxes than they paid over to the Romans.
> His fellow countrymen rejected Levi as a crook.
> Jesus does not reject Levi.
> Jesus invites Levi to be among his closest friends.
> Levi invites Jesus to a party in his house.

Dance/drama

- Act out the response of the villagers, who have been cheated by Levi, when they hear about his new friend Jesus.
- Devise a dance about being rejected and then accepted.

Games

- Play games which involve being rejected or excluded and the attempt to regain acceptance, like 'Piggy in the middle'.

EXPLORING WITH ADULTS

Introduction
Arrange the chairs in the room for the group. Remove some chairs so that there are insufficient chairs for everyone to sit down. Ask those who have no chair to describe their feelings of rejection.

Experience
- What kind of people are rejected in your community?
- When have you felt rejected?
- How did this rejection affect your life?

Scripture
Read MARK 2, 13-17
- What does this story say about Jesus' relationship with Levi?
- How do you interpret this story about Levi for today?
- What does this story say about God's dealings with men and women?

Integration
- How does God deal with rejects today?
- How has God accepted you?
- How has God's acceptance affected your life?

Application
- What can the church do to value people who feel rejected?
- How can you accept people who feel rejected?
- How can the Peace express acceptance of everyone?

CELEBRATING TOGETHER

Welcoming children

Make space during the service for the display of the children's work on rejects to be viewed and discussed. If the children have prepared drama about the response of the villagers to Levi's acceptance by Jesus, this may be presented after the Gospel reading.

All age activity

Invite members of the congregation to bring something to the service which they regard as a reject, but which could be useful to others and which could be sold through a local charity shop. Others may prefer to bring something which they have made from rejects. Display these rejects and craft work in the church. The following ideas can be explored in buzz groups, discussion or teaching:

- our experience of accepting and transforming rejects;
- people we know who are good at transforming rejects;
- the fate of rejects if they are not transformed;
- God's acceptance of rejects;
- the church's responsibility to accept rejects.

Teaching point

People are often rejected by others. Sometimes they are rejected because they behave badly or dishonestly, as Levi had done. Sometimes they are rejected because of their race or handicap. Jesus accepts rejects and rehabilitates them.

WORSHIP RESOURCES

Prayer

Merciful Lord,
grant to your faithful people pardon and peace;
that we may be cleansed from all our sins
and serve you with a quiet mind;
through Jesus Christ our Lord.

Readings

Old Testament - HOSEA 14, 1-7
New Testament - PHILEMON 1, 1-16
Gospel - MARK 2, 13-17

Hymns and songs

Come and Praise

- 26 There is singing in the desert
- 36 God is love; his the care
- 39 O Lord, all the world belongs to you
- 102 You can't stop rain from falling down

Hymns Ancient and Modern New Standard

- 122 How sweet the name of Jesus sounds
- 244 Hark, my soul! it is the Lord
- 247 I heard the voice of Jesus say
- 362 'Forgive our sins as we forgive'
- 383 Jesus, whose all-redeeming love
- 489 Lord God, your love has called us here
- 530 With joy we meditate the grace

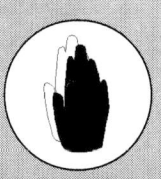

21
Feeling hungry

PREPARATION

Bible theme

The king and the kingdom: temptation (1ST SUNDAY IN LENT)

Lent prepares for Good Friday, when through his death and resurrection Christ brings salvation to all men and women. Only because he is nothing less than truly God can Christ do God's work of salvation. Only because he is nothing less than truly human can Christ save other men and women. The church safeguards this great mystery in the belief that Jesus Christ is both truly God and truly man. In the Sundays of Lent, which prepare for the events of Holy Week, the church's lectionary celebrates the manhood of Christ. On the first Sunday in Lent this point is made explicitly in the New Testament reading, which stresses that Jesus shared our 'same flesh and blood' and that 'he had to be made like these brothers of his in every way.' Then the Gospel readings for the first four Sundays in Lent illustrate different ways in which Jesus experienced and handled basic human needs and emotions. Today's Gospel reading draws attention to Jesus' need for food and the experience of hunger. In the Old Testament reading Jesus' way of dealing with his hunger is contrasted with that of the first Adam in the garden of Eden. We can begin to experience the significance of the gospel narrative about Jesus' period of fasting in the wilderness by exploring our own reactions to hunger and thirst.

Aims
- to build on our experiences of feeling hungry and thirsty;
- to help us understand hunger and thirst as basic human needs;
- to see that Jesus shared our feelings of hunger and thirst.

Hearing the scriptures

GENESIS 2, 7-9 AND 3, 1-7

The early chapters of Genesis tell of God's creation of the first man and the first woman, their disobedience and their fall from grace. Because of Adam's disobedience all who share Adam's common humanity share his experience of being cut off from God.

HEBREWS 2, 14-18

The letter to the Hebrews is concerned to give an account of how Christ restored the relationship between God and men and women, broken by Adam's disobedience. This is only possible, says the author, since Christ was truly human like Adam and like ourselves.

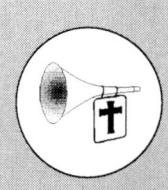

MATTHEW 4, 1-11

The story of the temptations shows Jesus in the same human predicament as the first Adam, tempted by Satan. While Adam gives in to temptation, Jesus withstands. The first temptation, as described by Matthew, builds on the basic human need for food and the experience of hunger.

EXPLORING WITH CHILDREN

Starting

Organise the room to make the children feel hungry when they arrive. For example, display adverts for food and pictures accompanying recipes in magazines; set out bowls of crisps which the children can see, but are not yet allowed to touch; make cooking smells; play in the background a recording of 'Food glorious food' or something similar. Discuss the children's feelings of hunger. Draw out ideas of:

- what makes them feel hungry;
- when they feel hungry;
- what feeling hungry is like;
- hunger makes you feel faint, light headed, tired, cross;
- hunger makes you feel sad, worried;
- food is a basic human need;
- food gives energy, warmth, life.

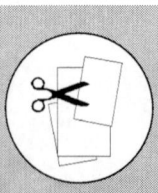

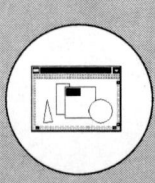

Making

Give the children the opportunity to make a display about feeling hungry. Here are some suggestions.

- Make pancakes following Shrove Tuesday.
- Collect food adverts from magazines and display them, with the heading 'Jesus felt hungry'.
- Make a chart showing daily foods for healthy living.
- Design a series of pictures about Jesus' temptations.
- Do some cooking to make cooking smells.

Doing

- Ask a runner to talk about feelings of hunger and thirst on a long run.
- Invite a nurse or doctor to talk about healthy eating.
- Invite someone who has undertaken a proper fast to talk about it.
- Smell different kinds of food while blindfolded and try to guess what they are.
- Taste different kinds of food while blindfolded and try to guess what they are.
- Find out about Shrove Tuesday customs.
- Find out about fasting during Lent.
- Look at pictures of Jesus' temptations in the wilderness.

Display headings

- Today's theme is Jesus' temptation in the wilderness.
- Hunger and thirst are basic human needs.
- Jesus shared our feelings of hunger and thirst.
- Jesus is fully human like us.
- Our project today is about feeling hungry.

Using the bible

The story of Jesus in the wilderness (MATTHEW 4, 1-11)

Help the listeners to hear in this story how Jesus shared common human feelings, like hunger, and how Jesus dealt with such experiences.

> Jesus is alone in the wilderness.
> Jesus fasts for forty days and forty nights and is very hungry.
> The devil tempts Jesus to turn stones into bread.
> Jesus refuses to use his power to satisfy his own hunger.
> The devil tempts Jesus to jump from the temple.
> Jesus refuses to win support by spectacular stunts.
> The devil tempts Jesus to gain power by serving him.
> Jesus refuses to use the power of evil.
> Jesus is tempted like us, but does not give in.

Dance/drama
- Devise a dance about the feelings of hunger and thirst.
- Prepare a radio interview with the devil after he has failed to tempt Jesus.

Games
- Hold a pancake race.

EXPLORING WITH ADULTS

Introduction
Bring in a tray loaded with food and drink and place it on a low table in the centre. Do not pour the drink or offer the food. Ask the group how they feel.

Experience
- What makes you feel hungry?
- How do you feel when you are hungry?
- What effect does hunger have on you?

Scripture
Read MATTHEW 4, 1-11
- What does this story say about Jesus' human needs?
- How do you interpret this story about Jesus' temptations for today?
- How does this story suggest that Jesus is like us?

Integration
- Why does the church fast in Lent?
- Why might you fast in Lent?
- How does fasting help you to identify with Jesus during Lent?

Application
- How can the church use Lent to prepare for Easter?
- What can you do in Lent to prepare for Easter?
- How can fasting before the eucharist help you prepare for the service?

CELEBRATING TOGETHER

Welcoming children
Make space during the service for the display of the children's work on feeling hungry to be viewed and discussed. Invite the children to tell the congregation how they felt hungry at the beginning of their project. Let them display the mouth-watering pictures of food and bring cooking smells into the service. If they have prepared a dance on the theme of hunger and thirst, this can be shared after the second sentence of the Gospel reading which says, 'And he fasted forty days and forty nights, and afterwards he was hungry.'

All age activity
Invite members of the congregation to miss their breakfast and to come to the service fasting. When they arrive at church present them with a hotel style breakfast menu card and invite them to tick what they would most like for breakfast if they were staying in a hotel. The following ideas can be explored in buzz groups, discussion or teaching:

- our experiences of feeling hungry and thirsty;
- images of hunger and thirst from films and television;
- how hunger changes our attitudes and feelings;
- fasting in the Christian tradition;
- Jesus' experiences of hunger in the wilderness.

Teaching point
In the Sundays of Lent the church celebrates the manhood of Jesus. Only because he is truly human can Jesus save other men and women. The human Jesus shares our basic human needs of hunger and thirst.

WORSHIP RESOURCES

Prayer

Almighty God,
whose Son Jesus Christ
fasted forty days in the wilderness,
was tempted as we are, and yet did not sin:
Give us grace to discipline ourselves
in obedience to your Spirit,
and, as you know our weakness,
so may we know your saving power;
through Jesus Christ our Lord.

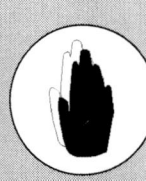

Readings

Old Testament - GENESIS 2, 7-9 AND 3, 1-7
New Testament - HEBREWS 2, 14-18
Gospel - MATTHEW 4, 1-11

Hymns and songs

Come and Praise

  27 There's a child in the streets
  51 Our father, who art in heaven
  65 When I needed a neighbour were you there, were you there?
  91 You can build a wall around you

Hymns Ancient and Modern New Standard

  56 Forty days and forty nights
113 Father hear the prayer we offer
247 I heard the voice of Jesus say
334 A man there lived in Galilee
378 Jesus, good above all other
415 Praise and thanksgiving
518 Walking in a garden

22

Feeling sad

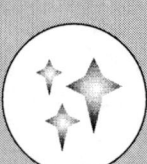

PREPARATION

Bible theme

The king and the kingdom: conflict (2ND SUNDAY IN LENT)

The second Sunday in Lent continues to explore the humanity of Jesus. Again the theme is expressed explicitly in the New Testament reading which stresses that 'every spirit which acknowledges that Jesus the Christ has come in the flesh is from God.' Today's Gospel reading draws attention to Jesus feeling sad and weeping. Here Jesus' sadness is caused by the failure of God's people to live their lives in the way God desires for them. Jesus sees and reacts to the same situation which God sees in the Old Testament reading, namely that 'all men had lived corrupt lives on earth.' We can begin to experience the significance of the gospel narrative about Jesus' feelings of sadness by exploring our experiences of sadness and weeping.

Aims

- to build on our experiences of feeling sad;
- to help us understand sadness as a basic human emotion;
- to see that Jesus shared our feelings of sadness.

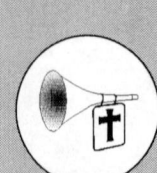

Hearing the scriptures

GENESIS 6, 11-22

According to the early chapters of Genesis, the disobedience of men and women frustrates God's plans for the creation. The biblical tradition portrays God as sad and as angry because of their sin and disobedience. However, God never gives up in the struggle to save and to reform the creation. Here, in the story of the great flood, the emphasis is not on God's punishment of the wicked, but on the salvation which God offers to the whole of creation, including 'creatures of every kind', through love for Noah. In this sense, God employs sadness and anger creatively.

1 JOHN 4, 1-6

The first letter of John seems to have been written to counter the early heresy which argued that Jesus was not really and fully man. Those who hold this view John describes as 'false prophets who represent not God but the Antichrist.'

LUKE 19, 41-48

Luke's gospel sees Jesus' arrival at Jerusalem as a particular climax to his ministry, since Jerusalem stands for the spiritual centre of God's chosen people. When he arrives, Jesus recognises that God's people are not ready and prepared for his visit. Jesus recognises the inevitability of the destruction which awaits the city. He is sad and weeps over it.

EXPLORING WITH CHILDREN

Starting

Ask the children to draw a sad face and then display the faces around the room. Invite the children to walk round the room, to stand in front of each face and to talk about the reasons for the face looking sad. Draw out ideas of:

- how you recognise a sad face;
- sad eyes and sad mouths;
- tears and crying;
- occasions when the children feel sad;
- tears when something is lost;
- tears when something is broken;
- tears when people are unkind to you;
- tears when you suffer pain.

Making

Give the children the opportunity to make a display about feeling sad. Here are some suggestions.

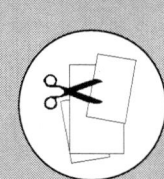

- Make a list beginning, 'sadness is …'.
- Look through magazines for pictures which make you feel sad and prepare a collage with the heading, 'Jesus wept'.
- Make sad face masks which the children can wear.
- Make badges of sad faces so all the congregation can have one.
- Design a picture of Jesus weeping over Jerusalem.

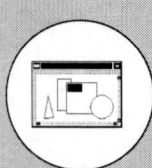

Doing

- Invite some members of the church to talk about times when they have been sad.
- Watch a sad excerpt from a children's cartoon video.
- Go for a walk or drive to spot things which make Jesus sad today.
- Find out why purple is used in church during Lent.
- Read the confession from the communion service and discuss the feeling of sadness there.

Display headings

- Today's theme is conflict.
- Sadness and tears are basic human feelings.
- We all know what it is to feel sad.
- Jesus shared our feelings of sadness.
- Jesus wept.
- Jesus is fully human like us.
- Our project today is about feeling sad.

Using the bible

The story of Jesus arriving in Jerusalem (LUKE 19, 41-48)

Help the listeners to hear in this story how Jesus shared common human feelings, like sadness, and what made Jesus experience such feelings.

> People are already coming to Jerusalem for the annual festival.
> The Passover festival celebrates how God rescued people in the past.
> Jesus arrives and sees the city in the distance.
> Jesus has come to rescue God's people again.
> But Jesus knows the people in the city are not ready for him.
> Jesus is sad because the people have rejected God's plan for them.
> Jesus weeps over the city.
> Jesus goes into the temple and teaches there.

Dance/drama

- Mime Jesus' journey towards Jerusalem, his sight of the city in the distance and his weeping.
- Devise a dance about feeling sad and weeping.

Games

- Play a competitive game where children are gradually excluded. When they are excluded they have to sit by themselves with their eyes closed. Discuss their feelings of isolation and sadness.

EXPLORING WITH ADULTS

Introduction
Give the group a selection of newspapers, including local papers. Ask them to cut out pictures or articles that make them feel sad.

Experience
- What is your experience of feeling sad?
- How do you express your feelings of sadness?
- What effect does sadness have on you?

Scripture
Read LUKE 19, 41-48
- What does this story say about Jesus' sadness over the city?
- How do you interpret this story about Jesus' sadness for today?
- What does this story say about Jesus' humanity?

Integration
- What makes Jesus sad in our world?
- Why might Jesus weep over your community?
- Why might Jesus weep over you?

Application
- How can the church express its sadness over sin?
- How can you express sadness over sin?
- How can the Confession be used to recognise what makes Jesus weep?

CELEBRATING TOGETHER

Welcoming children

Make space during the service for the display of the children's work on feeling sad to be viewed and discussed. Display the children's drawings of sad faces and invite the children to tell the congregation stories about why the faces are sad. If the children have prepared a dance about feeling sad and weeping, this can be shared during the Gospel reading immediately after the words, 'he wept over it'.

All age activity

Invite members of the congregation to bring a picture of someone looking sad, possibly clipped from a newspaper or magazine. Display these pictures around the church. If the children have made enough badges of sad faces, these can be given to the congregation as they come into church or at an appropriate point during the service. The following ideas can be explored in buzz groups, discussion or teaching:

- our experiences of feeling sad;
- images of sadness from television or films;
- how sadness changes our attitudes and outlook;
- Jesus' sadness at entering Jerusalem;
- what makes Jesus sad in today's world.

Teaching point

During Lent we recall that Jesus experienced and handled basic human feelings. He shares our feelings of sadness. When he entered Jerusalem, Jesus wept because God's people were not ready to respond to God's invitation held out to them.

WORSHIP RESOURCES

Prayer

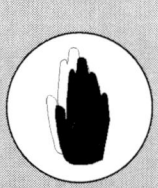

Lord God Almighty,
your Son prayed for his disciples,
that in all the conflicts of the world
you would deliver them from the power of the devil:
Strengthen us to resist every assault and temptation,
and to follow you, the only God;
through Jesus Christ our Lord.

Readings

Old Testament - GENESIS 6, 11-22
New Testament - 1 JOHN 4, 1-6
Gospel - LUKE 19, 41-48

Hymns and songs

Come and Praise
- 24 Go, tell it on the mountain
- 57 Think of all the things we lose
- 68 Kum ba yah
- 89 Guess how I feel

Hymns Ancient and Modern New Standard
- 177 Thy kingdom come, O God
- 210 Oft in danger, oft in woe
- 217 Be thou my guardian and my guide
- 246 Just as I am, without one plea
- 362 Forgive our sins as we forgive
- 474 In Adam we have all been one
- 480 Let us break bread together on our knees

23

Feeling hurt

PREPARATION

Bible theme

The king and the kingdom: suffering (3RD SUNDAY IN LENT)

The third Sunday in Lent continues to explore the humanity of Jesus. Today's Gospel reading draws attention to Jesus' experience of suffering. 'The Son of Man,' Jesus says, 'is destined to suffer grievously.' In the Old Testament reading the sacrifice of Isaac illuminates Jesus' suffering and sacrifice on the cross. In the New Testament reading Paul argues that he is happy to accept suffering in the service of Christ. We can begin to experience the significance of the gospel narrative about Jesus' feelings of suffering by exploring our own experiences of feeling hurt.

Aims

- to build on our experiences of feeling hurt;
- to help us understand pain as a basic human experience;
- to see that Jesus shared our feelings of pain.

Hearing the scriptures

GENESIS 22, 1-13

This story illustrates Abraham's complete obedience to God. God's earlier promise to Abraham was to make him the father of many nations through his only son Isaac. Abraham is now willing to put all this at risk in obedience to God's new demand to offer Isaac in sacrifice. Having tested Abraham's obedience, God rescues Isaac and provides a ram for sacrifice in his place. The early church saw in this story a prophecy of the cross. Just as Abraham handed over his only son to death in obedience to God and received him back again alive, so God hands over the only begotten Son of God to death for the sins of the world and raises him back to life.

COLOSSIANS 1, 24-29

In writing to the Colossians, Paul argues that the Christian apostle and missionary must be willing to accept suffering for the sake of the gospel. He writes, 'It is now my happiness to suffer for you.'

LUKE 9, 18-27

In the first chapters of the gospels the disciples have the opportunity to hear Jesus' teaching and to observe his actions. Now Jesus asks them to interpret what they have seen and heard. Peter recognises that Jesus is the Messiah. Jesus accepts this title, but also immediately qualifies it. He is not the warrior Messiah, whom some were expecting. Jesus is not to escape the consequence of being fully human through some glorious messianic victory. Rather he is 'destined to suffer grievously, to be rejected by the elders and chief priests and scribes and to be put to death.'

EXPLORING WITH CHILDREN

Starting

Show the children a home or school first aid box. Ask them what they expect to find inside and then slowly unpack the box, discussing the purpose and use of different articles. Draw out ideas of:

- experiences of being hurt;
- fall in the play ground;
- nose bleed;
- toothache;
- insect bite;
- the use of plaster, bandages, etc.;
- disinfectant, salve, etc.;
- medicine, pills, etc.

Making

Give the children the opportunity to make a display about feeling hurt. Here are some suggestions.

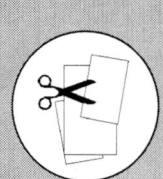

- Make a list of the different hurts the children have experienced.
- Make a collage of advertisements for plasters, medicines, etc., with the heading 'Jesus suffered pain'.
- Design a series of pictures of children receiving first aid.
- Prepare a book to illustrate the treatment of minor illnesses and injuries, like sore throats, wasp stings, grazed knees, etc.
- Make a chemist shop in a corner of the church.

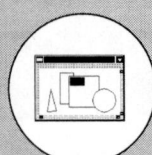

Doing

- Visit a chemist shop to see the display of medicines, plasters, etc.
- Visit the local health centre or hospital to talk with a member of staff.
- Invite a nurse, doctor or member of St John's Ambulance to talk about his or her work.
- Invite someone who has a leg in plaster or arm in sling to talk about it.
- Watch a video of a hospital programme.

Display headings

- Today's theme is suffering.
- Pain and suffering are basic human experiences.
- We all know what it is to feel hurt.
- Jesus shared our feelings of pain and suffering.
- Jesus is truly human like us.
- Our project today is about feeling hurt.

Using the bible

Jesus explains his own suffering and hurt to the disciples (LUKE 9, 18-27)

Help the listeners to hear in this story how Jesus shared common human experiences like suffering, and how Jesus faced up to such suffering.

> Jesus and the disciples have lived and worked together for some time.
> Jesus asks the disciples two questions.
> First he asks, 'Who do the crowds think I am?'
> The crowds think Jesus is a great man, like Elijah the prophet or John the Baptist.
> Second he asks, 'Who do you think I am?'
> Peter said, 'You are the Messiah, chosen by God to lead God's people.'
> Jesus explains that he is not a miraculous leader.
> He is a leader who will suffer pain and be put to death on the cross.
> Then he will be raised up on the third day.
> Jesus' followers too must accept suffering.

Dance/drama

- Devise a dance about suffering pain and recovery.
- As a TV news reporter, interview some of the crowd and some of the disciples, asking them who they think Jesus is and whether he really experiences pain and suffering.

Games

- Create a board game where the penalties and advantages are to do with pain and recovery, for example, 'grazed knee, go back four spaces', 'sore throat, miss a turn', 'leg in plaster, throw a six to move', 'your cold is better, take an extra turn'.

EXPLORING WITH ADULTS

Introduction
Display some newspaper cuttings of human suffering. Ask the group how they react to these pictures.

Experience
- What are your experiences of suffering?
- How do you feel about suffering?
- What effect does your suffering, or someone else's suffering, have on you?

Scripture
Read LUKE 9, 18-27
- What does this teaching say about Jesus' understanding of Messiahship?
- How do you interpret Jesus' teaching about his suffering for today?
- What does this story say about the purpose of Jesus' suffering?

Integration
- How does God use Jesus' suffering?
- How do Christians today share Jesus' suffering?
- How do you share Jesus' suffering?

Application
- How can the church express Jesus sharing human suffering?
- How can you express Jesus sharing human suffering?
- How can the cross be used in worship to proclaim today's theme?

CELEBRATING TOGETHER

Welcoming children

Make space during the service for the display of the children's work on feeling hurt to be viewed and discussed. If the children have prepared drama on the TV reporter interviewing the crowd and disciples, this can be presented immediately before the Gospel reading. The children might also interview some of the adult members of the congregation. Structure the prayers and intercessions around the theme of pain and suffering. If the children have prepared dance on suffering, this can be shared after the Invitation to Prayer.

All age activity

Invite members of the congregation to bring a picture of someone feeling hurt, possibly clipped from a newspaper or magazine. Display these pictures around the church. Also invite the congregation to place particular concerns with suffering on the intercession board. The following ideas can be explored in buzz groups, discussion or teaching:

- our experiences of feeling hurt;
- images of suffering from film and television;
- how suffering changes our attitudes and outlook;
- Jesus' acceptance of suffering;
- Jesus' concern with suffering in today's world.

Teaching point

When Peter and the disciples recognised that Jesus was the Messiah, Jesus began to explain to them what that meant. He was not a superhuman wonder worker, but someone truly human like themselves. He would suffer pain and he would be put to death; and God would raise him to life on the third day.

WORSHIP RESOURCES

Prayer

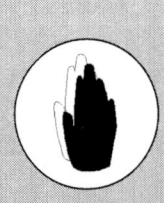

Lord God,
your Son Jesus Christ suffered
before he entered his glory:
Make us willing to deny ourselves,
take up the cross, and follow in his footsteps,
that we may share in his eternal joy;
who lives and reigns with you
and the Holy Spirit, now and for ever.

Readings

Old Testament - GENESIS 22, 1-13
New Testament - COLOSSIANS 1, 24-29
Gospel - LUKE 9, 18-27

Hymns and songs

Come and Praise

    25 When Jesus walked in Galilee
    48 Father, hear the prayer we offer
    49 We are climbing Jesus' ladder
    74 Sad, puzzled eyes

Hymns Ancient and Modern New Standard

    68 O sacred head, surrounded
  117 Praise to the holiest in the height
  141 The head that once was crowned with thorns
  237 Take up thy cross, the saviour said
  335 A stranger once did bless the earth
  487 Lord Christ, we praise your sacrifice
  530 With joy we meditate the grace

24 Feeling loved

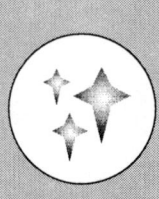

PREPARATION

Bible theme

The king and the kingdom: transfiguration (4TH SUNDAY IN LENT)

The fourth Sunday in Lent continues to explore the humanity of Jesus. Today's Gospel reading draws attention to Jesus' close relationship with God the Father and to his experience of being loved by the Father. Through this close relationship of love, the divine glory shines and is seen and recognised by Jesus' close companions. The Old Testament reading describes how Moses also was allowed to draw close to God and how 'the skin of his face shone because he had been speaking with the Lord.' In the New Testament reading Paul contrasts Moses' experience of closeness to God with the experience which we can share by being joined with Christ. Because we believe in Jesus' humanity we also believe that we can share with him in his closeness to the Father. We can begin to experience the significance of the gospel narrative about Jesus' close relationship with the Father by exploring our own experiences of feeling loved.

Aims

- to build on our experiences of feeling loved;
- to help us understand love as a basic human experience;
- to see that Jesus shared our experience of feeling loved.

Hearing the scriptures

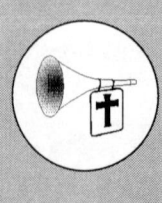

EXODUS 34, 2935

The book of Exodus tells of Moses' close relationship with God and how God gave the law to the people through Moses. The people knew that Moses had been speaking with God because 'the skin of his face shone.' The account of the transfiguration of Christ in the gospels is clearly influenced by this tradition about Moses.

2 CORINTHIANS 3, 4-18

Paul contrasts the age of Moses with the age of Jesus, the law which Moses gave with the freedom brought by Christ, and the glory which faded from Moses with the greater degree of glory we grow into in Christ.

LUKE 9, 28-36

Today's Gospel reading concerning the transfiguration follows on immediately from last Sunday's Gospel reading concerning the recognition of Jesus as Messiah and the prophecy of suffering. The transfiguration sets the seal of God's approval on Jesus' suffering. According to Luke's account, Moses and Elijah explicitly talk with Jesus about his 'departure' or death. According to Matthew's account God's voice addresses Jesus from the cloud and says, 'This is my son, my loved one.' At key points in his life, like his baptism and transfiguration, Jesus is assured of the Father's love.

EXPLORING WITH CHILDREN

Starting

Make a large outline of a heart on the floor, perhaps using strips of red paper, and invite the children to sit inside the heart with the teachers and leaders. Discuss their experiences of feeling loved. Draw out ideas of:

- being loved by brothers and sisters;
- being loved by friends;
- being loved by parents and grandparents;
- being loved in the church;
- signs of being loved;
- enjoying being together;
- enjoying doing things together;
- giving and receiving;
- warmth and comfort.

Making

Give the children the opportunity to make a display about feeling loved. Here are some suggestions.

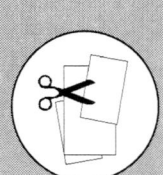

- Make a list beginning 'love is …'.
- Make happy face masks which the children can wear.
- Make a collage of people looking happy and loved, with the heading 'this is my son, my loved one'.
- Make badges of hearts with the motto 'Jesus loves me', so all the congregation can have one.
- Design a picture of the transfiguration.
- Make a huge heart which can be suspended from the rafters of the church.

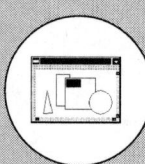

Doing

- Invite a mother to bring her young baby and tell how the baby experiences love.
- Invite members of the congregation to talk about their experiences of feeling loved.
- Look at pictures of children enjoying themselves with friends, family, school, church, etc.
- Invite the children to bring photographs of themselves taken when they have felt loved.
- Take the children on a trip or visit when they can feel especially loved by the group, teachers and leaders.

Display headings

- Today's theme is transfiguration.
- We all need to feel loved.
- Jesus shares our need to feel loved.
- Jesus felt the father's love.
- Jesus is truly human like us.
- God said 'This is my son, my loved one'.
- Our project today is about feeling loved.

Using the bible

The story of the transfiguration (LUKE 9, 28-36)
Help the listeners to hear in this story how Jesus felt close to God and how God assures Jesus that he is loved.

> This passage follows on directly from last week's Gospel reading.
> Jesus takes Peter, James and John into the hills to pray.
> Jesus' face starts to shine.
> Jesus' clothes become dazzling white.
> Moses and Elijah, great men of the past, are seen with Jesus.
> A cloud overshadows them.
> A voice speaks from the cloud, 'This is my son, my loved one'.
> Jesus feels God's love very closely at times like this in his life.

Dance/drama

- Develop choral speech with a chorus on the idea, 'love is …'.
- Devise a dance about feeling loved.

Games

- Play farmer's in his den to help the younger children feel included and loved.

EXPLORING WITH ADULTS

Introduction
Display some photographs showing loving relationships between people. These could include parents with a new born baby. Ask the group when they feel loved.

Experience
- What are the signs of being loved?
- What does it feel like to be loved?
- How does being loved change people?

Scripture
Read LUKE 9, 28-36
- What does this story say about the love between Jesus and the father?
- How do you interpret this story about Jesus' transfiguration for today?
- How did Jesus experience his father's love?

Integration
- How do people experience God's love today?
- How do you experience God's love today?
- What effect does God's love have on your life?

Application
- What can the church do to demonstrate God's love to people?
- How can you share God's love with others?
- How can the Peace be shared as a demonstration of God's love?

CELEBRATING TOGETHER

Welcoming children

Make space during the service for the display of the children's work on feeling loved to be viewed and discussed. If the children have devised a dance about feeling loved this can be presented after the Gospel reading. If the children have prepared choral speech on the idea 'love is ...' this can be shared before the Peace and the Peace used to express the love of Christ among the congregation.

All age activity

Invite members of the congregation to bring a picture of someone feeling loved, possibly clipped from a newspaper or magazine. Display these pictures around the church. If the children have made enough badges of hearts, these can be given to the congregation as they come into church or at an appropriate point during the service. During the Ministry of the Word, members of the congregation can be invited to add to the children's list 'love is ...'. The following ideas can be explored in buzz groups, discussion or teaching:

- our experiences of feeling loved;
- images of feeling loved from films and television;
- how feeling loved changes our attitudes and outlook;
- Jesus' experience of God's love;
- Jesus' concern for love in today's world.

Teaching point

The story of the transfiguration draws attention to Jesus' close relationship with God the Father and to his experience of being loved by the Father. Like all men and women, Jesus needed to feel loved.

WORSHIP RESOURCES

Prayer

Almighty God,
whose Son was revealed in majesty
before he suffered death upon the cross:
Give us faith to perceive his glory,
that we may be strengthened to suffer with him,
and be changed into his likeness
from glory to glory;
who lives and reigns with you and the Holy Spirit,
one God, now and for ever.

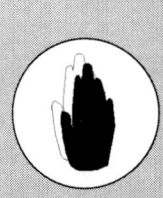

Readings

Old Testament - EXODUS 34, 29-35
New Testament - 2 CORINTHIANS 3, 4-18
Gospel - LUKE 9, 28-36

Hymns and songs

Come and Praise

   11 For the beauty of the earth
   16 When God made the garden of creation
   27 There's a child in the streets
   36 God is love; his the care
 101 In the bustle of the city

Hymns Ancient and Modern New Standard

 131 Love divine, all loves excelling
 133 Immortal love for ever full
 318 'Tis good, Lord, to be here
 365 God is love, let heav'n adore him
 407 O God in heaven, whose loving plan
 441 Christ upon the mountain peak

25

Feeling free

PREPARATION

Bible theme
The king and the kingdom: the victory of the cross (5TH SUNDAY IN LENT)
Through the victory of the cross God sets the people free, free from sin and free from the barriers which separate men and women from God. This message of freedom is conveyed in the Old Testament reading through Moses' call to liberate the people of Israel from their slavery in Egypt. In the Gospel reading Jesus meditates on the victory of his death over evil and how his cross liberates all whom he draws to himself. In the New Testament reading Paul stresses how baptism into the death and resurrection of Christ frees his followers from the consequences of sin and frees them to live in relationship with God. We can begin to experience the significance of the bible's teaching about the victory of the cross by exploring our own experiences of feeling free.

Aims
- to build on our experiences of feeling free;
- to help us understand the freedom which God wants for us;
- to see Jesus' death as God's way of setting the people free.

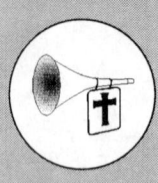

Hearing the scriptures
EXODUS 6, 2-13
The Exodus from Egypt stands at the heart of the religious life of the Old Testament. This is a story which is repeated every year at the festival of Passover, as all successive generations of Jewish people step into the shoes of their ancestors whom God graciously freed from slavery and led into the promised land. This is faith in a God who sets the people free. God says to the Israelites, 'I am the Lord. I will release you from your labours in Egypt. I will rescue you from slavery there. I will redeem you with arm outstretched and with mighty acts of judgement.'

COLOSSIANS 2, 8-15
Paul reminds the Colossians how once they were separated from God, 'dead because of your sins.' In baptism, however, they were buried with Christ and also 'raised to life with him through your faith in the active power of God.' This is true freedom.

JOHN 12, 20-32
In John's gospel the crucifixion is the hour of glory, the time of judgement and the final victory. Jesus says, 'when I am lifted up from the earth, I shall draw all people to myself.' Those whom Christ draws to himself share his freedom.

EXPLORING WITH CHILDREN

Starting
Begin by asking the children to work together to produce a large mural of a cage. When the mural is finished, ask them to imagine that they are trapped alone inside the cage. Draw out ideas of:

- restricted movement;
- lack of things to see;
- lack of things to do;
- lack of food and drink;
- lack of power to get out;
- lack of freedom to do what you want.

Then discuss their feelings when someone comes along to rescue them. Draw out ideas of:

- new found freedom;
- the power to do what they want;
- gratitude towards the rescuer;
- what they would most want to do once set free.

Making
Give the children the opportunity to make a display about feeling free. Here are some suggestions.

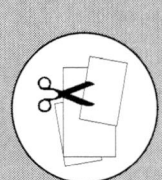

- Make a model of a cage.
- Design a picture of the Israelites as slaves.
- Choose pictures which illustrate freedom, including birds, animals, adults and children, with the heading, 'Jesus sets us free'.

- Make a list beginning 'freedom is …'.
- Design and cut out a set of cardboard keys, with the text 'Jesus unlocks and frees', so that all the congregation can have one.
- Organise a display of old keys.

Doing

- Invite someone who has been lost or trapped to talk of their experience of being rescued and set free.
- Look at pictures of birds or animals in cages.
- Look at pictures of slavery.
- Watch a video about finding freedom.
- Find out about the United Nations Freedom Charters.

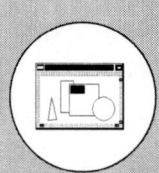

Display headings

- Today's theme is the victory of the cross.
- God sets the Israelites free from slavery.
- God wants us to be free.
- Jesus sets us free.
- Our project today is about feeling free.

Using the bible

The story of God's plans to rescue the Israelites from slavery (EXODUS 6, 2-13)
Help the listeners to hear in this story the great liberating promise that God wishes to set us free.

> The Israelites are slaves in Egypt.
> They are not free to do what they want.
> They are not free to go where they want.
> They are forced to give slave labour.
> God hears the groanings of the people.
> God sets out to set the people free.
> God calls Moses to lead the people to freedom.
> Moses tells the Israelite people of God's plans.
> The people are so depressed by their slavery that they do not believe Moses.

Dance/drama

- Devise a dance about being trapped and set free.
- Develop a play about the Israelites as slaves in Egypt.

Games

- Play freeze tag where the children are 'frozen' and set free by a touch.

EXPLORING WITH ADULTS

Introduction
Take the group outside, if possible into a garden. Ask what it feels like to have space and to be free.

Experience
- What things (or relationships) prevent people feeling free?
- What prevents you from feeling free?
- What is it like to feel free?

Scripture
Read Exodus 6, 2-13
- What does this story say about God's freeing of the Israelites?
- How do you interpret this story about freeing slaves for today?
- What does this story say about how God liberates men and women?

Integration
- From what do Christian people need freeing today?
- What are your experiences of being freed by God?
- How does Christ's death free you?

Application
- How can the church show God's power to set people free?
- How can you show God's power to set people free?
- How can the Absolution help us to be aware that God sets us free?

CELEBRATING TOGETHER

Welcoming children

Make space during the service for the display of the children's work on feeling free to be viewed and discussed. If the children have prepared drama about the Israelites as slaves, this can be shared immediately before the Old Testament reading. If they prepared dance on the theme of freedom, this can be shared immediately after the New Testament reading. If they have made keys for the congregation, these can be given out immediately after the Gospel reading, which ends 'I shall draw all people to myself.'

All age activity

Invite members of the congregation to bring something which speaks to them of freedom, for example, a poem about bird flight, a book about a wartime escape, a picture of wide open space. During the Peace invite them to discuss what they have chosen and to discover who has chosen similar things. Display these symbols of freedom around the church. The following ideas can be explored in buzz groups, discussion or teaching:

- our experiences of feeling free;
- images of freedom from films and television;
- how feeling free changed our attitudes and outlook;
- how Jesus sets us free;
- the needs of today's world to be liberated by Jesus.

Teaching point

Through the victory of the cross God sets the people free, free from sin and from the barriers which separate men and women from God.

WORSHIP RESOURCES

Prayer

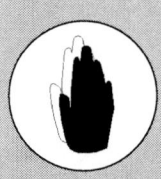

Grant, O merciful Lord,
that, as you saved the human race
by the cross and passion of your Son Jesus Christ;
so, trusting in the power of his sacrifice,
we may share in the glory of his victory;
through Jesus Christ our Lord.

Readings

Old Testament - Exodus 6, 2-13
New Testament - Colossians 2, 8-15
Gospel - John 12, 20-32

Hymns and songs

Come and Praise
- 22   I danced in the morning
- 29   From the darkness came light
- 39   O Lord, all the world belongs to you
- 98   You shall go out with joy

Hymns Ancient and Modern New Standard
- 67   When I survey the wondrous cross
- 129 Lord Jesus, think on me
- 141 The head that once was crowned with thorns
- 142 Hail to the Lord's anointed
- 361 For the healing of the nations
- 391 Lord Jesus Christ
- 395 Lord of all power, I give you my will

26

Fan club

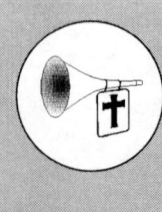

PREPARATION

Bible theme
The way of the cross (PALM SUNDAY)
Palm Sunday begins the events of Holy Week with Jesus coming to Jerusalem. The Gospel reading from Matthew tells of Jesus entering Jerusalem, 'riding on an ass, riding on the foal of a beast of burden.' The crowds go wild with excitement, shout Jesus' praises and cut branches from the trees to spread in his path. He receives a hero's welcome from a huge fan club. The Old Testament reading from Zechariah gives the prophecy which Jesus' entry into Jerusalem fulfils. The New Testament reading from Philippians looks forward to the day when the whole world unites to join Jesus' fan club, when 'at the name of Jesus every knee should bow.' We can begin to experience the significance of the Palm Sunday entry into Jerusalem by exploring our own images and experiences of fan clubs.

Aims
- to build on our experiences of fan clubs;
- to help us develop our personal commitment to Jesus;
- to see the Palm Sunday procession as Jesus' fan club.

Hearing the scriptures
ZECHARIAH 9, 9-12
Zechariah prophesies that the Messiah will come to Jerusalem in victory, but also in humility. The ass is a sign of humility in marked contrast to the fine horse of the warrior king.

PHILIPPIANS 2, 5-11

In this passage Paul is probably quoting an early Christian hymn on the nature of Christ. In his original glory Christ was the possessor of the divine nature. Through humility and obedience he became subject to human limitations and even to death. Now God has exulted him to the highest place where he will receive praise from 'every tongue'.

MATTHEW 21, 1-13

In this entry into Jerusalem, Jesus makes full use of prophetic imagery to show that he is the Messiah. The choice of the ass deliberately fulfils the prophecy of Zechariah, chosen for the Old Testament reading. The people recognise his claim and respond accordingly. His fan club shouts verses from Psalm 118, 'Hosanna to the Son of David!' 'Blessed is he who comes in the name of the Lord!' They spread their cloaks on the road, just as an earlier generation had done to welcome Jehu as king. They spread the way with palms, just as an earlier generation had done to welcome Simon Maccabeus after one of his most notable victories.

EXPLORING WITH CHILDREN

Starting

Borrow football supporters' scarves and hang them one side of the room; borrow posters of pop stars and hang them the other side of the room. Encourage the children to talk about going to a football match or pop concert, or watching them on television. Give particular attention to the supporters and fan club. Draw out ideas of:

- being a member of a fan club;
- what makes people want to join;
- signs of membership, like badges and scarves;
- time devoted to supporting team or star;
- excitement of seeing team or star;
- journeys made to support team or star;
- how the fan club cheers, waves, etc.

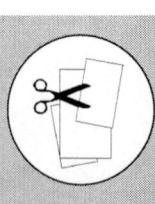

Making

Give the children the opportunity to make a display about fan clubs. Here are some suggestions.

- Organise a display of fan club materials.
- Make a collage of the Palm Sunday procession.
- Make a poster of football or pop star fans.
- Make palm crosses so they can be given to Jesus' fan club at the service.
- Make wavers from stiff paper for a Palm Sunday procession.
- Make shakers to use in the Palm Sunday procession.
- Make banners for the Palm Sunday procession.

Doing

- Watch a video of fans at a football match or a pop concert.
- Invite someone to talk about a local supporters club for football, cricket, school teams, etc.
- Ask children who belong to a fan club to bring some of their membership materials.
- Invite a member of the congregation who belongs to a fan club to talk about his or her interest.
- Go and cheer a local team.

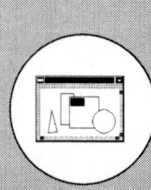

Display headings

- Today's theme is the way of the cross.
- Fan clubs support their teams.
- Fan clubs support their heroes.
- The crowd was Jesus' fan club on Palm Sunday.
- Jesus invites us to join his fan club.
- Our project today is about fan clubs.

Using the bible

The story of Jesus' entry into Jerusalem on Palm Sunday (MATTHEW 21, 1-13)
Help the listeners to hear in this story the great shouts of praise from Jesus' fan club.

> Jesus and his disciples have been travelling towards Jerusalem for some days.
> Jesus stops at the village of Bethphage.
> Jesus asks his disciples to fetch a donkey for him.
> An ancient prophet described the king riding on a donkey as a sign of peace.

Jesus completes his journey on the donkey.
The crowd and Jesus' fan club go wild with excitement.
They spread their cloaks in the road.
They cut branches from the trees to wave and spread in Jesus' path.
They shout 'Hosanna to the Son of David'.

Dance/drama
- Prepare a procession for Palm Sunday, using banners, shakers, wavers, palm crosses, etc. The children may like to dress up. Try to borrow a donkey.
- Devise a rhythmic shout of hosanna.

Games
- Invite the children to take turns in 'performing' before the group. The group acts as their fan club.

EXPLORING WITH ADULTS

Introduction
Display any objects which show membership of a fan club, for example, a scarf from a football club. Ask the group to describe fan club membership.

Experience
- What are your experiences of fan clubs?
- How do fan clubs treat their stars?
- Why might you join a fan club?

Scripture
Read MATTHEW 21, 1-13
- What does this story say about people's response to Jesus?
- How do you interpret this story about Jesus' followers for today?
- How is commitment expressed to Jesus by his followers?

Integration
- How is Jesus welcomed by Christians today?
- How do you welcome Jesus in your life?
- What do you do to show your commitment to Jesus?

Application
- How can the church express its commitment to Jesus on Palm Sunday?
- How do you express your commitment to Jesus on Palm Sunday?
- How can the Prayer of Thanksgiving express our commitment on Palm Sunday?

CELEBRATING TOGETHER

Welcoming children
Make space during the service for the display of the children's work on fan clubs to be viewed and discussed. If the children have prepared a rhythmic shout of hosanna, this can be incorporated within the Prayer of Thanksgiving.

All age activity
Begin the service by equipping the congregation with the palm crosses, shakers and wavers made by the children, and invite the congregation to share in Jesus' fan club. Then begin the Palm Sunday procession. It is most effective if the opening of the service can take place in the church hall, school or another church and then process through the streets to complete the service in the parish church. At an appropriate point in the service invite the congregation to reflect on their experience of taking part in the Palm Sunday procession. The following ideas can be explored in buzz groups, discussion or teaching:

- our experience of walking through the streets in procession;
- the reactions of other people to us;
- how the procession witnessed to the Gospel;
- how churchgoers can best witness their allegiance to Christ.

Teaching point
On Palm Sunday the crowd unites as a fan club to give Jesus a hero's welcome to the city of Jerusalem.

WORSHIP RESOURCES

Prayer

> Almighty and everlasting God,
> in your tender love towards us
> you sent your Son our Saviour Jesus Christ
> to take our human nature,
> and to suffer death upon the cross;
> Grant that following the example
> of his patience and humility
> we may be made partakers in his resurrection;
> through Jesus Christ our Lord.

Readings

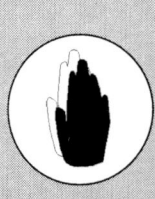

> Old Testament - ZECHARIAH 9, 9-12
> New Testament - PHILIPPIANS 2, 5-11
> Gospel - MATTHEW 21, 1-13

Hymns and songs

Come and Praise

> 33 Praise the Lord in the rhythm of your music
> 40 Praise him, praise him
> 45 The journey of life
> 128 Trotting, trotting through Jerusalem

Hymns Ancient and Modern New Standard

> 61 Ride on! ride on in majesty!
> 63 My song is love unknown
> 328 All glory, laud, and honour
> 337 All praise to thee, for thou, O king divine
> 345 Christ is the king! O friends rejoice
> 443 Christian people, raise your song
> 459 Give me joy in my heart, keep me praising

27 Spring

PREPARATION

Bible theme
The resurrection of Christ (EASTER DAY)
In pre-Christian times the word 'Easter' was associated with the Goddess of spring and the rebirth of the natural world after the death and barrenness of the winter months. In the Christian church Easter celebrates the resurrection of Christ and the Christians' participation in his resurrection. The Gospel reading tells the story of the first Easter Sunday and the empty tomb. In the New Testament reading Paul spells out the significance of the Easter resurrection to the followers of Christ. The Old Testament reading takes Isaiah's psalm of praise and reapplies it to the Easter resurrection of Christ. We can begin to experience the significance of the bible's teaching about the resurrection of Christ by exploring our own experiences of Spring time.

Aims
- to build on our experiences of spring;
- to help us understand spring as a season of new life;
- to see Easter as new life for Jesus and as new life for all God's people.

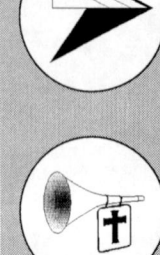

Hearing the scriptures
ISAIAH 12, 1-6
The Israelite people looked back to the Exodus from Egypt as the supreme point in history when God intervened to save them. In chapter 11 Isaiah has announced a new Exodus for God's people. Now in chapter 12, Isaiah provides two short psalms of praise to God for this new saving act. The church has applied these psalms to the resurrection of Christ.

1 Corinthians 15, 12-20

In the first eleven verses of this chapter, Paul sets out his evidence for the resurrection of Christ, recounting the early resurrection appearances. Now he argues that Christ's resurrection is the 'first fruits' and guarantees that the rest of the human race can be raised in Christ.

John 20, 1-18

John tells the story of the first Easter Sunday with less drama than Matthew. Mary Magdalen, Peter and the other disciple (usually thought to be John) find the empty tomb. John saw the empty tomb and believed. Mary does not understand until she sees the risen Lord and he addresses her by name.

EXPLORING WITH CHILDREN

Starting

Go out for a walk. Look for the signs of spring; listen to the sounds of spring; sniff the smells of spring. Look for signs of new life. Draw out ideas of:

- migratory birds returning and singing;
- birds building nests and laying eggs;
- grass growing through cracks in the paving stones;
- new life in the ponds: frog spawn and tadpoles;
- crocuses growing out of seemingly dead corms;
- new growth in grass and plants;
- buds opening on trees;
- hibernating animals waking;
- hares and rabbits in evidence;
- lambs in the meadows;
- brightness of the sky.

Making

Give the children the opportunity to make a display about spring. Here are some suggestions.

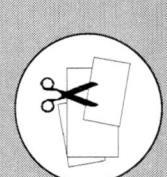

- Collect moss, twigs, flowers to make an Easter garden.
- Decorate hens' eggs as a sign of Easter; use a red dye.
- Grow cress seeds in an empty egg shell.
- Germinate beans on blotting paper.
- Make Easter cards, showing symbols of spring and new life.

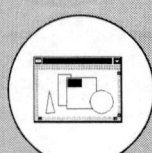

Doing
- Produce pictures of spring.
- Bring a bunch of spring flowers.
- Invite someone to talk about their experience and feelings of springtime.
- Look at a bird's nest.
- Look at different sorts of eggs.
- Look at seeds growing.

Display headings
- Today's theme is the resurrection of Christ.
- New Life comes out of death.
- Easter is an old name for the Goddess of spring.
- Spring comes out of winter.
- Easter Sunday comes out of Good Friday.
- Mary comes to the empty tomb.
- The Lord is risen: he is risen indeed. Alleluia!
- Our project today is about spring.

Using the bible
The story of Mary, Peter and John going to the empty tomb (JOHN 20, 1-18)
Help the listeners to hear in this story the powerful discovery of the empty tomb and the recognition of Jesus himself.

> Mary comes early to the tomb.
> It is still dark.
> The stone has been taken away.
> Mary goes to tell the others.
> She does not understand what has happened.
> Peter and John go into the tomb.
> They see the burial cloth and believe.
> Mary still does not understand; she is outside weeping.
> Jesus calls her by name, 'Mary'.
> She goes to the others and says 'I have seen the Lord.'

Dance/drama
- Devise a dance to illustrate the growth of a seed into a healthy plant.
- Devise a dance to explore the experience of a hibernating animal waking up in spring.
- Act out the coming of Mary, Peter and John to the empty tomb.

Games
- Freeze tag enables the children to experience freezing and unfreezing, suspending animation and becoming reanimated.

EXPLORING WITH ADULTS

Introduction
Take a short walk and look, sniff and feel the spring. Ask the group to describe their experiences of spring.

Experience
- What is your experience of spring?
- What new life do you experience in spring?
- How do you feel in spring?

Scripture
Read JOHN 20, 1-18
- What does this story say about the resurrection of Jesus?
- How do you interpret this story about Jesus' resurrection for today?
- What is the effect of Jesus' resurrection on Mary and Peter?

Integration
- What is the new life that Jesus experiences?
- What does this new life of Jesus mean to you?
- How do you experience Jesus' resurrection in your life?

Application
- How can the church witness to the new life in Jesus?
- How can your actions witness to the new life in Jesus?
- How can the eucharist witness to the new life in Jesus?

CELEBRATING TOGETHER

Welcoming children
Make space during the service for the display of the children's work on spring to be viewed and discussed. If the children have prepared a dance to explore the experience of a hibernating animal waking up in spring, this can be shared immediately after the Gospel reading. If the children have made Easter cards or painted Easter eggs, these can be presented to members of the congregation. Invite the children to assemble around the Easter garden for one of the hymns.

All age activity
Invite members of the congregation to bring something which speaks to them of the spring. This may include budding branches, flowers, photographs or pictures of springtime scenes. After the Gospel reading invite them to discuss what they have brought and to find someone who has brought something quite similar. The following ideas can be explored in buzz groups, discussion or teaching:

- our experiences of spring;
- images of springtime promoted by the media;
- how springtime can affect our feelings and attitudes;
- how the resurrection of Jesus promises a new start like spring;
- how we can share with others the excitement of the resurrection.

Teaching point
We see today how in the mystery of creation life is renewed in the spring. Today Jesus' resurrection from the dead brings new life to God's people.

WORSHIP RESOURCES

Prayer

All praise to you, our God,
you raised your Son in triumph from the grave
conquering sin and death,
and opening for all people the way to eternal life:
Grant us so to die daily to sin
that we may rise and live with him
in the joy of his resurrection;
who lives and reigns with you and the Holy Spirit,
one God, now and for ever.

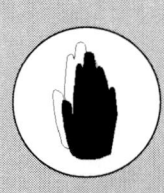

Readings

Old Testament - ISAIAH 12, 1-6
New Testament - 1 CORINTHIANS 15, 12-20
Gospel - JOHN 20, 1-18

Hymns and songs

Come and Praise

- 22   I danced in the morning
- 29   From the darkness comes light
- 39   O Lord, all the world belongs to you
- 130 All in an Easter garden

Hymns Ancient and Modern New Standard

- 75   The day of resurrection!
- 77   Jesus Christ is risen today
- 79   Christ the Lord is risen again
- 428 Thine be the glory
- 451 Early morning, 'Come prepare him'
- 501 Now the green blade riseth from the buried grain
- 518 Walking in a garden

28 Butterflies

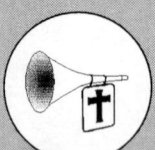

PREPARATION

Bible theme

The upper room (1ST SUNDAY AFTER EASTER)

The theme of the first Sunday after Easter is the power of Christ's resurrection to bring about change. In the Gospel reading the disciples were hiding behind locked doors in fear. Jesus changes their fear to joy. Later, he changes Thomas' doubts to faith. In the New Testament reading Peter emphasises how the Christian's suffering is changed to joy. The Old Testament reading is a psalm of praise to God for changing defeat into victory, slavery into freedom. We can begin to experience the significance of the bible's teaching about the power of the risen Christ to bring about change in the lives of his followers by exploring our own understanding of caterpillars and butterflies.

Aims

- to build on our experiences of caterpillars and butterflies;
- to help us understand change and transformation;
- to see the resurrection of Jesus as the source and power for change and transformation.

Hearing the scriptures

EXODUS 15, 1-11

This is the great song of praise offered to God by Moses and the Israelites for the safe crossing of the Red Sea. At Easter the Christian church re-applies this song of Moses and the Israelites in thanksgiving for the resurrection of Christ. As the exodus transformed slavery into freedom, so Christ's resurrection brings new life to God's people.

1 PETER 1, 3-9

Peter describes the power of the resurrection to bring about change in our lives. The resurrection brings us new birth, a living hope and salvation for our souls.

JOHN 20, 19-29

John describes the power of the risen Christ to bring about change in the lives of the early disciples. On the first day of the week they were full of fear and hiding behind locked doors. Jesus comes to them, proclaims peace to them and changes their fear into joy. A week later Jesus comes again. Now he changes Thomas' doubt into faith.

EXPLORING WITH CHILDREN

Starting

Bring some pictures of butterflies, their eggs, larvae, pupae and caterpillars. Discuss the life cycle of the butterfly and the changes that take place. Draw out ideas of:

- the butterfly lays tiny eggs;
- from the egg comes the caterpillar;
- the caterpillar eats and grows;
- it changes into a chrysalis covered in skin;
- the butterfly takes shape inside the skin;
- the butterfly emerges;
- the butterfly flies away to freedom and to lay eggs.

Making

Give the children the opportunity to make a display about butterflies. Here are some suggestions.

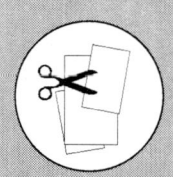

- Draw a diagram showing the life cycle of a butterfly.
- Design a collage of butterflies in a garden.
- Design a collage of the disciples in the upper room.
- Make small butterfly brooches.
- Make models of butterflies using bright tissues to display in church as mobiles.

Doing

- Use the book The Hungry Caterpillar as a stimulus.
- Produce pictures of other creatures which change shape as they develop, for example, spawn/tadpole/frog, egg/cygnet/swan.
- Discover where to find the eggs or chrysalis of butterflies.
- Visit a butterfly farm.

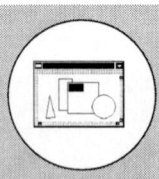

Display headings
- Today's theme is the upper room.
- Caterpillars change into butterflies.
- Jesus is changed by his resurrection.
- Jesus changes the disciples' fear into joy.
- Jesus changes Thomas' doubt into faith.
- Our project today is about butterflies.

Using the bible
The story of the disciples in the upper room and Jesus coming to them (JOHN 20, 19-29). Help the listeners to hear in this story the powerful transformation experienced by the disciples as they come face to face with the risen Christ.

> The disciples meet in secret behind locked doors.
> Their feelings include sadness, fear, anger, despair.
> Jesus comes and says 'Peace be with you'.
> The disciples' fear is changed to joy.
> Thomas is not there and refuses to believe.
> A week later Jesus comes again and says 'Peace be with you'.
> Thomas' doubt is changed into belief.

Dance/drama
- Devise a dance to explore the life cycle of the butterfly and celebrate the freedom of it.
- Act out the story of the upper room.

Games
- Play statues; when the music stops the children have to freeze in their current position. When the music starts they can come to life.

EXPLORING WITH ADULTS

Introduction
Listen to a record of resurrection music. You might use an extract from The Messiah. Ask the group to describe their experience of the change brought about by Christ's resurrection.

Experience
- What experiences change people's lives?
- What events have changed your life?
- How have people changed your life?

Scripture
Read JOHN 20, 19-29
- What does this story say about the impact of the resurrection on the disciples?
- How do you interpret this story about the upper room for today?
- What does this story say about the risen Christ's power to change people?

Integration
- How are people changed by the risen Christ today?
- How has the risen Christ changed your life?
- What effect has the risen Christ had on your daily life?

Application
- How can the church proclaim Christ's power to transform lives?
- How can you help others experience Christ's transforming power?
- How can the ancient Eastertide affirmation

    The Lord is risen

    He is risen indeed,

  be most effectively used in worship?

CELEBRATING TOGETHER

Welcoming children
Make space during the service for the display of the children's work on butterflies to be viewed and discussed. Hang the mobiles of butterflies prominently in church. The dance of the butterflies can make a powerful introduction to the Gospel reading, especially if this reading is presented in dramatic form.

All age activity
Invite members of the congregation to draw or paint a picture of a butterfly or to make a mobile featuring butterflies. Display these prominently in the church. The following ideas can be explored in buzz groups, discussion or teaching:

- occasions when butterflies have created an impression on us;
- how we felt about making a butterfly to bring to church;
- the feelings and images butterflies engender in us;
- why the butterfly is a symbol of transformation;
- how the disciples were changed by their meeting with the risen Christ.

Teaching point
The life cycle of the butterfly illustrates how change occurs in the natural world. Jesus' resurrection brings about a profound change in the lives of his followers when he greets them in the upper room.

WORSHIP RESOURCES

Prayer

Almighty God,
who in your great mercy made glad the disciples
with the sight of the risen Lord:
give us such knowledge of his presence with us,
that we may be strengthened and sustained
by his risen life
and serve you continually in righteousness and truth;
through Jesus Christ our Lord.

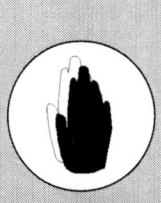

Readings

Old Testament - EXODUS 15, 1-11
New Testament - 1 PETER 1, 3-9
Gospel - JOHN 20, 19-29

Hymns and songs

Come and Praise

- 27 There's a child in the streets
- 29 From the darkness comes light
- 53 Peace, perfect peace, is the gift of Christ our Lord
- 55 Colours of day dawn into the mind
- 129 Jesus in the garden

Hymns Ancient and Modern New Standard

- 74 O sons and daughters let us sing!
- 82 Jesus lives! thy terrors now
- 349 Come, risen Lord, and deign to be our guest
- 412 O Lord, we long to see your face
- 424 The first day of the week
- 428 Thine be the glory, risen, conquering son

29

Bread

PREPARATION

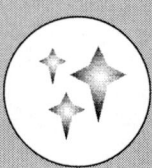

Bible theme

The Emmaus road (2ND SUNDAY AFTER EASTER)
The key idea which links the three readings is the feast prepared for God's people and through which God's presence is made known to them. In the Old Testament reading Isaiah looks forward to the time when God will prepare this feast. The Gospel reading shows the two disciples recognising Jesus' presence as he breaks bread to share with them. The New Testament reading speaks of this great feast as a wedding supper. We can begin to enter the disciples' experience of encountering the risen Christ in the breaking of bread by exploring our own experiences of bread.

Aims

- to build on our experiences of bread;
- to help us understand the bread of communion;
- to see the breaking of bread as the sacrament through which the risen Christ makes his presence known.

Hearing the scriptures

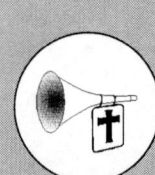

ISAIAH 25, 6-9
The prophet Isaiah is looking forward to the deliverance and ingathering of Judah. On that day God will prepare a great feast with the best food and the richest wines. Then people will say, 'See, this is our God for whom we have waited to deliver us.'

REVELATION 19, 6-9
John's vision also sees the climax of God's saving work as a feast, this time as the wedding feast of the Lamb. The climax of this passage is the invitation, 'Blessed are those who are invited to the wedding-supper of the Lamb.' The church continues to use these words as an invitation to communion.

LUKE 24, 13-35

This resurrection appearance on the Emmaus Road is related only by Luke. Like an early eucharist, ministry of the word is followed by ministry of sacrament. On the journey they studied the scriptures and began to fit parts of the jigsaw together; but it was not until the bread was broken that Christ was fully revealed. This feast at Emmaus both reenacted the last supper and looked forward to the great wedding supper of the Lamb.

EXPLORING WITH CHILDREN

Starting

Bring pictures of different kinds of bread or, better still, bring real bread in different shapes, sizes and types: white, brown, granary, wholemeal, sliced, matzot, chappati. Draw out ideas of:

- how bread is made;
- the flour, yeast, dough, oven, etc. used in making bread;
- the smell of newly baked bread;
- how different types of bread vary;
- the different ways in which bread is eaten;
- bread which the children remember and times when it has tasted especially good;
- how bread is a basic food.

Making

Give the children the opportunity to make a display about bread. Here are some suggestions.

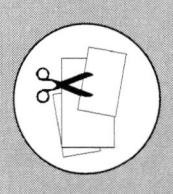

- Bake bread, some of which can be used for the eucharist and some can be shared with the congregation during or after the service (NB use quick rise yeast).
- Make matzot and chappatis.
- Design a collage of different types of bread.
- Design an advert for the different ways bread can be eaten, including different sandwich fillings.

Doing

- Collect adverts of bread from magazines.
- Look at bread wrappers.
- Invite someone to talk about making bread, ideally a local baker.
- Look at pictures of bread making in this country and in other parts of the world.
- Look at pictures of people eating bread in different cultures.
- Collect recipes for making different types of bread.

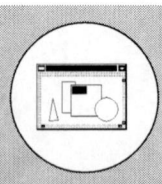

Display headings

- Today's theme is the Emmaus road.
- Bread is a common and important part of life.
- Jesus takes bread.
- Jesus blesses bread.
- Jesus breaks bread.
- Jesus shares bread.
- The disciples recognise Jesus at the breaking of bread.
- Our project today is about bread.

Using the bible

The story of the walk to Emmaus (LUKE 24, 13-35)

Help the listeners to hear in this story the great disclosure as the disciples recognise Jesus when he broke the bread.

> It is Easter day.
> The travellers know about the crucifixion, not yet the resurrection.
> They talk about what has been happening in Jerusalem.
> The stranger joins the travellers.
> The stranger explains the scriptures to them.
> They invite the stranger to share supper with them.
> During the meal the stranger:
> - takes bread,
> - blesses bread,
> - breaks bread,
> - shares bread.
> They recognise Jesus' presence with them.

Dance/drama

- Devise a dance about bread in the making. One child, or group of children, is the cook and other children represent each of the ingredients which are gradually added and mixed together. The mixture is put into the oven, where it rises and spills over the tin.
- Act out the journey on the Emmaus Road and the supper.

Games

- Create a board-game about making a loaf of bread. Use ideas like 'good weather for harvest, go on six spaces', 'rain at harvest, miss a turn', 'oven not hot enough, go back two spaces', 'oven too hot, go back to start', etc.

EXPLORING WITH ADULTS

Introduction
Bring in a new loaf of bread. Break it and share it with the group. Ask them to describe the importance of bread in their lives.

Experience
- Why is bread an important daily food?
- How did you feel receiving the broken bread?
- What did the experience of sharing the broken bread say to you?

Scripture
Read LUKE 24, 13-35
- What does this story say about how Jesus is recognised?
- How do you interpret this story of breaking bread for today?
- What does breaking bread tell us about the presence of Christ?

Integration
- How is bread used in the eucharist?
- How is the bread linked with the presence of Christ?
- How is Christ present for you in the eucharist?

Application
- How can the church proclaim Christ's presence through breaking bread?
- How can you proclaim Christ's presence through breaking bread?
- How can the breaking of bread be emphasised in the eucharist?

CELEBRATING TOGETHER

Welcoming children
Make space during the service for the display of the children's work on bread to be viewed and discussed. If the children have prepared dance about making bread, this can follow the gospel most effectively. When the bread 'rises' it overflows and the children can move into the congregation to share some of the bread which they have baked with the worshippers. Some of the bread can also be used for the eucharist.

All age activity
Invite members of the congregation to bring to the service something to do with bread, for example a baking tin, a recipe, a picture, a poem or a text from scripture. After the Gospel reading invite them to display and discuss these items. The following ideas can be explored in buzz groups, discussion or teaching:

- our experiences of eating fresh bread;
- images of bread throughout the world;
- our experiences of sharing bread in the eucharist;
- our meeting with the risen Jesus in the breaking of bread.

Teaching point
The loaf of bread stands right at the centre of Christian worship. When Jesus broke bread at Emmaus his disciples recognised his presence with them. We, too, come to recognise Jesus' presence at the eucharist.

WORSHIP RESOURCES

Prayer

Almighty God,
your Son Jesus Christ after his resurrection
appeared to his disciples on the Emmaus Road,
and made himself known in the breaking of bread:
Open our eyes that we may know him
in all his redeeming work;
who lives and reigns with you and the Holy Spirit,
one God, now and for ever.

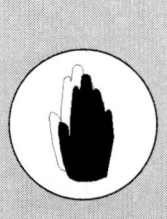

Readings

Old Testament - ISAIAH 25, 6-9
New Testament - REVELATION 19, 6-9
Gospel - LUKE 24, 13-35

Hymns and songs

Come and Praise

  45 The journey of life
  47 One more step along the world I go
  75 I saw the man from Galilee

Hymns Ancient and Modern New Standard

  84 The Lord is risen indeed!
214 Guide me, O thou great redeemer
262 Alleluia! sing to Jesus!
263 Lord, enthroned in heavenly splendour
349 Come, risen Lord, and deign to be our guest
357 Father, we thank thee who hast planted
439 Christ is the heavenly food that gives
480 Let us break bread together on our knees

30

Fish

PREPARATION

Bible theme
The lake side (3RD SUNDAY AFTER EASTER)
The readings continue the theme of the resurrection appearances. In the New Testament reading Paul lists the key resurrection appearances on which his faith rests. In the Gospel John tells of the appearance by the lake and how the risen Jesus reverses the disheartened disciples' feelings of failure. In the Old Testament reading Isaiah emphasises how God intends to replace disappointment with joy. We can begin to enter into the disciples' experience of meeting with the risen Christ at the lake side by drawing on our own experiences of fish and fishing.

Aims
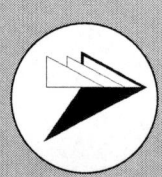
- to build on our experiences of fish;
- to help us understand the fish as a Christian symbol;
- to see the link between the appearances at the lake side and the eucharist.

Hearing the scriptures

ISAIAH 61, 1-7
Isaiah announces that the spirit of the Lord has come upon him to bring a message of good news to the people in exile, 'to comfort all who mourn, to give them garlands instead of ashes, oil of gladness instead of mourners' tears.' The word 'good news' is the same word which Christians translate as 'gospel'.

1 CORINTHIANS 15, 1-11
There were those in Corinth who denied the resurrection of the dead. In this passage Paul reminds them of the tradition which he handed on to them. He includes a short creed 'that Christ died for our sins according to the scriptures, that he was buried, that he was raised on the third day according to the scriptures.' Then he lists the appearances to 1) Peter, 2) the twelve, 3) the 5000, 4) James, 5) all the apostles, 6) Paul himself.

JOHN 21, 1-14

Some of the disciples had returned to their work as fishermen. This night they had caught nothing. In the morning Jesus joins them, but they recognise him only after they have landed a large catch. Jesus invites them to share breakfast with him and hosts a fellowship meal. This story had a great influence on early Christian art, where the eucharist was pictured as a meal presided over by Christ with fish and bread on the table. The fish also becomes a key secret sign in the early church, whereby Christians could recognise each other in times of persecution. The Greek word for fish, ICHTHUS, makes up the initial letters for 'Jesus Christ God's Son Saviour.'

EXPLORING WITH CHILDREN

Starting

Bring some fishing pictures: anglers by the river bank, small fishing boats in harbour, deep sea fishing boats. Talk about who has been fishing and what it is like. Draw out ideas of:

- different types of fishing: rod, net, trawler, etc.;
- the life of the fishermen: those who fish for fun and those who fish for a living;
- different types of fish: shapes, weight, etc.;
- fish as a rich food resource;
- different ways of cooking fish: frying, grilling, baking, boiling, barbecuing.

Making

Give the children the opportunity to make a display about fish. Here are some suggestions.

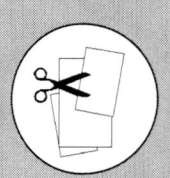

- Make a fish for each member of the congregation: two or three dimensional.
- Make a net and fill it with model fish.
- Make a model of the shore, boats, fish and fishermen.
- Make banners with the fish sign, the Greek word 'ICHTHUS' and the words 'Jesus', 'Christ', 'God's Son', 'Saviour'.
- Design a collage showing Jesus presiding over a feast or eucharist with bread and fish on the table.

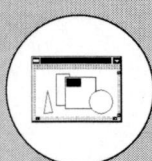

Doing
- Collect adverts of fish.
- Visit a fishmongers: smell, look and handle the fish.
- Visit a fish farm or market.
- Go on a fishing or angling trip.
- Watch fishermen or anglers, in real life by a local river or lake or on television.
- Cook some fish and feast on it.

Display headings
- Today's theme is the lake side.
- After the crucifixion the disciples return to their trade as fishermen.
- The risen Jesus meets with the disciples by the lake side.
- The risen Jesus shares a meal of bread and fish with the disciples.
- The fish became a secret sign in the early church.
- The Greek word for fish is ICHTHUS.
- Our project today is about fish.

Using the bible
The story of the meeting with Jesus at the lake side (JOHN 21, 1-14)
Help the listeners to hear in this story the great disclosure as the disciples recognise Jesus.

> The disciples return to their familiar, normal working life as fishermen.
> They had been fishing all night long.
> They had failed to catch any fish.
> The unexpected visitor appears on the shore.
> He advises them to try again.
> The advice from the shore results in a huge catch.
> They recognise the stranger.
> They share a breakfast of bread and fish.
> New courage comes as old friendships are renewed.

Dance/drama
- Act out the return of the disciples to their work as fishermen, the night time fishing trip, Jesus' arrival by the lake side, the catch and the shared breakfast.
- Devise a dance about the despair of the fishermen, working all night without catching anything, the excitement of landing a huge catch and the happiness of sharing breakfast with Jesus.

Games
- Suspend a small magnet at the end of a string and bamboo cane 'fishing-line'; attach paperclips to small paper fish and go fishing.

EXPLORING WITH ADULTS

Introduction
Display some examples of the Christian fish sign, such as car stickers and brooches. Ask the group why the fish sign is used and what it means.

Experience
- Where have you seen the fish sign?
- What is the significance of the fish sign?
- How do you feel wearing or displaying the fish sign?

Scripture
Read JOHN 21, 1-14
- What does this story of the lakeside say about resurrection life?
- How do you interpret this story about Jesus' resurrection appearance for today?
- What is the significance of the meal for the disciples?

Integration
- Why is a meal at the centre of the Christian faith?
- How is the risen Christ linked to the fish sign?
- How does displaying the fish sign declare faith?

Application
- How can the fish sign be used in the life of your church?
- How can the fish sign be used in your own life?
- How can the eucharist reflect the meal at the lakeside?

CELEBRATING TOGETHER

Welcoming children

Make space during the service for the display of the children's work on fish to be viewed and discussed. The dance of despair at catching nothing and the delight in landing a full catch and recognising Jesus can help to interpret the Gospel reading. A cardboard fish can be given to each member of the congregation as they enter. The congregation are then invited to write their names on the fish which are collected during the service in the net made by the children. The net is put on the altar as a sign of commitment.

All age activity

Invite members of the congregation to bring something which speaks to them of fish or fishing. Anglers may choose to bring their rod and line; cooks may choose to bring a fish recipe. Others may choose to bring a picture, a poem or a text from scripture. After the Gospel reading invite them to display and discuss these items. The following ideas can be explored in buzz groups, discussion or teaching:

- our experiences of fishing;
- our experiences of cooking fish;
- our experiences of sharing a fish meal;
- the disciples' meeting with the risen Jesus as they share a breakfast of bread and fish.

Teaching point

The fish became an important symbol to the early church. After his resurrection Jesus shared a meal of bread and fish with his disciples. The Greek word for fish, ICHTHUS, makes up the initial letters for 'Jesus Christ God's Son Saviour.'

WORSHIP RESOURCES

Prayer

Almighty God,
you raised your Son from death
to be the resurrection and the life for all believers:
Raise us to true life in him,
that we may seek the things which are above,
where Christ reigns with you and the Holy Spirit,
for ever.

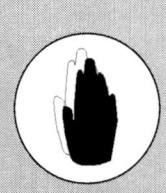

Readings

Old Testament - Isaiah 61, 1-7
New Testament - 1 Corinthians 15, 1-11
Gospel - John 21, 1-14

Hymns and songs

Come and Praise

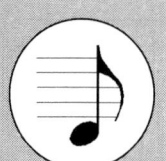

- 19 He's got the whole world, in his hand
- 25 When Jesus walked in Galilee
- 32 Thank you, Lord, for this new day
- 84 Waves are breaking on the shore

Hymns Ancient and Modern New Standard

- 80   Alleluia, alleluia, hearts to heaven and voices raise.
- 83   Love's redeeming work is done
- 235 O Jesus, I have promised
- 427 The Son of God proclaim
- 428 Thine be the glory, risen, conquering Son
- 431 We have a gospel
- 533 You, living Christ, our eyes behold

31 Mender

PREPARATION

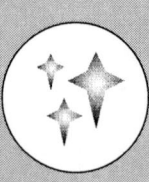

Bible theme
The charge to Peter (4TH SUNDAY AFTER EASTER)
The key idea which links the three readings is the way in which Christ's resurrection brings restoration. In the Old Testament reading Isaiah proclaims that God restores his chosen city of Jerusalem. In the New Testament reading restoration is offered to the church in Laodicea. In the Gospel reading Jesus offers restoration to Peter and recommissions him. We can begin to experience the significance of the bible's teaching about restoration by exploring our own experiences of mending and of the mender.

Aims
- to build on our experiences of mending and restoring things;
- to help us understand ideas of mending and restoring relationships;
- to see Christ's resurrection as bringing mending and restoration.

Hearing the scriptures
ISAIAH 62, 1-5
The prophet Isaiah proclaims that God will reverse the fortunes of Jerusalem and restore the city as a sign of God's supremacy in the world. At the time of writing, people looked at Jerusalem and called her 'forsaken' and 'desolate'. When God restores the city they will call her 'hephzibah' (which means 'my delight is in her') and 'beulah' (which means 'married').

REVELATION 3, 14-22
The church in Laodicea is severely criticised for being 'lukewarm, wretched, pitiable, poor, blind, and naked.' The severe criticism is followed by an invitation to accept the restoration which Christ can bring.

JOHN 21, 15-22

Earlier in the gospel narrative Peter had played a central part in the work and commitment of the disciples. At Jesus' trial, however, Peter's commitment had been tested and failed. He had denied his Lord three times. Now after the resurrection, Jesus offers Peter the chance of making a three fold affirmation of commitment in place of the three fold denial. Peter's personal restoration carried with it the responsibility to share Christ's pastoral concern for his followers.

EXPLORING WITH CHILDREN

Starting

Bring something which is broken, for example, a toy which is obviously broken or no longer works. Talk about the children's experiences of things breaking and needing repair. Concentrate on the people who do the work of repair. Draw out ideas of:

- the shoemaker reheeling shoes;
- the clockmaker repairing a watch;
- the RAC or AA mechanic attending a breakdown;
- parents repairing a cycle tyre puncture;
- parents repairing a broken electric fuse;
- the toy repairer in the 'dolls hospital'.

Making

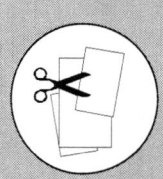

Give the children the opportunity to make a display about the mender. Here are some suggestions.

- Repair a cycle tyre puncture.
- Make a collage of people who mend, using bits of the things they mend in the collage, for example, a piece of a clock for the clockmaker, or an old piece of shoe leather for the shoemaker.
- Mend something that is broken.
- Sew on a button that has come off a garment.
- Make a display of tools used for mending.

Doing

- Collect examples of things that are broken: toys, clocks, vases, etc.
- Look at pictures of things that are broken.
- Visit a building which is being repaired or restored.
- Watch a shoemaker or clockmaker at work.
- Invite someone from a local garage to talk about their work repairing cars.
- Talk with a member of the congregation who likes repairing things at home.

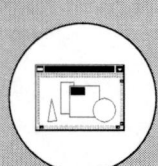

Display headings

- Today's theme is the charge to Peter.
- The clockmaker mends the broken watch.
- The shoemaker puts a new heel on the shoe.
- The RAC or AA mends the broken car.
- Peter had broken his trust with Jesus.
- Jesus mends his relationship with Peter.
- Our project today is about the mender.

Using the bible

The gospel story of Peter and Jesus (JOHN 21, 15-22)
Help the listeners to hear in this story the great sense of restoration which Peter experienced.

> Peter (Simon) is chosen to be a disciple (MARK 1, 16-17).
> Peter is given special responsibility and privileges by Jesus (MATTHEW 16, 17-19).
> Peter falls asleep in Gethsemane before Jesus is arrested (MARK 14, 37-39).
> Peter denies that he knows Jesus three times (MARK 14, 66-72).
> Now Jesus asks Peter three times whether he loves him.
> Jesus charges Peter three times to feed his sheep.
> Peter, who broke his trust with Jesus, is now restored.

Dance/drama

- Devise a dance about the breakdown of a car, the gradual grinding to a stop, the frustration of it being broken and the feeling of restoration when the mechanic repairs it.
- Act out the scene at Jesus' trial when Peter denied Jesus three times; bring out his sorrow and shame.
- Act out the scene when Jesus mends the relationship with Peter; bring out Peter's anxiety and subsequent joy.

Games
- Play mechanical toys. A small proportion of the children are appointed as menders; when the music starts the others pretend to be mechanical toys; when the music stops the toys break down; when the music restarts the menders need to touch each broken toy to signal its repair.

EXPLORING WITH ADULTS

Introduction
Display a pair of worn out shoes in need of repair. Ask the group how things and people are restored.

Experience
- What are your experiences of restored relationships?
- How do you feel about such experiences?
- How are you affected by restored relationships?

Scripture
Read JOHN 21, 15-22
- What does this story say about Jesus restoring relationship with Peter?
- How do you interpret this story about Peter for today?
- What does this story say about Jesus' action in broken relationships?

Integration
- Where is mending and restoration needed in people's lives today?
- How does Jesus bring mending and restoration today?
- How have you experienced Jesus' power to mend and restore?

Application
- How can the church help to mend and restore broken lives?
- How can you help to mend and restore broken lives?
- How can the Absolution be used as an act of restoration?

CELEBRATING TOGETHER

Welcoming children

Make space during the service for the display of the children's work on the mender to be viewed and discussed. If the children have prepared a short dramatic presentation based on Peter's threefold denial of Jesus at the trial, this can provide a powerful prelude to the Gospel reading. At the Peace a special point can be made of restoring broken relationships. Before the Peace a short dance can emphasise the feeling of being broken; after the Peace the dance can recommence, now emphasising the feeling of being restored.

All age activity

Invite members of the congregation to bring something which is broken and needs the attention of the mender, for example, a watch or clock. During the Peace invite them to discuss what they have brought and what would be needed to mend these broken objects. Display these items around the church. The following ideas can be explored in buzz groups, discussion or teaching:

- our experiences of breaking down on the road and the need for the repair services;
- our experiences of things which have broken down at home and the need to have them mended;
- our own skills in mending;
- broken relationships and how they are mended;
- Peter's experience of restoration.

Teaching point

During Jesus' trial Peter had denied him three times. Today we hear how Jesus mends that broken relationship after the resurrection. Just as Peter had denied him three times, now Jesus gives Peter the opportunity to affirm his love for him three times.

WORSHIP RESOURCES

Prayer

Almighty God,
you have given us your Son Jesus Christ
to be the way, the truth and the life:
Help us in faith to follow him as your apostles did,
and bring us to eternal life;
through Jesus Christ our Lord.

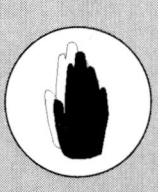

Readings

Old Testament - ISAIAH 62, 1-5
New Testament - REVELATION 3, 14-22
Gospel - JOHN 21, 15-22

Hymns and songs

Come and Praise

- 25   When Jesus walked in Galilee
- 39   O Lord, all the world belongs to you
- 51   Our father, who art in heaven
- 102   You can't stop rain from falling down

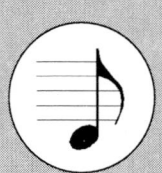

Hymns Ancient and Modern New Standard

- 115   Dear Lord and father of mankind
- 235   O Jesus, I have promised
- 244   Hark, my soul! it is the Lord
- 317   Thou art the Christ, O Lord
- 362   'Forgive our sins as we forgive'
- 391   Lord Jesus Christ
- 509   Rise and hear! the Lord is speaking

32
Sons and daughters

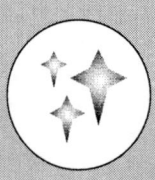

PREPARATION

Bible theme

Going to the father (5TH SUNDAY AFTER EASTER)

All three readings draw on the image of God as father. In the Old Testament reading Hosea portrays God talking with the people like a betrayed husband and a disobeyed father. In the New Testament and Gospel readings both Paul and John speak about Jesus' relationship with the father and imply that we too enjoy the status of God's sons and daughters. We can begin to experience the significance of the bible's teaching about God as father by exploring our own experiences of being sons and daughters.

Aims

- to build on our experiences of being sons and daughters;
- to help us understand Jesus as the Son of God;
- to help us appreciate our relationship with God as sons and daughters.

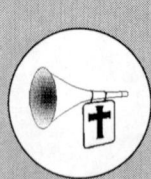

Hearing the scriptures

HOSEA 6, 1-6

Through his relationship with his unfaithful and adulterous wife, Hosea understands how God feels about the relationship with the chosen people. In verses 1-3 the people decide to 'return to the Lord', but in verses 4-6 God expresses distrust of their sincerity. What God is looking for is not their sacrifices, but 'the knowledge of God'. The Hebrew word translated 'the knowledge of God', hesed, means the kind of close relationship which enables one person to get right inside another person's thoughts and feelings. According to the Gospel reading, this is the kind of relationship Jesus has with the father.

1 CORINTHIANS 15, 21-28

Paul speaks of Jesus as the second Adam. According to Genesis, Adam was made in God's own image and in this sense Adam is the son of God. Adam spoils that image and through Adam's disobedience death enters the world. Jesus, the second Adam, restores the image of sonship and through Jesus' obedience comes the resurrection: 'for as in Adam all die, so also in Christ shall all be made alive.'

JOHN 16, 25-33

In John's gospel, Jesus' close relationship with the father is the basis on which his followers also enjoy their close relationship with the father. Feelings of distance from God are replaced by the direct access which is the privilege of members of God's family.

EXPLORING WITH CHILDREN

Starting

Play the card game of Happy Families (preferably a set using people rather than animals). Draw out ideas of:

- how we recognise each family;
- how brothers and sisters look alike;
- how children and parents look alike;
- other ways in which children are like their parents:
    - the way they talk;
    - the way they walk;
    - their attitudes and ideas.

Making

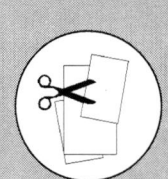

Give the children the opportunity to make a display about sons and daughters. Here are some suggestions.

- Ask each child to draw a picture of himself or herself and of one parent. Mount these pictures in a large collage with a picture of Jesus at the centre.
- Use pictures from magazines to make banners of 'Happy Families'.
- Make enough sets of Happy Family cards so that every child and adult in the congregation can have one card. Choose obvious family identities (for example, hair colour, style of dress) with a number of mothers, fathers, sons and daughters in each family.
- Make a collage showing scenes from Jesus' life which give clues about the character of the father.

Doing

- Collect pictures of animals and their young.
- Collect pictures of children and their parents.
- Invite the children to bring photographs of themselves and their parents.
- Invite a mother and father from the congregation to bring their young baby.
- Invite someone from a local 'family business' (for example, a local builder or baker) to talk about following in their parents' footsteps into the business.

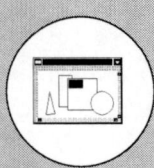

Display headings

- Today's theme is about going to the father.
- Jesus is the Son of God.
- We believe in a God like Jesus.
- In Jesus we see what God is like.
- We are called to be God's sons and daughters.
- Our project today is about sons and daughters.

Using the bible

Talk about how we recognise God the father by looking at Jesus. Invite the children to talk about some of the characteristics of Jesus' life and ministry and what these say about God the father; for example:

> Jesus heals the lame.
> Jesus gives sight to the blind.
> Jesus restores hearing to the deaf.
> Jesus befriends outcasts.
> Jesus forgives sinners.
> Jesus teaches his disciples.

Dance/drama

Devise a set of short sketches in which some of the children adopt the role of parents and others the role of children. Use costumes and mannerisms to show the family likeness.

Games

Play animal families by giving each child an animal picture. The pictures are in groups so that there are about six copies of the same picture. By making the noise of the animal, children try to find the rest of their family.

EXPLORING WITH ADULTS

Introduction
Display some family photographs. Ask the group to discover the relationships between the people.

Experience
- How important are parents in shaping their children's lives?
- How do you feel about this relationship?
- What effect does this relationship have on your life?

Scripture
Read JOHN 16, 25-33
- What does this teaching say about the relationship between Jesus and the father?
- How do you interpret this teaching about Jesus and the father for today?
- What does this teaching say about the disciples' relationship with the father?

Integration
- What does it mean to be a son or daughter of God?
- How are you a son or daughter of God?
- What effect does the relationship have on your life?

Application
- How can the church live as children of God?
- How can your life show you are a son or daughter of God?
- How can the Peace express that all present are children of God?

CELEBRATING TOGETHER

Welcoming children
Make space during the service for the display of the children's work on sons and daughters to be viewed and discussed. If they have prepared short sketches in which some of the children adopt the role of parents and others the role of children, these can be shared before the scripture readings in order to illustrate the secular experiences on which the image of God as father is based.

All age activity
Distribute the Happy Family cards made by the children to the congregation as they come in: give the mother and father cards to the adults and the son and daughter cards to the children, making sure that adults and children from the same family do not get cards which belong to the same set of cards. At the Peace invite the children and adults to seek out those who have cards belonging to the same family as they do. Some may like to mime their family identity. The following ideas can be explored in buzz groups, discussion or teaching:

- our experiences as sons and daughters;
- contemporary images of sons and daughters;
- the strengths and limitations of calling God father;
- how Jesus helps us to see God the father.

Teaching point
Jesus talked about God as father. Through his life and ministry Jesus the Son gives us glimpses of what God the father is like. Through the power of Jesus' resurrection we, too, are called to live as sons and daughters of God our father.

WORSHIP RESOURCES

Prayer

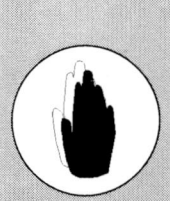

Lord Jesus Christ,
you returned to the glory of your father,
and sent the Holy Spirit to be with us for ever:
May we, knowing his presence and power,
be led into the way of truth
and come to the glory of your kingdom;
where you live and reign
with the father and the Holy Spirit,
one God, now and for ever.

Readings

Old Testament - HOSEA 6, 1-6
New Testament - 1 CORINTHIANS 15, 21-28
Gospel - JOHN 16, 25-33

Hymns and songs

Come and Praise
- 23 Jesus, good above all other
- 36 God is love; his the care
- 66 In Christ there is no east or west
- 69 I belong to a family, the biggest on earth
- 86 The bell of creation is swinging

Hymns Ancient and Modern New Standard
- 102 My God, how wonderful thou art
- 117 Praise to the holiest in the height
- 199 Immortal, invisible, God only wise
- 353 Eternal ruler of the ceaseless round
- 358 Father, who in Jesus found us
- 440 Christ is the world's light, he and none other

33

Kings and queens

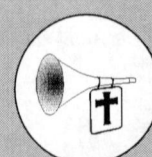

PREPARATION

Bible theme

The ascension of Christ (SUNDAY AFTER ASCENSION DAY)
The key idea which links the three readings is kingship. In the Old Testament reading Daniel's vision describes the enthronement of 'one like a son of man.' In the New Testament reading the writer of the letter to the Ephesians speaks of Christ's kingly rule. The Gospel reading is Luke's account of the ascension: the imagery of the ascension celebrates the kingship of Christ. We can begin to experience the significance of the bible's teaching about the kingship of Christ by exploring our own images of kings and queens.

Aims

- to build on our ideas about the authority of kings and queens;
- to develop our understanding of the kingship of Jesus;
- to see the ascension as a proclamation of Jesus' kingship.

Hearing the scriptures

DANIEL 7, 9-14
The book of Daniel offers God's people a vision of hope. The changing foreign rulers under which they are living are symbolised by a sequence of beasts. God, symbolised as the ancient of days, will take power away from these inhuman rulers and invest power in the humane kingdom of God's people, symbolised as a man taking over rule from the beasts. Later Christian understanding applied this prophecy to the kingship of Christ and gave Christ the title 'Son of Man'.

EPHESIANS 1, 15-23

Christ's rule is described as supreme, above all other earthly and heavenly rulers. He is 'supreme Lord over all things.' The image in verse 20 of sitting at God's right hand is taken from Psalm 110, a psalm associated with the ceremonies of royal initiation.

LUKE 24, 45-53

The story of the ascension enables Luke to provide a link between his two books. He ends his gospel with a brief reference to the ascension; then he begins the Acts of the Apostles with a more extended account. The ascension affirms the kingship of Christ.

EXPLORING WITH CHILDREN

Starting

Look at products which carry the royal crest and the royal assent, 'By appointment to HM the Queen', like some tins of syrup, packets of sugar, etc. Look at stamps and coins which bear the head of the sovereign. Draw out ideas of:

- why coins and stamps carry the sovereign's head;
- why some products carry the royal crest;
- the importance and authority of the sovereign;
- the honour and majesty of the sovereign;
- what kings and queens do.

Making

Give the children the opportunity to make a display about kings and queens. Here are some suggestions.

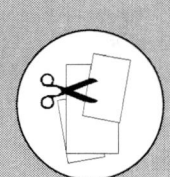

- Make crowns with bright jewels.
- Make royal robes for a procession.
- Design a collage of the royal family.
- Display a collection of products carrying the royal crest.
- Design an invitation to a royal occasion, suitably illuminated and sealed.
- Organise a display of stamps showing the royal head.
- Make a pattern by rubbing the surface of coins showing the royal head.

Doing
- Look at pictures of the royal family, or a royal function like a Buckingham Palace garden party.
- Invite someone from the congregation who has seen or met a member of the royal family to talk about the occasion.
- Visit somewhere associated with the royal family.
- Look for the royal crest in the local neighbourhood, or on products in a local shop.
- Look to see if there is a royal crest in the local church.

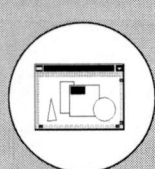

Display headings
- Today's theme is the ascension of Christ.
- The queen's authority is shown on stamps and coins.
- The queen's coat of arms is carried on famous tins and packets.
- Jesus is king.
- The ascension celebrates the kingship of Jesus.
- Our project today is about kings and queens.

Using the bible
The story of the ascension of Jesus (LUKE 24, 45-53)
Help the listeners to hear in this story of the ascension the enthronement of Jesus as king.

> Jesus meets with the disciples after the resurrection.
> Jesus promises them the power of the Holy Spirit.
> Jesus commissions them to proclaim the gospel, starting in Jerusalem and then moving out to the ends of the earth.
> The disciples are left to carry on Jesus' work.
> Jesus is enthroned.
> Jesus is given authority to rule over everything and all people.

Dance/drama
- Select music which evokes the pomp and dignity of a royal occasion and develop a stately dance.
- Act out a series of short interviews for television with the disciples immediately after the ascension.

Games
- Play 'dress the queen or king'. Assemble two sets of regal clothes (robe, crown, chain of office, etc.). Divide the children into two groups and assign each child a number within the groups. When their number is called the two children (one from each group) race to robe in the regal clothes. The winner gets a point for their team.

EXPLORING WITH ADULTS

Introduction
Display some memorabilia of the coronation. Ask the group about symbols of kingship.

Experience
- What is your experience of royalty?
- How do you feel about the honour and respect given to royalty?
- How do you understand the image of Jesus ruling as king?

Scripture
Read LUKE 24, 45-53
- What does this story of the ascension say about Jesus as king?
- How do you interpret this story about Jesus' ascension for today?
- What does the ascension say about Jesus' relationship with men and women?

Integration
- What evidence is there that Jesus rules in the world today?
- What evidence is there that Jesus rules in your life today?
- How does the world respond to Jesus' kingship?

Application
- How can the church witness to Jesus' kingship?
- How can you witness to Jesus' kingship?
- How can your worship express Jesus' kingship?

CELEBRATING TOGETHER

Welcoming children

Make sure there is space during the service for the display of the children's work on kings and queens to be viewed and discussed. At the Offertory invite the congregation to take a coin out of their pocket or handbag, to look at the sovereign's face on the coin, and then to give the coin in a special collection, taken by the children. Make the procession for the Offertory a royal occasion with appropriate music and dance. The offering of the coins at the altar symbolises Jesus' kingship even over earthly kings and queens.

All age activity

Invite members of the congregation to bring something which speaks to them of kings and queens, for example, a coronation mug, a souvenir stamp, a picture of a royal procession. After the Gospel reading invite them to discuss what they have brought and to discover who has brought similar things. Display these symbols of kings and queens around the church. The following ideas can be explored in buzz groups, discussion or teaching:

- our images of kings and queens;
- media images of royalty;
- the strengths and limitations of seeing Jesus as king;
- the feast of the ascension.

Teaching point

The ascension speaks of Christ being enthroned as king in the same way as Psalm 110 spoke of the enthronement of the Jewish kings:

> The Lord said to my lord:
> 'Sit on my right hand.'

WORSHIP RESOURCES

Prayer

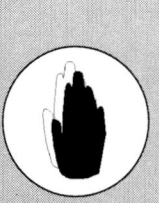

Eternal God, the king of Glory,
you have exalted your only Son
in great triumph to your kingdom in heaven:
Leave us not comfortless,
but send your Holy Spirit to strengthen us
and exalt us to the place
where Christ is gone before,
and where with you and the Holy Spirit
he is worshipped and glorified,
now and for ever.

Readings

Old Testament - DANIEL 7, 9-14
New Testament - EPHESIANS 1, 15-23
Gospel - LUKE 24, 45-53

Hymns and songs

Come and Praise

- 20 Come, my brothers, praise the Lord, alleluia
- 21 Come and praise the Lord our king, hallelujah
- 34 Praise to the Lord, the almighty
- 95 Rejoice in the Lord always

Hymns Ancient and Modern New Standard

- 139 Rejoice! the Lord is king!
- 141 The head that once was crowned with thorns
- 147 Crown him with many crowns
- 148 At the name of Jesus
- 431 We have a gospel to proclaim
- 460 Give to our God immortal praise
- 533 You, living Christ, our eyes behold

34 Wind

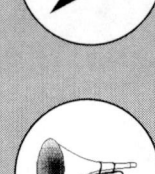

PREPARATION

Bible theme
PENTECOST (PENTECOST)

All three readings speak of God's power working like wind, breath or the Spirit. The close relationship between the ideas of wind, breath and spirit is demonstrated by the fact that the same word is used for all three, both in the Hebrew language of the Old Testament (ruach) and the Greek language of the New Testament (pneuma). We can begin to experience the significance of the bible's teaching about God the Spirit by exploring our own experiences of wind.

Aims
- to build on our ideas of wind;
- to develop our idea of wind as an image of the Holy Spirit;
- to see Pentecost as the feast of the Holy Spirit.

Hearing the scriptures
EZEKIEL 37, 1-14

According to the Hebrew creation story in Genesis, God 'breathed' into Adam's 'nostrils the breath of life.' Ezekiel remembers this when he is writing for the people of God at a time when they are in exile as prisoners of war. They feel desolate, dispirited, as if life itself has gone out of them. The key to Ezekiel's vision in verse 5 is that God will bring new life to the dry bones of the people: 'I will put breath into you, and you shall live.'

ACTS 2, 1-11

This is Luke's account of the coming of the Holy Spirit to the early church, after the period of waiting following the ascension. According to Luke's understanding, it is the presence of the Holy Spirit which constitutes the early church as God's people and makes them the legitimate heirs of the Old Israel where the Holy Spirit had dwelt in earlier times. The key image in verse 2 is 'the rush of a mighty wind.'

John 14, 15-26

In John's gospel Jesus promises the gift of the Holy Spirit to his followers. He says, 'The Holy Spirit, whom the Father will send in my name, will teach you all things and will remind you of everything I have said to you.'

EXPLORING WITH CHILDREN

Starting

Go outside to experience the wind through feeling and seeing its power and effects. Get children talking about the wind and its power. Discuss how they experience the wind and how they know it is there. Draw out ideas of:

- the sounds of the wind: whistling, banging, sweeping;
- the feel of the wind: caressing, soothing, pushing;
- the smell of the wind: spreading scents of animals and flowers;
- the power of the wind: sailing a boat, drying washing, driving windmills, turning weather vanes, dispersing seeds, moving trees, blowing smoke.

Making

Give the children the opportunity to make a display about the wind. Here are some suggestions.

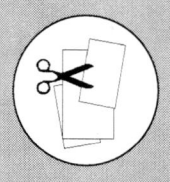

- Make wind chimes.
- Make a weather vane using yoghurt pots and bamboo canes.
- Make wind instruments.
- Use your wind instruments and recorders to make wind music.
- Make hand windmills or model windmills.
- Make kites and fly them.

Doing

- Borrow from the Red Cross or St John's Ambulance a 'Resuscitating Annie', or ask an officer of one of these societies to visit and demonstrate. Perhaps the children can try giving the breath of life to the 'doll'.
- Go and look at a windmill.
- Visit a sailing centre.
- Find some seeds dispersed by wind, for example, dandelions.
- Invite a member of the community to talk about their experience of sailing.
- Go and fly a kite.
- Blow up balloons.
- Sail a model boat.

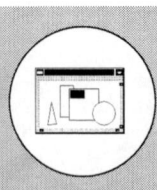

Display headings

- Today's theme is Pentecost.
- In Hebrew, ruach means both Spirit and wind.
- In Greek, pneuma means both Spirit and wind.
- The Holy Spirit came to the disciples like a rushing wind.
- You cannot see the wind but you can feel its effects.
- Our windmill, kites, weather vanes and balloons speak to us of the Holy Spirit.
- Our project today is about wind.

Using the bible

The story of Pentecost/Whitsun (ACTS 2, 1-11)

Through this story help the listeners to share the disciples' experience of God's presence as the wind.

> In Jerusalem the Jewish people are celebrating their festival of Pentecost.
> Jesus' friends are meeting together.
> They experience God's presence like wind.
> They experience God's presence like fire.
> The power of the Holy Spirit changes fear to faith.
> The disciples go to tell others.

Dance/drama

- Imagine the wind is getting up and blowing through a forest picking up the leaves and throwing them into the air. It then drops them. Express these ideas in dance.
- Devise a dance about the valley of dry bones.

Games

- Divide into teams. Make a symmetrical shape of a bird or butterfly for each team. The teams use newspapers to fan their bird or butterfly up and down the room in a form of relay race.

EXPLORING WITH ADULTS

Introduction
Invite someone to play a wind instrument. Ask the group about the experience of the instrument 'coming alive' through the breath of the player.

Experience
- What is your experience of wind bringing something to life?
- When are you aware of the power of the wind?
- How do you feel on a windy day?

Scripture
Read ACTS 2, 1-11
- What does this story say about the Holy Spirit?
- How do you interpret this story about Pentecost for today?
- What is the effect of the presence of the Holy Spirit?

Integration
- Why is wind used as an image of the Holy Spirit?
- How does this image help you to understand the Holy Spirit?
- How do you know the Holy Spirit is present in you?

Application
- How can the church witness to the Holy Spirit?
- How can you witness to the Holy Spirit in your life?
- Develop a response to the reading from Acts affirming the presence of the Holy Spirit.

CELEBRATING TOGETHER

Welcoming children
Make space during the service for the display of the children's work on the wind to be viewed and discussed. The church can be decorated with all that has been made. Balloons and kites can be hung around the church. A dance on the valley of dry bones can follow very powerfully from the reading of that lesson. If wind instruments have been made, make a special point of sharing this music. Balloons can be suspended from the rafters and let down immediately after the Blessing, inviting the congregation to take them home.

All age activity
Invite the congregation to bring something from home which speaks to them about the power of wind, for example, a wind-chime, a wind instrument, a weather vane, a model glider, a model sailing boat, or an appropriate picture. Before the scripture readings invite them to discuss what they have chosen and to display the objects in appropriate groupings. The following ideas can be explored in buzz groups, discussion or teaching:

- our experiences of the wind;
- the different moods of the wind;
- the creative and the destructive face of the wind;
- the experience of God as wind;
- the first Pentecost for the disciples.

Teaching point
We often speak about God in picture language. The picture which tells us most about God the Holy Spirit is that of the wind.

WORSHIP RESOURCES

Prayer

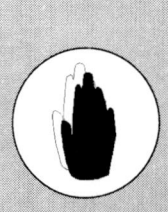

Almighty God,
who on the day of Pentecost
sent the Holy Spirit to the disciples,
filling them with joy
and with boldness to preach the Gospel:
Send us out in the power of the same Spirit
to witness to your truth,
and to draw all people to the fire of your love;
through Jesus Christ our Lord.

Readings

Old Testament - EZEKIEL 37, 1-14
New Testament - ACTS 2, 1-11
Gospel - JOHN 14, 15-26

Hymns and songs

Come and Praise

- 7   All creatures of our God and king
- 19   He's got the whole world, in his hand
- 63   Spirit of God, as strong as the wind
- 107   You've got to move when the Spirit says move

Hymns Ancient and Modern New Standard

- 92   Come, thou Holy Spirit, come
- 154   Gracious Spirit, Holy Ghost
- 156   Come down, O love divine
- 157   Breathe on me, breath of God
- 471   Holy Spirit, come, confirm us
- 478   Let every Christian pray
- 504   On the day of Pentecost

35

Space travel

PREPARATION

Bible theme
The Trinity (TRINITY SUNDAY)
The full nature of God is a mystery which men and women have struggled to grasp and to express. The doctrine of the Trinity affirms that God has been made known in the world in three characteristic ways, as Father, Son and Holy Spirit. The way the early church chose to express this doctrine was in terms of 'three persons in one God.' The readings for Trinity Sunday all emphasise the mystery of God. We can begin to experience the significance of the bible's teaching on the mystery of God by exploring the feelings generated by the mystery of outer space and the wonder of space travel.

Aims
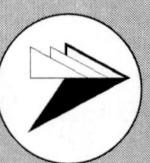
- to build on our ideas about the vastness and mystery of space;
- to develop our response of awe and wonder at the mystery of space;
- to see Trinity Sunday as a celebration of the mystery of God.

Hearing the scriptures
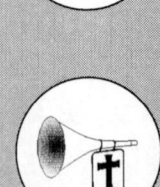
ISAIAH 6, 1-8
Isaiah describes the vision of God through which he received his call to be a prophet. His vision emphasises the mystery and wonder of God. He sees God 'sitting on a throne, high and lifted up.' The awe and majesty is emphasised by the heavenly creatures who surround God and the clouds of incense which serve to partially hide God. Even the seraphim stand in awe of God and worship with the acclamation:

> Holy, holy, holy is the Lord of hosts;
> the whole earth is full of his glory.

EPHESIANS 1, 3-14

This passage is chosen because it makes reference to the three persons of the Trinity. The writer begins this letter to the Ephesians by praising God the Father for the great work God has done through Jesus Christ and sealed in the individual Christian by the Holy Spirit. This is the mystery of the Christian faith.

JOHN 14, 8-17

In his last conversation with the disciples before his passion, the Jesus of John's gospel discusses the mystery of his close relationship with the Father: 'to have seen me is to have seen the Father.' Jesus also promises the indwelling presence of the Spirit.

EXPLORING WITH CHILDREN

Starting

Play some music which suggests the mystery and grandeur of space (for example, Gustav Holst's suite, 'The Planets'). Show a chart of the sky at night and encourage the children to talk about their experience of seeing the night sky. Draw out ideas of:

- the vastness of space;
- some of the names of the stars, constellations and planets;
- the mystery and wonder of space;
- the excitement of space travel;
- the feeling of awe when we consider space;
- our smallness in comparison with space.

Making

Give the children the opportunity to make a display about outer space and space travel. Here are some suggestions.

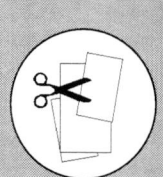

- Build a space rocket from cardboard boxes.
- Make space helmets which the children can wear.
- Create a space ship control deck.
- Design a glorious backcloth of bright silver stars and planets on a dark background.
- Make a model of the solar system, using different size balls and dowelling.
- Draw pictures of the groups of stars.

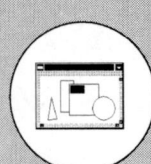

Doing
- Look at pictures of the night sky.
- Look at photographs taken from satellites or space probes.
- Watch a video about space travel.
- Visit a planetarium.
- Look through a telescope.
- Invite someone who is interested in astronomy to talk about it.
- Make a special evening session to look at the stars at night.

Display headings
- Today's theme is the Trinity.
- Holy, holy, holy is the Lord of Hosts.
- The sky at night reminds us of the vastness of God's universe.
- Space speaks of the mystery of God.
- Trinity Sunday proclaims the mystery of God.
- Our project today is about space travel.

Using the bible
The story of Isaiah's vision in the temple (ISAIAH 6, 1-8)
Help the listeners to hear in this story Isaiah's great vision of the mystery and wonder of God.

> Isaiah is sad at the death of the king.
> He is in the temple and has a vision of God.
> The foundations of the temple shake.
> The temple is filled with smoke.
> The seraphim shout, 'Holy, holy, holy is the Lord'.
> Isaiah feels small and insignificant.
> God appoints Isaiah to be a prophet.
> Isaiah responds, 'Here I am! Send me!'.

Dance/drama
- Act out life at the space station, in the space capsule, preparing for lift-off, and landing on the moon.
- Devise a dance to express the mystery of unknown space.

Games
- Use computer games based on the idea of space travel.

EXPLORING WITH ADULTS

Introduction
Go outside and look at the vastness of space. Ask the group how they feel about space travel.

Experience
- How do you feel when you look at the vastness of space?
- How do you react to satellite pictures of space?
- How do these experiences affect your life?

Scripture
Read ISAIAH 6, 1-8
- What does this story say about the holiness of God?
- How do you interpret this story about Isaiah's vision for today?
- What does this story say about the nature of God?

Integration
- How do people react to the holiness of God?
- How do you react to the holiness of God?
- How does the holiness of God affect your life?

Application
- How can the church witness to the holiness of God?
- How can you witness to the holiness of God?
- How can a sense of holiness be promoted in your worship?

CELEBRATING TOGETHER

Welcoming children

Make space during the service for the display of the children's work on outer space and space travel to be viewed and discussed. If a creative dance has been devised to express the mystery of unknown space, this dance could be used twice in the service: after or during the Old Testament reading to illustrate the hymn 'Holy, holy, holy' and during the Prayer of Thanksgiving when the same words reappear.

All age activity

Invite members of the congregation to bring something which speaks to them of the awesomeness and mystery of outer space, for example, a picture of the night sky, a poem or a piece of music. After the Old Testament reading invite them to discuss what they have chosen and to arrange a display in the church. The following ideas can be explored in buzz groups, discussion or teaching:

- our awareness of the mystery of outer space;
- how we communicate our feelings about awe and mystery;
- how experiences of awe and mystery change our outlook on life;
- how the bible communicates the mystery of God;
- the mystery of the Trinity.

Teaching point

When we look at God's universe we glimpse the mystery of God. The Christian doctrine of the Trinity speaks of the mystery, wonder and greatness of God.

WORSHIP RESOURCES

Prayer

Almighty and eternal God,
you have revealed yourself
as Father, Son and Holy Spirit,
one holy and undivided Trinity,
and live and reign in the perfect unity of love:
Keep us in this faith,
that we may know you in all your ways,
and evermore rejoice in your eternal glory,
who are three Persons in one God
now and for ever.

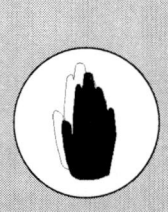

Readings

Old Testament - ISAIAH 6, 1-8
New Testament - EPHESIANS 1, 3-14
Gospel - JOHN 14, 8-17

Hymns and songs

Come and Praise

- 7 All creatures of our God and king
- 12 Who put the colours in the rainbow?
- 13 O praise him!
- 98 You shall go out with joy

Hymns Ancient and Modern New Standard

- 95 Holy, holy, holy! Lord God almighty!
- 181 May the grace of Christ our saviour
- 199 Immortal, invisible, God only wise
- 353 Eternal ruler of the ceaseless round
- 355 Father all-powerful, thine is the kingdom
- 520 We give immortal praise
- 532 Ye watchers and ye holy ones

36

Teams

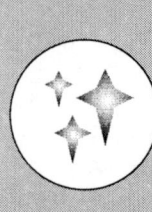

PREPARATION

Bible theme
The people of God (2ND SUNDAY AFTER PENTECOST)
All three readings emphasise how God's people are called to be a special community. In other words, God's church is not simply a loose association of individuals, but a team of people who live and work closely together. Each of the readings uses a different image for this community or team. The Old Testament reading from Exodus speaks of God's call to the people of Israel to be 'a holy nation.' The New Testament reading from 1 Peter applies this same image to the church, 'you are a chosen nation,' and also develops the idea of individual Christians being built together into a temple, 'as living stones.' The Gospel reading from John speaks of the organic unity between branches and the vine. We can begin to experience the bible's teaching about the people of God by exploring our own experiences of teams.

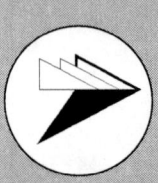

Aims
- to build on our experience of being part of a team;
- to develop our ideas of the church as the team of God's people;
- to meet some of the people in the local church who make up God's team.

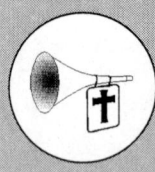

Hearing the scriptures
EXODUS 19, 1-6
This passage comes after the Exodus from Egypt and immediately before the giving of the law at mount Sinai. God makes a special bond with Israel to be 'a holy nation.' In this sense 'holy' means 'belonging to God.'

1 PETER 2, 1-10
It is likely that this section of 1 Peter was originally addressed to those who had just been baptised, as part of the baptism liturgy. Individuals are baptised one by one, but after baptism they become part of God's community. A range of images are used to describe this community: 'living stones', 'a spiritual temple', 'a holy nation', 'a people claimed by God.'

JOHN 15, 1-5

John's gospel does not describe the institution of the eucharist at the last supper before Jesus' arrest. In its place John describes the final teaching which Jesus gave to his disciples; at the heart of this teaching comes the image about the vine: 'I am the vine and you are the branches.'

EXPLORING WITH CHILDREN

Starting

Begin with a game of tug-of-war, but create a deliberate imbalance by having the teacher on one side and varying numbers of children on the other side. Draw out ideas of:

- the need for team work;
- the added strength of a team;
- the way in which members of a team need to pull together.

Now ask the children to form two (or more) teams of equal size and play a team game, for example using a bean bag. Draw out ideas of:

- individuals working together to make up a team;
- individuals have different abilities in the team;
- the role of the leader of the team;
- the need to encourage the slower members.

Talk about the people who make up the team of the local church:

- bell ringers who call people to worship;
- choristers who lead the singing;
- churchwardens who look after the building;
- sidespersons who welcome visitors;
- Sunday school teachers who nurture the young;
- cleaners who keep the church tidy;
- grass cutters who keep the churchyard tidy;
- PCC members who make decisions for the church;
- organist who provides the music;
- vicar who leads the services.

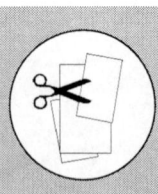

Making

Give the children the opportunity to make a display about teams. Here are some suggestions.

- Design a banner for the local church team.
- Make a set of badges, arm bands, or caps for members of the team to wear.
- Draw up a list of all the different 'jobs' which contribute to the life of the local church.
- Design a collage of all the different people who are the local church.
- Draw a picture of a large vine.
- Draw a picture of a team (a football match, a boat race, a hockey team).

Doing

- Go to watch a team game.
- Watch a video of a team game.
- Invite a member of the church who is part of a local team (football or hockey, etc.) to talk about their team.
- Visit a vineyard or someone who has a vine growing in the garden.
- Invite some members of the church to talk about their particular jobs in the church, for example, organist, bell ringers, etc.

Display headings

- Today's theme is the people of God.
- The people of God work together like a team.
- A team is composed of many individuals.
- Christ is the leader (head) of his team, the church.
- Our project today is about teams.

Using the bible

Jesus uses the vine to teach about God's people being a team (JOHN 15, 1-5)

Help the listeners to hear in this great image from John's gospel how we all form part of the same vine nourished by Jesus himself.

> Vines are trailing plants.
> Vines need training and support.
> The branches produce a mass of leaves and grapes.
> The grapes are picked for food and to make wine.
> The grapes only grow because the branches are part of the vine.
> Jesus said that members of the church are linked to him as their vine.

Dance/drama
- Devise a dance about a growing vine.
- Interview the people who have special responsibilities or jobs in the local church (for example, organists, cleaners, bell ringer, vicar) and tape record a short 'radio programme' or prepare something 'live' for the service. This could be based on the radio programme 'Down Your Way'. Let the people interviewed choose a hymn or something similar.

Games
- Play any team game which is a favourite of the group, for example, rounders, ball games, etc.

EXPLORING WITH ADULTS

Introduction
Involve the group in doing a church job, like stapling the church magazine or news sheet. Ask the group how they feel about working together as a team.

Experience
- What is your experience of the church as a team?
- How does it feel to be part of that team?
- How does belonging to the church team affect your life?

Scripture
Read JOHN 15, 1-5
- What does this teaching say about relationships among the people of God?
- How do you interpret this teaching about the vine for today?
- What does this teaching say about discipleship?

Integration
- In what ways is your church a team?
- How is team work expressed in your church?
- How do you feel about being part of the church team?

Application
- How can your church work best as a team?
- What can you contribute to the teamwork of your church?
- How can worship reflect the teamwork of the people of God?

CELEBRATING TOGETHER

Welcoming children
Make space during the service for the display of the children's work on teams to be viewed and discussed. If the children have prepared a short 'radio programme' on the people who make up the local team at church, this can be presented immediately after the Gospel reading.

All age activity
Invite the members of the congregation to bring something which speaks to them of team spirit, identity or activity, for example, the colours worn by a local football team. Invite them to talk about the teams to which they have belonged and the experience of team collaboration. Make a display of these items. The following ideas can be explored in buzz groups, discussion or teaching:

- our experiences of being part of a team;
- our images of team work;
- how the local church works as a team;
- how the church worldwide is united as a team in Christ;
- how the image of the vine speaks of God's people being a team.

Teaching point
We see today how as many individuals we work together to become the people of God, with Christ as our team leader, the head of the church.

WORSHIP RESOURCES

Prayer

Almighty and eternal God,
you have called us to be your people:
Bring us to closer unity and fellowship
with you and one another,
so that every member of your church
may serve you in holiness and truth;
through our Lord and Saviour Jesus Christ.

Readings

Old Testament - EXODUS 19, 1-6
New Testament - 1 PETER 2, 1-10
Gospel - JOHN 15, 1-5

Hymns and songs

Come and Praise

    20 Come, my brothers, praise the Lord, alleluia
    38 Now thank we all our God
    49 We are climbing Jesus' ladder, ladder
  146 We ask that we live and we labour

Hymns Ancient and Modern New Standard

  171 Thy hand, O God, has guided
  175 Ye that know the Lord is gracious
  208 O happy band of pilgrims
  350 Come, workers for the Lord
  353 Eternal ruler of the ceaseless round
  374 Help us to help each other, Lord
  376 In Christ there is no east or west

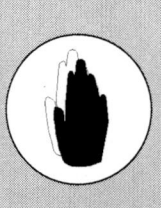

37

Baptism

PREPARATION

Bible theme
The life of the baptised (3RD SUNDAY AFTER PENTECOST)
The key idea which links the three readings is the kind of life which God's people are called to live. In the Old Testament reading the book of Deuteronomy reminds the people of the old covenant of the commandments God requires them to keep. They accepted these commandments when God led them out of Egypt. In the New Testament reading Paul reminds the people of the new covenant of God's expectations of them. They accepted these expectations when they were baptised. In the Gospel reading Jesus talks about the expectations he holds of his followers. While today's New Testament reading spells out the significance of baptism for the early church, it does not actually describe what took place in the ceremony of baptism. A helpful example from the New Testament is to be found in Acts 8, 26-38. We can begin to experience the significance of the bible's teaching about the life of the baptised by exploring our own experiences of baptism.

Aims
- to build on our ideas about baptism;
- to develop our understanding of baptism;
- to see baptism as an entry into the church.

Hearing the scriptures
DEUTERONOMY 6, 17-25
The people of Israel look back to the Exodus from Egypt as the time when God gave them the opportunity for a new way of life. The covenant God then made with them involved the acceptance and keeping of the law.

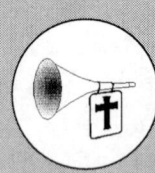

ROMANS 6, 3-11
For Paul baptism was the key moment when the individual was set free from the old way of life and enabled to share in the new life of Christ. Here Paul interprets baptism as a dying and rising with Christ. As adults are literally plunged under water they are buried with Christ; as they are raised up from the water they share in Christ's resurrection.

JOHN 15, 5-11

According to Paul, baptism means incorporation into Christ's risen body. A similar point is made in John's gospel by the image of the vine: the believer becomes a branch of Christ himself who is the true vine.

EXPLORING WITH CHILDREN

Starting

Look at the font or baptistry (or pictures of it) and talk about its use. Draw out ideas of:

- children brought by their parents to be baptised;
- the role of godparents;
- the promises made for the child;
- the special clothes and christening robes;
- the baptism of adults;
- the purpose of baptism;
- the use of water;
- the symbolism of water;
- baptism as a celebration.

Making

Give the children the opportunity to make a display about baptism. Here are some suggestions.

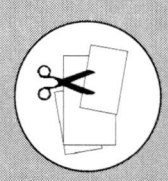

- Design a baptism card welcoming the next children to be baptised in the church.
- Make cards for those babies who were baptised some time ago, perhaps inviting them to a special service.
- Design and make a candleholder for the baptism candle.
- Make a model of a font.
- Design a collage of a baptism taking place in church.

Doing

- Look at the church's baptism register.
- Encourage children to bring photos of their own baptism.
- Collect items connected with baptism, for example, christening robes, cards, candles.
- Invite parents who have recently had their baby baptised to talk about it.
- Invite someone who was baptised as an adult to talk about it.
- Invite someone from the local Baptist church to talk about their way of baptising.

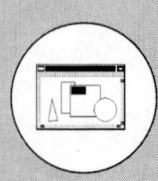

- Visit the Baptist church to look at the baptistry.
- Look at the baptism service in the modern service book.
- Attend a baptism service.

Display headings

- Today's theme is the life of the baptised.
- We join the church at our baptism.
- The water of baptism is the symbol of new life in Christ.
- Our project today is about baptism.

Using the bible
The story of Philip baptising the Ethiopian official (ACTS 8, 26-38)
Help the listeners to hear in this story the preparation and confession of faith required before baptism, and the commitment to a new quality of life made at baptism.

> The Ethiopian official is studying the scriptures and reading the prophet Isaiah.
> Philip teaches him and helps him to understand.
> He asks for baptism.
> Philip tests his faith (see verse 35, which sometimes appears as a footnote).
> He confesses his faith, 'I believe that Jesus Christ is the Son of God'.
> Philip baptises him.
> They both go down to the water for total immersion.

Dance/drama

- Act out a baptism service, using a doll or teddy bear, with children taking the parts of the priest, parents, godparents, friends, etc.
- Devise a dance about the experience of being baptised by Philip in the river, the total immersion, dying with Christ, rising to new life.

Games

- Take the children to a swimming pool and experience the water.

EXPLORING WITH ADULTS

Introduction
Look at any materials used by your church for baptism preparation and services. These might include leaflets of explanation and the cards given to parents. Ask the group to discuss their experiences of attending baptism services.

Experience
- What are the key symbols of baptism?
- How are these symbols used in the service?
- What do you think really takes place in a service of baptism?

Scripture
Read ACTS 8, 26-38
- What does this story say about baptism in the early church?
- How do you interpret this story about baptism for today?
- What is the relationship between baptism and new life?

Integration
- What difference does baptism make to a person's life?
- What difference does baptism make to your life?
- What difference does baptism make to the life of your church?

Application
- How can the church help parents nurture their children in faith?
- How can you help parents nurture their children in faith?
- How can baptismal vows be reaffirmed during the service?

CELEBRATING TOGETHER

Welcoming children
Make space during the service for the display of the children's work on baptism to be viewed and discussed. Ideally the service could include a baptism. The cards made by the children can be presented to the newly baptised baby. The dance on baptism and new life can be shared immediately after the baptism.

All age activity
Invite members of the congregation to bring something which speaks to them of their own baptism, for example, the baptism certificate, a baptismal robe, a baptismal gift, or a photograph. During the service invite them to share and discuss what they have brought and to organise a display in the church. The following ideas can be explored in buzz groups, discussion or teaching:

- baptisms we have attended, perhaps as parents or godparents;
- what we know or have been told of our own baptism;
- why the church baptises babies;
- adult baptism;
- the promises and commitment of baptism.

Teaching point
Through baptism we are joined to Christ, made members of his body the church and share in his risen life.

WORSHIP RESOURCES

Prayer

Lord God,
through our Saviour Jesus Christ
you have assured us of eternal life,
and in baptism have made us one with him:
Deliver us from the death of sin,
and raise us to new life in your love,
in the fellowship of the Holy Spirit,
by the grace of our Lord Jesus Christ.

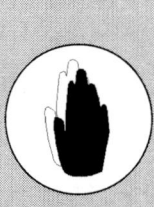

Readings

Old Testament - DEUTERONOMY 6, 17-25
New Testament - ROMANS 6, 3-11
Gospel - JOHN 15, 5-11

Hymns and songs

Come and Praise

- 2 Have you heard the raindrops drumming on the roof-tops?
- 58 At the name of Jesus
- 63 Spirit of God, as strong as the wind
- 95 Rejoice in the Lord always

Hymns Ancient and Modern New Standard

- 80 Alleluia, alleluia, hearts to heaven and voices raise
- 170 The church's one foundation
- 235 O Jesus, I have promised
- 342 Awake, awake: fling off the night!
- 402 Now is eternal life
- 446 Christians, lift up your hearts
- 452 Eternal God, we consecrate

38

Growing up

PREPARATION

Bible theme
The freedom of the sons and daughters of God (4TH SUNDAY AFTER PENTECOST)
The three readings explore God's relationship with the people of God. They illustrate how God gives the people choice and responsibility and how God wants them to mature and grow up to enjoy the full freedom, privilege and responsibility of being the sons and daughters of God. The Old Testament reading reminds us how God rescued the Hebrew people from slavery in Egypt and brought them to the freedom of the promised land. In the New Testament reading Paul argues that Christ rescues God's people from slavery to the law and offers them a share in the freedom of the sons and daughters of God. In the Gospel reading Jesus addresses his followers in the freedom of friends, not as servants. We can begin to experience the significance of the bible's teaching about the freedom of the sons and daughters of God by exploring our own experiences of growing up.

Aims
- to build on our experiences of growing up;
- to help us recognise our growing capabilities and self reliance;
- to see how God wants us to grow up and to use our growing capabilities responsibly;
- to appreciate our freedom and responsibility as the sons and daughters of God.

Hearing the scriptures
DEUTERONOMY 7, 6-11
Deuteronomy reminds the Hebrew people how God rescued them from slavery in Egypt. However, that new freedom which God offers to them remains conditional on obedience to the law.

GALATIANS 3, 23 TO 4, 7

Paul argues that Christ sets us free from the Old Testament law. Through our baptism into Christ we share in him the freedom of being God's sons and daughters: 'you are no longer a slave.' With this freedom, of course, comes responsibility.

JOHN 15, 12-17

In these chapters of John's gospel, Jesus is talking with his disciples immediately before the arrest and crucifixion: 'I shall not call you servants any more.... I shall call you friends.' As friends they are invited to share his close relationship with the Father.

EXPLORING WITH CHILDREN

Starting

Invite the children to bring photographs of themselves as babies and, if possible, some information about their weight and height at the time of their birth and at subsequent stages in their lives. Begin by numbering the photographs and displaying them around the room. Ask the children to guess who is in each photograph. Draw out ideas of:

- what helps them identify the photographs;
- what makes it difficult to identify the photographs;
- differences between the babies in the photographs and the children in the class;
- changes in size and weight;
- changes in expression;
- development of movement;
- development of speech;
- development of abilities.

Making

Give the children the opportunity to make a display about growing up. Here are some suggestions.

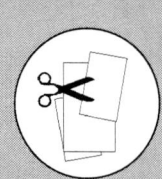

- Make a wall chart of weight and height, comparing the children now and as babies.
- Invite each child to draw a self portrait and to list around it the skills and abilities which they have acquired as they grow up.
- Design a poster comparing the dependence of baby birds and animals with their adult freedom.
- Make model figures demonstrating the skills which the children have acquired as they grow up.

Doing

- Make a list of the new things which the children have learnt.
- Make a list of the new things which the children can do.
- Make a list of the things which the children still must wait for, like driving the car.
- Discuss what the children would like to be or to do when they grow up.
- Invite some adults to talk about their experiences of growing up.
- Look at pictures of baby birds and animals, consider their dependence and the freedom into which they grow.

Display headings

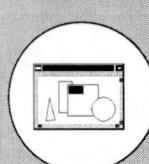

- Today's theme is the freedom of the sons and daughters of God.
- As we grow up we achieve new skills.
- As we grow up we gain greater self reliance.
- As we grow up we experience more freedom.
- As we grow up we accept greater responsibilities.
- Our project today is about growing up.

Using the bible

Jesus' conversation with the disciples (JOHN 15, 12-17)

Help the listeners to hear in this story how Jesus wished his disciples and followers to be aware of sharing the freedom of the sons and daughters of God.

> Jesus' disciples had spent three years with him.
> They had listened to his teachings.
> They had witnessed his healings.
> Now Jesus prepares them to carry on his ministry after his death.
> Jesus said they used to be learners, now they must be teachers.
> Jesus said they used to do what he told them, now they must act in his name.
> Just as Jesus has loved them, now they must love others.

Dance/drama

- Devise a dance about a baby bird growing up, leaving the nest and celebrating the freedom of flight.
- Act out the story of Jesus training his disciples and sending them out in his name.

Games

- Play games which test a skill the children have acquired as they grow up, like catching a soft ball, or rounders.

EXPLORING WITH ADULTS

Introduction
Display pictures of people at different stages in life, from infancy to old age. Invite the group to spend a short time in silence to meditate on the process of growing up. Ask them about their experiences of growing up.

Experience
- What are your memories of growing up?
- How do you feel about your growing up?
- What are the effects of your growing up?

Scripture
Read JOHN 15, 12-17
- What does Jesus' teaching say about the freedom of the children of God?
- How do you interpret this teaching about freedom for today?
- What does this teaching say about the responsibility of the children of God?

Integration
- What choice and responsibility does God give Christians today?
- What choice and responsibility has God given you?
- How has this choice and responsibility affected your life?

Application
- How can the church help Christians experience God's freedom?
- How can you experience God's freedom?
- How can your worship express the freedom of the children of God?

CELEBRATING TOGETHER

Welcoming children

Make space during the service for the display of the children's work about growing up to be viewed and discussed. If the children have written poems or prepared dance on growing up, these can be shared between the readings. Some of the children may like to talk about the early photographs of themselves and how they have grown up.

All age activity

Invite the members of the congregation to bring photographs of themselves at different stages of their lives. Some may like to make a poster about themselves growing up through life. Display these photographs around the church. During the service provide an opportunity for the congregation to look at these photographs and to see whether they can identify who they are. The following ideas can be explored in buzz groups, discussion or teaching:

- our experiences of growing up;
- the growing sense of freedom and of responsibility;
- how we mature;
- growing up into the likeness of Jesus;
- the freedom and the responsibility of being sons and daughters of God.

Teaching point

God gives us choice and responsibility. He wants us to mature and to grow up and enjoy the full freedom, privileges and responsibilities of being his sons and daughters.

WORSHIP RESOURCES

Prayer

Lord God,
you have sent the Spirit of your Son into our hearts,
and called us to the glorious liberty of your children:
Give us grace to use our freedom in your service,
and in our lives to follow in the footsteps
of our Lord and Master, Jesus Christ,
who lives and reigns with you and the Holy Spirit,
one God, now and ever.

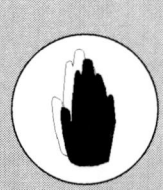

Readings

Old Testament - DEUTERONOMY 7, 6-11
New Testament - GALATIANS 3, 23 TO 4, 7
Gospel - JOHN 15, 12-17

Hymns and songs

Come and Praise

- 16 When God made the garden of creation
- 18 He gave me eyes so I could see
- 43 Give me oil in my lamp, keep me burning
- 66 In Christ there is no east or west
- 134 I planted a tree

Hymns Ancient and Modern New Standard

- 109 When all thy mercies, O my God
- 157 Breathe on me, breath of God
- 230 O for a heart to praise my God
- 430 We find thee, Lord, in others' need
- 440 Christ is the world's light, he and none other
- 473 I came with joy to meet my Lord

39

Money

PREPARATION

Bible theme
The new law (5TH SUNDAY AFTER PENTECOST)
The readings demonstrate the expectations which God has of the people of God. The Ten Commandments of the old law recited in the Old Testament reading show that these expectations do not stop with narrowly religious matters (the first four commandments), but include the whole of personal and social life (the other six commandments). In the New Testament reading Paul argues that God's expectations of the new law do not even stop with our personal and social actions, but include our motives and our thoughts. For the young man in the Gospel reading, the conflict comes between acknowledging God's expectations and his attachment to his wealth. Our response to the social and personal dimensions of God's expectations, too, must be tested against our attitudes towards money and possessions. We can begin to experience the significance of the bible's teaching about the new law by exploring our own attitudes to money.

Aims
- to build on our ideas of money;
- to develop our understanding of the proper use of money;
- to help us appreciate how excessive attachment to money and possessions can get in the way of fulfilling God's expectations.

Hearing the scriptures
EXODUS 20, 1-17
In the exodus from Egypt God showed kindness towards the people of God. Then at Sinai God makes known the terms which they have to meet if they are to continue to enjoy this favour. These terms include respect for people and for property as well as for God.

EPHESIANS 5, 1-10

Paul sums up the heart of the Christian understanding of the new law: 'try to be like Christ, and live in love as he loved you.' Such love must influence our attitudes towards people and possessions, for 'no one who is immoral, indecent or greedy will receive a share in the Kingdom of Christ.'

MATTHEW 19, 16-26

When the young man asks Jesus, 'what good must I do to gain eternal life?' Jesus first reminds him of the social dimensions of the old law. When the young man recognises that this is not the whole story, Jesus challenges him to examine his priorities. In the case of this young man, what stands in the way of meeting God's expectations is his commitment to material possessions and money.

EXPLORING WITH CHILDREN

Starting

Have an assortment of coins and bank notes left over from foreign holidays. Invite the children to look at them and sort them by shape, colour, country of origin, etc. Draw out ideas of:

- coins and bank notes;
- cheques, travellers cheques, credit cards, etc.;
- the names of the coins;
- what is written on the coins;
- the spending value of the coins;
- what the children would like to buy with the money;
- the things money cannot buy, like health, happiness, friends, etc.

Making

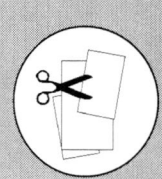

Give the children the opportunity to make a display about money. Here are some suggestions.

- Make a display of coin rubbings.
- Make a display of foreign coins and bank notes.
- Make a display of advertising material from banks, building societies, post office savings, etc.
- Design a collage of things you can buy.
- Design a collage of things you cannot buy.
- Draw a pie graph of pocket money spending.
- Build a bank in a corner of the church.

Doing

- Discuss pocket money and how to budget it.
- Visit a bank.
- Visit a shopping centre.
- Invite someone who works in a bank to talk about their work.
- Look at newspapers and see how much emphasis is given to money in adverts, news and the financial pages.
- Invite voluntary workers to explain what they do and why they do it without pay.
- Invite members of a religious order to speak about their vows of poverty.
- Find out about Charles Dickens' story of Scrooge.

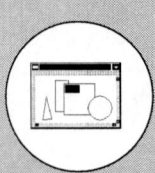

Display headings

- Today's theme is the new law.
- We need money to buy food, clothes and a home to live in.
- Many of the good things in life cannot be bought with money.
- God wants us to use our money responsibly.
- Jesus challenges our attitudes to money.
- Our project today is about money.

Using the bible

The story of Jesus and the rich young man (MATTHEW 19, 16-26)

Help the listeners to hear in this story the conflict which the young man experiences between his attachment to money and his desire to learn from Jesus' teaching and example.

> The young man comes to Jesus for advice.
> He sees that Jesus has the secret of the good life.
> He asks Jesus, 'How should I live my life?'
> Jesus first tells him to keep God's commandments.
> The young man replies that he has kept God's commandments.
> The young man wants to do better than that.
> Jesus says he should share his possessions and money.
> The young man is very sad.
> The young man loves his possessions and money too much to share them.

Dance/drama

- Act out the story of the young man coming to Jesus and his feelings as he goes away.
- Devise a dance about a miser who later changes his attitudes and shares his money.

Games
- Use coins to play tippet. The children place one coin on a table or floor and press the edge with a second coin to see how far they can make the first coin move. Experiment with different coins and different surfaces.

EXPLORING WITH ADULTS

Introduction
Display advertisements from colour magazines, illustrating a range of expensive consumer products. Ask the group to reflect on the central place given to money in today's society.

Experience
- What is your experience of using money?
- How do you feel about talking about money?
- How does money affect how you live?

Scripture
Read MATTHEW 19, 16-26
- What does this story say about Jesus' attitude to the young man?
- How do you interpret this story about the young man today?
- What are God's expectations of priorities for men and women?

Integration
- What would Jesus say to people about priorities today?
- What would Jesus say to you about your use of money?
- How would Jesus' comments affect your use of money?

Application
- How can the church respond to this teaching of Jesus today?
- How can you respond to this teaching of Jesus today?
- How can the Offertory help express commitment to today's theme?

CELEBRATING TOGETHER

Welcoming children
Make space during the service for the display of the children's work on money to be viewed and discussed. Give special prominence in the service to taking and offering the collection. The children's display of money can be included in the procession for the Offertory. If the children have prepared drama on the Gospel reading or dance on the theme of the changed miser, these can be presented immediately before the Offertory.

All age activity
Invite members of the congregation to bring some examples of foreign currency or old coins. Before the Offertory invite them to display and discuss what they have brought. Encourage them to find others who have brought similar coins or bank notes. The following ideas can be explored in buzz groups, discussion or teaching:

- the importance attributed to money in today's society;
- the pressure on people to spend and live on credit;
- the rival attractions of money and Jesus' teaching;
- God's claim over our wealth.

Teaching point
Today's readings show how God expects his people to live their lives. God's new law touches every part of our lives. The young man in the gospel reading turned away because he was unwilling to accept God's claims over his wealth.

WORSHIP RESOURCES

Prayer

Lord God,
your love reaches out to all people,
and you have commanded us to follow your Son our Saviour:
Give us grace to do your will,
and to share in your Church's mission
to proclaim the gospel of your love to all the world;
through Jesus Christ our Lord.

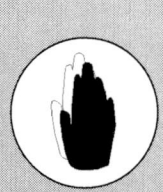

Readings

Old Testament - EXODUS 20, 1-17
New Testament - EPHESIANS 5, 1-10
Gospel - MATTHEW 19, 16-26

Hymns and songs

Come and Praise

- 24 Go, tell it on the mountain
- 25 When Jesus walked in Galilee
- 28 Said Judas to Mary
- 39 O Lord, all the world belongs to you
- 75 I saw the man from Galilee

Hymns Ancient and Modern New Standard

- 238 Blest are the pure in heart
- 287 O Lord of heaven and earth and sea
- 296 Rejoice, O land, in God thy might
- 371 Good is our God who made this place
- 432 What does the Lord require
- 495 Lord, to you we bring our treasure

40
Railway turntables

PREPARATION

Bible theme
The new person (6TH SUNDAY AFTER PENTECOST)
The message of the bible is that God holds out the offer of a new beginning to those who turn to God. Those who accept this invitation become new men and women living in relationship with God. In the Old Testament reading the people of Israel who turn to God accept the new standards of life set out in 'the book of the covenant'. This new relationship with God is sealed through the blood of sacrifice. In the New Testament reading Christians who turn to God accept the qualities of life God desires, like compassion and kindness. Their new relationship with God is sealed through the water of baptism. In the Gospel reading the prodigal son turns his back on his old way of life and returns to his father. His new relationship is sealed in the celebration meal. We can begin to experience the significance of the bible's teaching about the need for changing direction and becoming new people by exploring the image of railway turntables.

Aims
- to build on our ideas of railway turntables;
- to develop our understanding of changing direction;
- to see how God invites us to turn round.

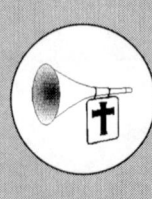

Hearing the scriptures
EXODUS 24, 3-11
In Exodus chapter 20 Moses received the law from God. Now in Exodus chapter 24 Moses makes sure that the people have heard God's words. The people hear and accept. 'All the words which the Lord has spoken we will do,' they say. Their new relationship with God is sealed through the blood of sacrifice.

COLOSSIANS 3, 12-17
For the Christian the sign of repentance and new life is not the blood of sacrifice, but the water of baptism. In early tradition adults were baptised by total immersion and after baptism they put on a special robe. Here that robe is seen to symbolise the new style of life expected of God's people, 'compassion, kindness, lowliness, meekness, and patience.'

LUKE 15, 11-32
After squandering his inheritance in reckless living, the prodigal son sees the foolishness of his ways, repents and turns round to go home to his father. Through his father's acceptance and welcome, the son becomes a new person and begins a new life.

EXPLORING WITH CHILDREN

Starting
Set up a straight stretch of model railway track which includes a turntable at one end. Demonstrate how the engine uses the turntable to turn round and to come back in the opposite direction. Draw out ideas of:

- the engine being set in its track;
- the engine has to keep going in the same direction;
- the need for the engine to face the other way to come back;
- the opportunity given by the turntable for the engine to turn round;
- what would happen if there were no turntable in the layout.

Making
Give the children the opportunity to make a display about railway turntables. Here are some suggestions.

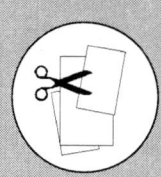

- Design a model railway layout, using turntables.
- Make a large model of a turntable.
- Make a poster of Thomas the Tank Engine or Gordon the Big Engine on a turntable.
- Make a series of pictures telling the story of the prodigal son.
- Make posters about famous Christian men and women who turned round their style of life.

Doing

- Watch a video of Thomas the Tank Engine which includes a turntable.
- Visit a railway museum to look at the turntable.
- Invite a railway enthusiast to talk about turntables.
- Discover how Dick Whittington heard the bells telling him to turn back.
- Study some famous Christian men and women who turned round their style of life.
- Invite someone who feels that he or she has changed direction because of meeting Christ to talk with the children.

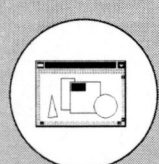

Display headings

- Today's theme is the new person.
- Railway engines need to turn round.
- Railway engines cannot turn without a turntable.
- God asks us to turn round to come to God.
- Our project today is about railway turntables.

Using the bible

The story of the prodigal son (LUKE 15, 11-32)

Help the listeners to hear in this story how the younger son turns round and becomes a new person reunited with his father.

> The son takes his share of the inheritance.
> He leaves home.
> He squanders his money on reckless living.
> He ends up penniless and hungry.
> He takes a lowly job looking after pigs.
> He is so hungry he would have eaten the pig-swill.
> He changes his mind and decides to return home.
> He retraces his steps.
> Instead of turning him away, his father gives him a big welcome.

Dance/drama

- Act out the story of the prodigal son.
- Devise a dance about an engine being turned on a turntable.

Games

- Play 'What's the time Mr Wolf?' where the wolf has to turn round quickly.

EXPLORING WITH ADULTS

Introduction
Borrow and display a model railway. Ask a member of the group to demonstrate the turntable. Ask the group how they have changed direction.

Experience
- What is your experience of changing direction?
- How do you feel about this experience?
- What difference did this experience make to your life?

Scripture
Read LUKE 15, 11-32
- What does this story say about the relationship between the father and the son?
- How do you interpret this story about the prodigal son for today?
- What does this story say about God's relationship with men and women?

Integration
- Why do people turn away from God?
- What turns people back to God?
- How has this happened in your life?

Application
- How can the church challenge people to turn to God?
- How can you challenge people to turn to God?
- What aspects in the eucharist can best challenge us to change direction?

CELEBRATING TOGETHER

Welcoming children
Make space during the service for the display of the children's work on railway turntables to be viewed and discussed. If the children have prepared drama on the theme of the prodigal son, this can be shared after the Gospel reading.

All age activity
Invite members of the congregation to bring something which speaks to them of changing direction, like the railway turntable. Before the Confession invite them to think about the need for changing direction in order to become the new people God wants us to become. At certain stages of the service invite the whole congregation to turn and face in a certain direction as a witness to their turning to God: for example, in place of the Creed they could turn to face the font in order to renew their baptismal vows; at the close of the service they could turn to face the church door for the words of the Dismissal, 'Go in peace to love and serve the Lord.' The following ideas can be explored in buzz groups, discussion or teaching:

- our experiences of changing direction;
- how our lives have been changed to become new people;
- how the prodigal son changed direction;
- how God welcomes us when we turn to God.

Teaching point
God holds out the offer of a new beginning to those who turn to God. But first God asks us to turn round away from our old way of life to face in a new direction.

WORSHIP RESOURCES

Prayer

Almighty God,
without you we are not able to please you:
Mercifully grant that your Holy Spirit
may in all things direct and rule our hearts;
through Jesus Christ our Lord.

Readings

Old Testament - EXODUS 24, 3-11
New Testament - COLOSSIANS 3, 12-17
Gospel - LUKE 15, 11-32

Hymns and songs

Come and Praise

- 39   O Lord, all the world belongs to you
- 44   He who would valiant be
- 47   One more step along the world I go
- 102 You can't stop rain from falling down

Hymns Ancient and Modern New Standard

- 115 Dear Lord and father of mankind
- 192 Praise, my soul, the king of heaven
- 231 O for a closer walk with God
- 246 Just as I am, without one plea
- 372 Have faith in God, my heart
- 383 Jesus, whose all-redeeming love
- 473 I come with joy to meet my Lord

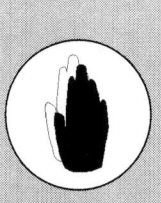

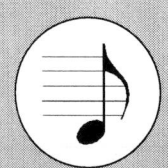

41

Teddy bears

PREPARATION

Bible theme

The more excellent way (7TH SUNDAY AFTER PENTECOST)

'The more excellent way' advocated by the bible is God's way of love. In the Old Testament reading the prophet Hosea describes God's relationship with Israel in terms of a father's love for his son; 'When Israel was a boy, I loved him.' In the New Testament reading Paul argues that love is the greatest of all Christian virtues: 'There are three things that last forever, faith, hope and love, but the greatest of them all is love.' In the Gospel reading Matthew presents a parable which illustrates both God's love for us and God's expectation that we should show love to others. We can begin to experience the significance of the bible's teaching about the more excellent way of love by exploring our own love for our teddy bear.

Aims

- to build on our present or previous love for our teddy bears;
- to extend our understanding of the teddy bear as a sign of love and acceptance;
- to help us see how God loves us and asks us to love others.

Hearing the scriptures

HOSEA 11, 1-9

The prophet Hosea comes to understand God's forgiving love for the people of God by thinking deeply about his own love for his family. Through his consistent love for his unfaithful wife, Hosea recognises God's consistent love for the unfaithful people. Now in this passage Hosea recognises that God treats the people of God patiently like a loving and forgiving father.

1 CORINTHIANS 12, 27 TO 13, 13

Whatever spectacular spiritual gifts the Christian community possesses, like prophecy and healing, these gifts are valueless unless the community is first characterised by love. Love is the greatest of God's gifts and of Christian virtues. The polished rhythm and style of chapter 13, 'The Hymn to Love', suggests that it existed before being used in this letter.

MATTHEW 18, 21-35

The parable of the unforgiving debtor demonstrates two things. First, it shows just how much God's love forgives us. Second, it shows how God expects our love to show the same forgiveness to others.

EXPLORING WITH CHILDREN

Starting

Invite the children to bring their teddy bears. Begin by asking the children to introduce their teddy bears to the other bears and settle the bears down to enjoy a picnic. Discuss their relationship with the teddy bears and that of their younger brothers and sisters. Draw out ideas of:

- teddy bears as long standing friends;
- their care for their teddy bears;
- their teddy bears' care for them;
- telling teddy bears our problems;
- teddy bears as a comfort in need;
- teddy bears are always there.

Making

Give the children the opportunity to make a display about teddy bears. Here are some suggestions.

- Display a collection of teddy bears.
- Design a collage of teddy bear pictures.
- Organise a display of teddy bear books.
- Make teddy bear masks for the children to wear.
- Make teddy bear glove puppets.
- Illustrate a story about a famous teddy bear.

Doing

- Invite someone from the congregation to talk about their own teddy bear, perhaps a specially old teddy bear.
- Invite someone to show how teddy bears are made.
- Visit a teddy bear museum or toy shop.
- Find out about the story of Super Ted's origins.
- Read a famous teddy bear story, like Winnie the Pooh or Paddington.
- Look at pictures of old teddy bears.

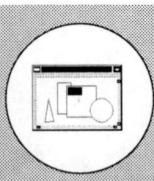

Display headings
- Today's theme is the more excellent way.
- Teddy bears love and accept us.
- Teddy bears go on loving and forgiving us.
- Teddy bears need us to love them.
- God loves us and wants us to love each other.
- Our project today is about teddy bears.

Using the bible
The story of the two debtors (MATTHEW 18, 21-35)
Help the listeners to hear in this story how God loves and forgives us and how God expects us to love and forgive others.

> This is a story about two men, let's call them John and Fred.
> John owes the king a great deal of money.
> The king demands that the money is repaid.
> John cannot pay.
> John pleads for more time.
> The king is kind and cancels the debt.
> Fred owes John a much smaller sum.
> Although the king has cancelled his debt, John demands his money from Fred.
> Fred cannot pay.
> Fred pleads for time.
> John refuses to give Fred time.
> The king is angry when he finds out and punishes John.
> God forgives us like the king.
> God expects us to love others and to forgive them.

Dance/drama
- Devise a dance about teddy bears.
- Prepare a radio interview with the king, the two debtors and those who have watched what has taken place.

Games
- Take your teddy bears out to play Pooh Sticks.

EXPLORING WITH ADULTS

Introduction
Display some teddy bears. Ask the group to remember incidents when their teddy bears were particularly important to them.

Experience
- What stories do you have about your teddy bear?
- How did you feel about your teddy bear as a child?
- How important is your teddy bear in your life?

Scripture
Read MATTHEW 18, 21-35
- What does this parable say about God's forgiving love?
- How do you interpret this parable about the debtor for today?
- What does this parable say about the nature of God?

Integration
- How is God's forgiving love experienced?
- How do you know that you are loved by God?
- How can you respond to God's love?

Application
- How can the church express God's gift of love to others?
- How can you express God's gift of love to others?
- How can the Peace express God's love for all?

CELEBRATING TOGETHER

Welcoming children

Make space during the service for the display of the children's work on teddy bears to be viewed and discussed. If the children have prepared drama on the theme of the two debtors, this can be presented after the Gospel reading.

All age activity

Invite the members of the congregation to bring their own teddy bears to the service. Leave plenty of time at the Peace for the congregation to introduce their teddy bears to each other and through their teddy bears to meet and to talk with people whom they do not know well. The following ideas can be explored in buzz groups, discussion or teaching:

- our relationships (past and present) with our teddy bears;
- how we learn about love and forgiveness from our teddy bears;
- how God can use the teddy bear to teach us about God's love for us;
- the lesson of love in the story of the two debtors

Teaching point

Love is the greatest of God's gifts. It is through being loved ourselves that we learn to love. It is through loving our teddy bears that we first learn to direct that love from ourselves to others.

WORSHIP RESOURCES

Prayer

Lord, you have taught us
that all our doings without love are worth nothing:
Send your Holy Spirit
and pour into our hearts
that most excellent gift of love,
the true bond of peace and of all virtues,
for without love
whoever lives is counted dead before you.
Grant this for the sake of your only Son
our Lord and Saviour Jesus Christ.

Readings

Old Testament - HOSEA 11, 1-9
New Testament - 1 CORINTHIANS 12, 27 TO 13, 13
Gospel - MATTHEW 18, 21-35

Hymns and songs

Come and Praise

- 27   There's a child in the streets
- 36   God is love; his the care
- 39   O Lord, all the world belongs to you
- 99   Love will never come to an end

Hymns Ancient and Modern New Standard

- 131   Love divine, all loves excelling
- 154   Gracious Spirit, Holy Ghost
- 156   Come down, O Love divine
- 362   'Forgive our sins as we forgive'
- 365   God is love: let heav'n adore him
- 374   Help us to help each other, Lord
- 528   Where love and loving-kindness dwell

42 Fruit

PREPARATION

Bible theme
The fruit of the Spirit (8TH SUNDAY AFTER PENTECOST)
God's people are recognised by the quality of their lives. In the Old Testament reading, through the prophet Ezekiel, the Spirit is promised to God's people to enable them to live by God's laws. In the New Testament reading, St Paul spells out the qualities of life expected of God's people and he calls these qualities the 'fruits of the Spirit.' In the Gospel reading Jesus commissions his followers 'to go out and to bear fruit.' Just as trees and plants are recognised by the kind of fruit they produce, so are God's people. We can begin to experience the significance of the bible's teaching about the fruit of the Spirit by exploring our own experiences of fruit.

Aims
- to build on our ideas of fruit;
- to help us understand how we identify trees and plants by the fruit they bear;
- to help us value the 'fruit' which God wants us to bear in our lives.

Hearing the scriptures
EZEKIEL 36, 24-28
God promises to restore the people after their exile and to re-establish them in their home land. God will give the people a new heart and make them responsive to the way of life God requires of them.

GALATIANS 5, 16-25 (22)
Paul contrasts the two different life styles of those who are guided by the Spirit and those who are not. Each life style has its own harvest. The fruits of the Spirit, says Paul, are life, joy, peace, patience, kindness, goodness, trustfulness, gentleness and self-control.

John 15, 16-27

In this part of his farewell discourse with the disciples before the crucifixion, according to John's gospel, Jesus describes himself as the real vine and the disciples as the branches. Now Jesus commissions those branches to bear fruit in his name. This fruit is seen in the quality of their lives: 'What I command you is to love one another.'

EXPLORING WITH CHILDREN

Starting

Cut up several different fruits into small bite-sized pieces, for example, apples, bananas, grapefruits, peaches. Invite the children to taste them and to describe the different tastes. Then ask them to name all the other fruits they know and write out a list of them. Draw out ideas of:

- different tastes;
- different colours;
- different textures;
- times of year when different fruits grow;
- different types of trees, bushes, vines, etc.;
- different countries of origin;
- how you can tell which fruit is which;
- how you can tell the different trees by their fruits.

Making

Give the children the opportunity to make a display about fruit. Here are some suggestions.

- Make a display of labels from fresh, canned, frozen and dried fruits.
- Make a huge collage tree, bearing many different fruits.
- Design a map of the world where different fruits are grown.
- Make banners showing the fruits of the Spirit.
- Make a fruit salad to share in church.
- Make home-made lemonade from real lemons.

Doing

- Go for a walk and see what fruits you can identify.
- Visit an orchard.
- Arrange to go and pick soft fruits.
- Collect fruit wrappers.
- Visit a fruit market or shop.

- Buy and share some unusual fruits.
- Discuss the qualities you like in your best friends.
- Talk about someone you admire and identify their good qualities or good fruit.

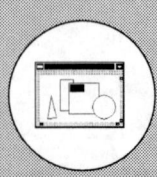

Display headings
- Today's theme is the fruit of the Spirit.
- Each tree produces its own kind of fruit.
- We recognise trees by the fruit they produce.
- Our project today is about fruit.

Using the bible
The story of the gardener and the vine (JOHN 15, 1-10)
Help the listeners to hear in this story Jesus' clear expectation that we should all bear fruit of the Spirit.

> The gardener chooses and plants the vine.
> The vine is watered.
> The vine is carefully trained against the wall.
> The vine is pruned.
> The vine produces fruit.
> The grapes ripen in the sun.
> The grapes are harvested.
> Jesus says his disciples should be like that and bear fruit.

Dance/drama
- Develop mime to demonstrate some of the fruits of the Spirit.
- Devise a dance to tell the story of the vine being planted, tended, growing and the grapes ripening and being harvested.

Games
- Play collective memory game: 'I went to the greengrocers and bought a....' Each child repeats and adds another fruit.

EXPLORING WITH ADULTS

Introduction
Display some biographies of famous Christians, such as Gladys Alyward or William Booth. Ask the group to describe the fruit of these Christian lives.

Experience
- What is your experience of someone living a Christian life?
- How does Christianity affect your life?
- How would you recognise the 'fruits of the Spirit'?

Scripture
Read JOHN 15, 1-10
- What does Jesus' teaching say about how good fruit is produced?
- How do you interpret this teaching about the vine for today?
- What is the fruit which God desires?

Integration
- What are the 'fruits of the Spirit'?
- Which 'fruit' do you desire in your life?
- How would this affect your life?

Application
- How can the church show the 'fruits of the Spirit'?
- How can you show the 'fruits of the Spirit' in your life?
- How can the Peace be used to proclaim Christ's command 'love one another'?

CELEBRATING TOGETHER

Welcoming children
Make space during the service for the display of the children's work on fruit to be viewed and discussed. If the children have produced banners about the fruits of the Spirit, these can be held during the New Testament reading. If they have produced mime on this theme it can be shared after the New Testament reading.

All age activity
Invite members of the congregation to bring a piece of fruit to the service. During the service invite them to group the fruit around the appropriate trees or plants, so that, for example, all the apples are together in an apple orchard. Arrange to share some fruit with all the congregation during or after the service as symbol of the way they all share in the fruits of the Spirit. The following ideas can be explored in buzz groups, discussion or teaching:

- our experiences of different fruits, where and how they grow;
- our experiences of growing and nurturing fruit;
- how you can tell if a tree or plant is sound;
- the fruits of the Spirit.

Teaching point
Just as we recognise trees by the fruit they produce, so we recognise God's people by the kind of lives they live. St Paul says that the fruits of the Spirit in our lives are love, joy, peace, patience, kindness, goodness, trustfulness, gentleness and self-control.

WORSHIP RESOURCES

Prayer
Almighty God,
who sent your Holy Spirit
to be the life and light of your church:
Open our hearts to the riches of his grace,
that we may bring forth the fruit of the Spirit,
in love and joy and peace;
through Jesus Christ our Lord.

Readings
Old Testament - EZEKIEL 36, 24-28
New Testament - GALATIANS 5, 16-25
Gospel - JOHN 15, 16-27

Hymns and songs
Come and Praise
- 53 Peace, perfect peace, is the gift of Christ our Lord
- 63 Spirit of God, as strong as the wind
- 70 Would you walk by on the other side
- 87 You gotta have love in your heart

Hymns Ancient and Modern New Standard
- 156 O Love divine
- 157 Breathe on me, breath of God
- 236 God be in my head
- 459 Give me joy in my heart, keep me praising
- 478 Let every Christian pray
- 503 Of all the Spirit's gifts to me
- 515 There's a Spirit in the air

43 Armour

PREPARATION

Bible theme
The armour of God (9TH SUNDAY AFTER PENTECOST)
Throughout the bible God promises to be with and to protect the chosen people, provided that they remain loyal. In the Old Testament reading God promises Joshua, 'I will not fail you or forsake you,' and equips Joshua for physical victory over those who stand in his way. The New Testament reading turns the imagery from physical to spiritual warfare, when Paul describes God's protection for the people as a whole suit of spiritual armour. In the Gospel reading Jesus, too, speaks of spiritual warfare when he recognises that the going will be tough for his followers and prays that the father will 'protect them from the evil one.' We can begin to experience the significance of the bible's teaching about the armour of God by exploring our own experiences of armour.

Aims

- to build on our ideas about the protective function of armour;
- to help us understand how God protects us;
- to help us desire to put on the armour which God offers to us.

Hearing the scriptures

JOSHUA 1, 1-9
Before Moses' death the Lord commissioned Joshua to lead the people into the promised land. Now Moses is dead, Joshua has to take up his commission. The Lord promises to be with Joshua as the Lord was with Moses: 'Be strong and of good courage ... for the Lord your God is with you wherever you go.'

EPHESIANS 6, 10-20
As God equipped Joshua to fight physical battles, so the Christian disciple is equipped to fight spiritual battles and to be victorious in God's name. The armour which God provides is truth, righteousness, the gospel of peace, faith, salvation and the word of God.

JOHN 17, 11B-19

This is part of Christ's high priestly prayer before the crucifixion. He prays for the disciples as they engage in their missionary task in a hostile world. As the world failed to understand Jesus, so it will fail to understand them. He prays that they may be equipped for the spiritual battle and protected 'from the evil one'.

EXPLORING WITH CHILDREN

Starting

See if it is possible to borrow some theatrical armour from a local resource centre, amateur dramatic society, or secondary school drama department. Begin the lesson wearing the armour. Let the children take it off and try it on themselves or find pictures of armour. Draw out ideas of:

- who wears armour;
- why they wear armour;
- names of different pieces of armour, like helmet and shield;
- protection for vulnerable parts of the body, like the head;
- other kinds of protective clothing;
- things we use to protect us like oven gloves;
- God's way of protecting us;
- the evils from which God protects us.

Making

Give the children the opportunity to make a display about armour. Here are some suggestions.

- Make a suit of armour, helmet and shield from cardboard and tin foil.
- Design a large collage of Roman soldiers in protective armour.
- Label a suit of armour with St Paul's descriptions from Ephesians 6, 10-20.
- Design a poster to recruit for God's army.
- Make a display of modern protective clothing, like crash helmets and oven gloves.
- Make a collage or model of St George in armour fighting the evil dragon.

Doing

- Visit a museum and look at armour.
- Look at modern armour like the crash helmet.
- Invite someone who wears protective clothing for their work to demonstrate what they wear and why.
- Visit a factory where the children have to wear protective clothing to look round.
- Look for heraldic armour in church, on monuments and memorials.

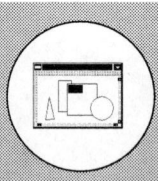

Display headings
- Today's theme is the armour of God.
- Armour protects the soldier from harm.
- We wear protective clothing to keep us from harm.
- The people of God are protected from harm.
- We are invited to put on the armour of God.
- God invites us to wear faith as our shield.
- Our project today is about armour.

Using the bible
Build up Paul's image of God's protective armour (EPHESIANS 6, 10-20)
Help the listeners to build up a graphic picture of the whole armour of God as developed by St Paul.

> St Paul tells us to protect ourselves from evil.
> St Paul warns us against doing evil, thinking evil, and being influenced by evil.
> St Paul advises us to make full use of the armour God gives us.
> Truth is a belt round your waist.
> Righteousness is your breast plate.
> The good news of peace is your shoes.
> Faith is your shield.
> Salvation is your helmet.
> The word of God is your sword.

Dance/drama
- Devise a dance to demonstrate the goodness of God overcoming evil. Let the good be symbolised by wearing armour.

Games
- Use different shapes of armour (say helmets or armbands) to distinguish team membership for a team game.

EXPLORING WITH ADULTS

Introduction
Display some examples of protective clothing, such as a kitchen apron, gardening gloves or a crash helmet. Ask the group to discuss why people need these pieces of equipment.

Experience
- What kinds of protective clothing do you possess?
- How is protective clothing useful to you?
- What are your experiences of needing protection?

Scripture
Read EPHESIANS 6, 10-20
- What does this teaching say about God equipping the Christian?
- How do you interpret this teaching about the armour of God for today?
- What does the reading say about God's presence with people?

Integration
- How does God protect people today?
- How does God protect you today?
- What does it mean to you to put on the whole armour of God?

Application
- How can the church put on the whole armour of God?
- How can you put on the whole armour of God?
- How can the whole armour of God be presented in worship?

CELEBRATING TOGETHER

Welcoming children
Make space during the service for the display of the children's work on armour to be viewed and discussed. If the children have prepared dance, dressed in armour, this can be shared immediately after the New Testament reading.

All age activity
Invite members of the congregation to bring any protective clothing which they possess, including oven gloves, crash helmets, goggles, etc. After the New Testament reading invite them to put on this protective clothing and to seek out individuals who have similar items. These items can then be displayed in the church. The following ideas can be explored in buzz groups, discussion or teaching:

- our experiences of protective clothing;
- our images of armour;
- how protective clothing and armour protect us;
- why St Paul speaks of the armour of God;
- how God's armour protects us.

Teaching point
St Paul describes God's presence with the people to be like a suit of armour which protects them from evil. We must put on the armour which God offers to us.

WORSHIP RESOURCES

Prayer

Almighty God,
you call us to your service:
Give us strength to put on the armour you provide
that we may resist the assaults of the devil,
and ever trust in the salvation
which you have promised us
in Jesus Christ our Lord.

Readings

Old Testament - JOSHUA 1, 1-9
New Testament - EPHESIANS 6, 10-20
Gospel - JOHN 17, 11B-19

Hymns and songs

Come and Praise
- 44 He who would valiant be
- 45 The journey of life
- 50 When a knight won his spurs in the stories of old
- 100 I may speak in the tongues of angels

Hymns Ancient and Modern New Standard
- 219 Soldiers of Christ, arise
- 220 Fight the good fight with all thy might!
- 221 Stand up, stand up for Jesus
- 333 Onward, Christian soldiers!
- 343 Be thou my vision, O Lord of my heart
- 353 Eternal ruler of the ceaseless round
- 516 This day God gives me

44

Monks and nuns

PREPARATION

Bible theme

The mind of Christ (10TH SUNDAY AFTER PENTECOST)

When men and women truly perceive themselves in relationship to God, they recognise their smallness compared with God's greatness, their ignorance compared with God's infinite wisdom. This is a truly humbling experience, and in discovering this humility the Christian disciple shares in the humility of Christ himself. In the Old Testament reading Job recognises humility before God. In the New Testament reading St Paul exhorts the Christian disciple to imitate the humility of Christ, while in the Gospel reading Jesus demonstrates his own humility by washing the disciples' feet. We can begin to experience the significance of the bible's teaching on the mind of Christ by exploring our own experiences and images of those who try to live especially close to Christ, like members of religious communities.

Aims

- to build on our experience of monks and nuns;
- to help us understand the monastic vows of poverty and obedience as signs of Christian humility;
- to help us want to follow Christ's example of humility.

Hearing the scriptures

JOB 42, 1-6

The story of Job is that of a man whose prosperity was followed by tragedy and suffering. In earlier chapters, Job has struggled to comprehend the mystery of suffering, failed in his struggle and railed against God. Now at the end of the book, Job recognises that he will never comprehend God's infinite wisdom and confronts the depth of his own ignorance. In so doing Job finds true humility.

PHILIPPIANS 2, 1-11

Paul exhorts his readers at Philippi to base their own lives and relationships one with another on Christ's example of humility. Paul drives his point home by quoting what is probably an early Christian hymn, in which Christ 'humbled himself, and in obedience accepted even death - death on a cross.'

JOHN 13, 1-15

John describes this event in the context of Jesus' last meal with the disciples before the crucifixion, the Last Supper. During supper Jesus washes his disciples' feet, a duty normally performed by servants before the meal, and then he interprets his action: 'If I, your Lord and master, have washed your feet, you also ought to wash one another's feet. I have set you an example: you are to do as I have done.'

EXPLORING WITH CHILDREN

Starting

Display some pictures of monks or nuns in their habits and invite the children to talk about what makes them different. Draw out ideas of:

- their clothes and what they wear;
- why they are called 'brother' and 'sister';
- their commitment to a religious community;
- their vows of obedience and poverty;
- the simplicity of their life style;
- the pattern of their prayer life.

Then concentrate on the well known figure of Mother Teresa and her sisters of charity in Calcutta, if possible using pictures of her work. Draw out ideas of:

- her life of service to others;
- her commitment to the poor;
- her work in the name of Christ.

Making

Give the children the opportunity to make a display about monks and nuns, concentrating especially on Mother Teresa of Calcutta. Here are some suggestions.

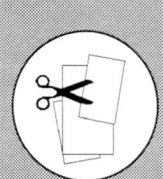

- Make simple monastic habits for the children to wear.
- Make a model of a medieval monastic community.
- Organise a display of pictures of monks and nuns.
- Design a collage about Mother Teresa's work.
- Make a mural about the washing of feet.

Doing
- Invite a member of a religious order to talk about his or her way of life.
- Visit a religious community and share their hospitality.
- Visit a monastic ruin.
- Find out about a famous monk or nun.
- Look up the service for 'the washing of feet' on Maundy Thursday (*Lent, Holy Week, Easter: services and prayers*, page 187).
- Invite someone who has attended a Maundy Thursday service with washing of feet to describe what happens.

Display headings
- Today's theme is the mind of Christ.
- Monks and nuns take vows of poverty and obedience.
- Jesus washes his disciples' feet.
- Jesus gives us an example of service and humility.
- Mother Teresa follows Jesus' example.
- Monks and nuns are signs of Christian humility.
- Our project today is about monks and nuns.

Using the bible
The story of Jesus washing the disciples' feet (JOHN 13, 1-15)
Help the listeners to hear in this story the great humility of Jesus and the invitation to become like him.

> This is Jesus' last meal with his friends.
> Judas is already waiting to betray him.
> Jesus gets up from the table.
> He takes a towel and fills a basin with water.
> He washes his disciples' feet.
> This is a job done by servants in a hot country where the roads are dusty.
> Peter feels uncomfortable about Jesus doing this.
> Jesus insists on washing Peter's feet.
> Jesus teaches his disciples to serve others by his own example.

Dance/drama
- Devise a dance about the washing of feet.
- Prepare a radio interview with Mother Teresa.

Games
- Play 'Simon says', to help the children experience the difficulty of following a leader.

EXPLORING WITH ADULTS

Introduction
Display books and pictures of Mother Teresa. Ask the group how being a nun has affected her life.

Experience
- What is your experience of monks and nuns?
- What does the way of life lived by monks and nuns say to you?
- How do you feel about monks and nuns as examples of Christ?

Scripture
Read JOHN 13, 1-15
- What does this story say about the mind of Christ?
- How do you interpret this story about washing feet for today?
- What does this story say about the life of discipleship?

Integration
- What does Christian humility mean to you?
- How would you recognise humility in a person's life today?
- What is the relationship between Jesus' action and your life?

Application
- How can the church best reflect the mind of Christ?
- How can you best reflect the mind of Christ in your life?
- How can the eucharist best reflect the mind of Christ?

CELEBRATING TOGETHER

Welcoming children

Make space during the service for the display of the children's work on monks and nuns to be viewed and discussed. If the children have made monastic costumes these can be worn throughout the service. Dressed as monks and nuns let the children serve as stewards welcoming the congregation and giving out books before the service. If the children have prepared dance about the washing of feet, this can be shared immediately after the Gospel reading. Ask for volunteers from the congregation to have their feet washed by the children during the service.

All age activity

Invite members of the congregation to bring something which speaks to them of the best characteristics of monks and nuns, perhaps something to do with Mother Teresa of Calcutta. During the peace invite them to discuss what they have brought and why. Arrange a display of these items. The following ideas can be explored in buzz groups, discussion or teaching:

- our experiences of monks and nuns;
- our image of Mother Teresa of Calcutta;
- the symbolism of the foot washing
- the power of including such symbolic acts in worship.

Teaching point

When men and women truly perceive themselves in relationship to God, they recognise their smallness compared with God's greatness. This is a truly humbling experience. In discovering this humility the Christian disciple shares in the humility of Christ himself.

WORSHIP RESOURCES

Prayer

Lord Jesus Christ,
you humbled yourself in taking the form of a servant,
and in obedience died on the cross for our salvation:
Give us the mind to follow you
and proclaim you as Lord and king,
to the glory of God the Father.

Readings

Old Testament - JOB 42, 1-6
New Testament - PHILIPPIANS 2, 1-11
Gospel - JOHN 13, 1-15

Hymns and songs

Come and Praise

    25 When Jesus walked in Galilee
    36 God is love; his the care
    39 O Lord, all the world belongs to you
    94 Make us worthy, Lord

Hymns Ancient and Modern New Standard

  148 At the name of Jesus
  156 Come down, O love divine
  230 O for a heart to praise my God
  238 Blest are the pure in heart
  374 Help us to help each other, Lord
  380 Jesus, Lord, we look to thee
  489 Lord God, your love has called us here

45
Cubs and brownies

PREPARATION

Bible theme
The serving community (11TH AFTER PENTECOST)
Throughout the bible individual people and groups of people are called to be servants of God. Through these people others are led to believe in God. Those whom God calls in this way can be recognised by their style of life as clearly as if they were wearing a special uniform. In the Old Testament reading Isaiah speaks of the Lord's servant who is recognised by his gentle leadership and justice. In the New Testament reading Paul describes himself and his companions as servants to the Christian community who are recognised by declaring the truth openly. In the Gospel reading Jesus says his disciples will be recognised by the love they have for one another. We can begin to experience the significance of the bible's teaching about identifying with the serving community by exploring our own experiences of identifying with groups like cubs and brownies.

Aims

- to build on our understanding of cubs and brownies;
- to help us understand how cubs and brownies are recognised by their uniform and by their commitment to serve others;
- to help us see how Christians are called to serve others and to be recognised by their love.

Hearing the scriptures
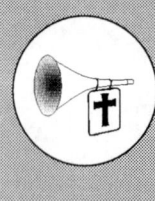
ISAIAH 42, 1-7
There are three writers responsible for different sections of the book of Isaiah. The second writer has a series of 'songs of the servant of God.' This section is part of the first of these songs. God's Spirit has been given to God's servant commissioning him to bring forth justice to the nations.

2 CORINTHIANS 4, 1-10

As the servant in Isaiah was called by God, so Paul sees that he and his fellow Christians have been called to be servants to God's people. As Isaiah's servant was empowered by God's spirit, so St Paul sees that his power to be God's servant, 'does not come from us, but is God's alone.'

JOHN 13, 31-35

After Judas has left the supper table Jesus commissions the disciples to continue his work, and to be his servants. As his servants, they are to be recognised by the love they have for one another, as clearly as if they were wearing a distinctive uniform.

EXPLORING WITH CHILDREN

Starting

Invite the children who belong to cubs and brownies to wear their uniforms and to talk about belonging to these groups. Draw out ideas of:

- how we recognise cubs and brownies;
- why they wear a uniform;
- the promises they make when joining;
- who leads the meetings;
- what they do at meetings;
- the promise to serve others.

Making

Give the children the opportunity to make a display about cubs and brownies. Here are some suggestions.

- Organise a display of scouting badges, uniforms, etc.
- Design a collage of a scout or guide camp.
- Draw a picture of a camp fire.
- Design a poster advertising bob-a-job week.
- Make a directory of local cub, brownie, scout and guide groups.
- Make a display of scouting promises.

Doing

- Invite local cub or brownie leaders to talk about their groups.
- Visit a scout or guide camp and see what these older children are doing.
- Invite scouts or guides to arrange an evening for the children, including a camp fire and singing.
- Invite members of adult uniform groups to talk about their work, for example St John Ambulance.
- Discuss how cubs, scouts, brownies and guides serve the community.

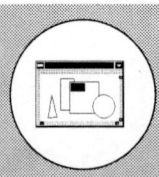

Display headings

- Today's theme is the serving community.
- Cubs and brownies are recognised by their uniforms.
- Cubs and brownies promise to serve the community.
- Jesus said, 'I give you a new commandment: love one another.'
- Our project today is about cubs and brownies.

Using the bible

The story of the last meal (JOHN 13, 31-35)

Help the listeners to hear in this story how Jesus' disciples will be recognised by their love for one another, just as if they were wearing a uniform.

> Jesus is sharing his last meal with the disciples.
> Judas, the betrayer, has already left the group.
> Jesus is now giving his final teaching to the eleven.
> His final command is 'love one another'.
> Jesus says 'just as I have loved you, you also must love one another'.
> Jesus says his disciples will be recognised by their love for one another, just like wearing a uniform.

Dance/drama

- Devise a dance about making a camp fire and the fun and fellowship around it.

Games

- Invite the cubs or brownies to teach the group one of their games.

EXPLORING WITH ADULTS

Introduction
Display some of the 'rule' books for the cubs and brownies. Ask the group to look through the books and discuss the aims of these organisations.

Experience
- What is your experience of cubs and brownies, scouts and guides?
- What is important about the uniform for the members?
- What is important about the uniform for people who are not members?

Scripture
Read JOHN 13, 31-35
- What does this teaching say about how disciples are recognised?
- How do you interpret this teaching about service for today?
- What does this story say about service as 'witness'?

Integration
- How are Christians recognised today?
- How do Christians express commitment to service today?
- How is your faith expressed in Christian service?

Application
- How can your church be the serving community?
- How can you contribute to the serving community?
- How can the Dismissal express commitment to service?

CELEBRATING TOGETHER

Welcoming children
Make space during the service for the display of the children's work on cubs and brownies to be viewed and discussed. Invite local cub, brownie, scout and guide groups to come to the service. Invite them to make a display of their activities in the church and to tell the congregation about their activities. Invite them to read the lessons, and to form the offertory procession, to contribute music or drama to the service.

All age activity
Invite members of the congregation who have had any personal involvement in the scouting movement to bring to the service something which speaks of that experience, for example, a photograph, cap, badge or a certificate. After the Gospel reading invite them to discuss what they have brought and to make a display. The following ideas can be explored in buzz groups, discussion or teaching:

- our experiences of scouts and guides;
- the importance of the uniform;
- how groups are recognised by their values or by their dress;
- how the Christian community is recognised;
- Jesus' command to love one another.

Teaching point
Just as cubs and brownies are recognised by their uniforms, so Christ's disciples are recognised by the love they have one for another.

WORSHIP RESOURCES

Prayer

Almighty God,
whose Son Jesus Christ has taught us
that what we do for the least of our brothers and sisters
we do also for him:
Give us the will to be the servant of others
as he was the servant of all,
who gave up his life and died for us,
but is alive and reigns with you and the Holy Spirit,
one God, now and for ever.

Readings

Old Testament - ISAIAH 42, 1-7
New Testament - 2 CORINTHIANS 4, 1-10
Gospel - JOHN 13, 31-35

Hymns and songs

Come and Praise

    63 Spirit of God, as strong as the wind
    65 When I needed a neighbour were you there, were you there?
    71 If I had a hammer, I'd hammer in the morning
    94 Make us worthy, Lord

Hymns Ancient and Modern New Standard

    235 O Jesus, I have promised
    239 Forth in thy name, O Lord, I go
    240 Teach me, my God and king
    377 In humble gratitude, O God
    395 Lord of all power, I give you my will
    421 Strengthen for service, Lord, the hands
    519 We are your people

46 Adverts

PREPARATION

Bible theme
The witnessing community (12TH SUNDAY AFTER PENTECOST)
The people whom God calls (Israel in the Old Testament and the Church of Christ in the New Testament) are commissioned to proclaim the good news about God to the whole world. They are to become God's messengers, God's adverts. In the Old Testament reading from Isaiah, God's servant lifts up his voice: 'Listen to me, you coasts and islands, pay heed, you peoples far away.' In the New Testament reading St Paul describes himself as Christ's ambassador through whom God himself speaks. In the Gospel reading Jesus prays not only for his disciples and followers but for those who are yet to hear the good news and who, through hearing the good news, will come to believe in him. We can begin to experience the significance of the bible's teaching about the witnessing community by exploring our own experience of adverts.

Aims
- to build on our experience of adverts;
- to help us understand how the Christian community is an advert for Christ;
- to help us to be fully part of the witnessing community.

Hearing the scriptures
ISAIAH 49, 1-6
This is the second of Isaiah's 'songs of the servant of God'. God's servant has chosen not simply to win back the elected people Israel, but to proclaim salvation to the whole world. The servant's message is to go out 'to earth's farthest bounds.'

2 CORINTHIANS 5, 14 TO 6, 2
St Paul discovered in Christ the good news that God was offering the human race a new beginning, a new start in relationship with God. Acceptance of this new beginning involves passing on the good news and proclaiming to others 'the message of reconciliation'.

JOHN 17, 20-26

This great prayer of Jesus in John 17 sums up his relationship with the Father and the mission of his disciples. During his earthly ministry Jesus has made the Father's name known and the disciples have believed. Now they and all Christian disciples must continue to proclaim the message of Jesus that others may also come to believe.

EXPLORING WITH CHILDREN

Starting

Invite the children to look through a pile of magazines, to choose the adverts which most appeal to them and to produce a collage display. Discuss what they like best in adverts and why. Draw out ideas of:

- the products promoted in adverts;
- sweets, foods and drinks frequently featured in adverts;
- furniture, curtains and home-making seen in adverts;
- adverts for cars;
- adverts for holidays;
- adverts for radios, televisions, videos, etc.;
- the humour of adverts;
- the exaggeration of truth in some adverts.

Making

Give the children the opportunity to make a display about adverts. Here are some suggestions.

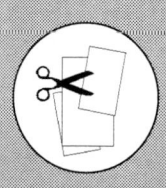

- Sort newspaper adverts into subject groups and make a bar chart showing their frequency.
- Design a poster to advertise your church.
- Draw an advert or write a jingle for your favourite ice cream.
- Display adverts for rival brands of the same product, for example different makes of cars, fish fingers, etc.
- Make a toy television showing adverts.

Doing

- Visit the local shopping centre and note the adverts.
- Watch some television adverts on video.
- Invite some adults to talk about their favourite adverts.
- Discuss the children's favourite adverts.
- Sing jingles from local radio adverts.
- Consider how the church advertises itself.

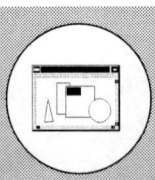

Display headings

- Today's theme is the witnessing community.
- Adverts catch our attention.
- Adverts want to convince us.
- Jesus wants us to be adverts for him.
- Our project today is about adverts.

Using the bible

The story of Jesus' prayer (JOHN 17, 20-26)

Help the listeners to hear in this story how Jesus prays that we will share in the work of witnessing to him.

> Jesus is in the upper room with his disciples.
> He is sharing his last meal with them.
> He prays to the Father.
> He prays for those who already are his close friends.
> He prays for those who will hear about him from his close friends.
> He prays that his friends will carry on his work.

Dance/drama

- Devise a 'television advert' for your church or for a favourite product.
- Devise a dance to show the impact of an advert on a family.

Games

- Display a series of adverts for familiar products around the room, masking out the names of the products. Number the adverts and invite the children to write a list of the products.

EXPLORING WITH ADULTS

Introduction
Record some adverts from the television and play them to the group. Ask them to discuss which is the most effective advert and why?

Experience
- What memorable advert have you seen?
- Why was the advert effective?
- How did the advert affect your life?

Scripture
Read JOHN 17, 20-26
- What does this teaching say about Jesus' witness to God?
- How do you interpret this teaching of Jesus for today?
- How does Jesus' witness to the father influence the disciples?

Integration
- How do Christians bear witness to their faith?
- How do you bear witness to your faith?
- How aware are you of being an advert for Christ?

Application
- How can the church become a better advert for Christ?
- How can you become a better advert for Christ?
- How can your worship become a better advert for Christ?

CELEBRATING TOGETHER

Welcoming children
Make space during the service for the display of the children's work on adverts to be viewed and discussed. If a display of adverts has been prepared with the names of the products masked out, the adult congregation can be invited to share in the children's game of identifying the products. If a 'television advert' has been prepared this can be shared during the Ministry of the Word.

All age activity
Invite members of the congregation to bring an advert which they find particularly powerful, or to design an advert of their own to advertise the church. Display these advertisements around the church. The following ideas can be explored in buzz groups, discussion or teaching:

- our favourite adverts;
- our reactions to adverts;
- adverts which have encouraged us to buy or to do something;
- how the church can advertise;
- how we can become better adverts for Jesus.

Teaching point
We are called to be the people of God; we are called to proclaim the good news about God to the whole world. We are to become God's messengers, God's adverts.

WORSHIP RESOURCES

Prayer

Eternal Lord,
you gave your apostles grace
to believe and to proclaim your word:
Grant that your Church may love and preach
the word which they believed,
and give to all people grace to come to you, the only God;
through Jesus Christ our Lord.

Readings

Old Testament - ISAIAH 49, 1-6
New Testament - 2 CORINTHIANS 5, 14 TO 6, 2
Gospel - JOHN 17, 20-26

Hymns and songs

Come and Praise

- 8 Let us with a gladsome mind
- 24 Go, tell it on the mountain
- 43 Give me oil in my lamp, keep me burning
- 93 Morning sun, morning sun

Hymns Ancient and Modern New Standard

- 72 Lift high the cross, the love of Christ proclaim
- 149 Ye servants of God, your master proclaim
- 239 Forth in the peace of Christ we go
- 422 Tell out, my soul, the greatness of the Lord
- 431 We have a gospel to proclaim
- 481 Let us talents and tongues employ
- 519 We are your people

47

Heroes and heroines

PREPARATION

Bible theme

The suffering community (13TH SUNDAY AFTER PENTECOST)

The church's portrait gallery of heroes and heroines looks rather different from the world's ideas of heroes and heroines. The New Testament reading paints a picture of the death of Stephen, the first Christian martyr and hero of the early church. The Old Testament reading paints a picture of the 'suffering servant', the hero of Isaiah. Suffering and martyrdom are key characteristics of the church's heroes and heroines. The Gospel reading shows Jesus linking the suffering of his followers with his own crucifixion and death. The crucifixion and resurrection show that Jesus himself shares their suffering and that beyond the suffering lies vindication. We can begin to experience the significance of the bible's teaching about the suffering community by exploring our own experiences of heroes and heroines.

Aims

- to build on our ideas about our own heroes and heroines;
- to develop our understanding about what makes heroes and heroines;
- to help us see the 'glorious company of martyrs' as the church's heroes and heroines.

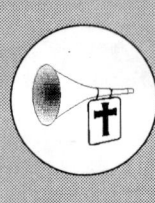

Hearing the scriptures

ISAIAH 50, 4-9A

This is the third of Isaiah's 'songs of the servant of God'. The others are to be found in 42, 1-4; 49, 1-6; and 52, 13 to 53, 12. Together these songs have been interpreted by the church to illuminate Jesus' suffering and death: 'I offered my back to those who beat me.... I did not hide my face from mocking and spitting.'

ACTS 7, 54 TO 8, 1

In the earlier part of chapter 7, Stephen has made a speech before the Sanhedrin, the Jewish council. What follows is the lynching of the first Christian martyr. Luke, who writes this account, deliberately draws parallels with Jesus' own death.

JOHN 16, 1-11

During his 'final discourses' with the disciples in John's gospel, Jesus prepares them both for his own death and for the persecution and suffering which will follow for them. The two are closely related.

EXPLORING WITH CHILDREN

Starting

Display around the room pictures of the children's heroes and heroines, for example, pop stars, footballers, television personalities. Use these pictures for a pencil and paper quiz. Number the pictures, ask the children to work in pairs and to write the names of the ones they recognise. Draw out ideas of:

- the identity of each picture;
- where the children have seen them before;
- the reason for the popularity of each individual;
- the attention given to these people by the media;
- what heroes and heroines have in common;
- how we look up to our heroes and heroines;
- how we try to copy our heroes and heroines.

Making

Give the children the opportunity to make a display about heroes and heroines. Here are some suggestions.

- Organise pictures of the children's heroes and heroines to be used as a quiz among the adult congregation.
- Make a zigzag book on the life of Stephen.
- Design a set of posters showing the martyrdom of Stephen and other Christian martyrs.
- Design a collage showing some of the children's heroes and heroines in context, for example the footballer at the football match, or the pop star at the pop concert.
- Make a pile of stones to symbolise the means of Stephen's death.

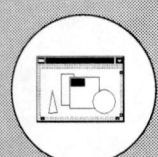

Doing

- Invite the children to bring pictures of their personal heroes and heroines.
- Invite a local 'hero' or 'heroine' to come to talk to the group.
- Find out about the lives and deaths of some of the martyrs.
- Visit churches dedicated to the martyrs.
- Invite someone to talk about martyrs in today's church.

Display headings

- Today's theme is the suffering community.
- Our heroes and heroines are people we admire.
- Martyrs are heroes and heroines of the church.
- Originally the word 'martyr' meant a 'witness'.
- Martyrs died for their faith.
- Stephen was the first Christian martyr.
- Our project today is about heroes and heroines.

Using the bible

The story of the stoning of Stephen (ACTS 7, 54 TO 8, 1)

Help the listeners to hear in this story the character of one of the great heroes of the early Christian church.

> Stephen is totally committed to Jesus.
> He confesses his faith without fear.
> His persecutors are very angry.
> They turn Stephen out of the city and stone him.
> Stephen says, 'Lord Jesus, receive my spirit'.
> Stephen says, 'Lord do not hold this sin against them'.
> Stephen is recognised as a hero of the early church.
> Stephen's feast day is 26 December.

Dance/drama

- Devise a short mime on 'Today's heroes and heroines'.
- Be a television camera crew and interview the bystanders following Stephen's death.

Games

- The children take it in turns to mime an activity characteristic of their hero or heroine; the other children have to guess who it is.

EXPLORING WITH ADULTS

Introduction
Display pictures of heroes and heroines. Pictures could include TV personalities, politicians and artists. Ask the group whom they admire and why.

Experience
- Who is your hero or heroine?
- How do you feel about this person?
- How does your admiration affect your life?

Scripture
Read ACTS 7, 54 - 8,1
- What does this story say about the heroes and heroines of the early church?
- How do you interpret this story about Stephen for today?
- How did Stephen follow in the steps of Jesus?

Integration
- Who are the heroes and heroines of the church today?
- How do the heroes and heroines of the church differ from those of the world?
- How do these heroes and heroines affect your life?

Application
- How can your church support those who suffer for Christ today?
- How can you support those who suffer for Christ today?
- How can the Prayers celebrate the heroes and heroines of the church?

CELEBRATING TOGETHER

Welcoming children
Make space during the service for the display of the children's work on heroes and heroines to be viewed and discussed. If the children's heroes and heroines have been displayed around the church, the congregation can be invited to name them. Before the scripture readings introduce pen portraits of some of the church's heroes. The drama interview would fit in well after the New Testament reading.

All age activity
Invite members of the congregation to bring a picture of someone whom they would place in their own gallery of heroes and heroines. During the service invite them to discuss their choice and then organise a display of these pictures in church. The following ideas can be explored in buzz groups, discussion or teaching:

- our personal heroes and heroines;
- what people look for in heroes and heroines;
- the heroes and heroines of the church;
- the suffering of Stephen.

Teaching point
The church's portrait gallery of heroes and heroines looks rather different from the world's ideas of heroes and heroines. Among the church's heroes and heroines are those who suffered and died for their faith, like St Stephen.

WORSHIP RESOURCES

Prayer

Lord God,
your blessed Son our Saviour
gave his back to the smiters
and did not hide his face from shame:
Give us grace to endure the sufferings of the present time
with sure confidence in the glory that shall be revealed;
through Jesus Christ our Lord.

Readings

Old Testament - Isaiah 50, 4-9a
New Testament - Acts 7, 54 to 8, 1
Gospel - John 16, 1-11

Hymns and songs

Come and Praise
- 44 He who would valiant be
- 46 My faith, it is an oaken staff
- 50 When a knight won his spurs in the stories of old
- 101 In the bustle of the city

Hymns Ancient and Modern New Standard
- 108 Sometimes a light surprises
- 112 God moves in a mysterious way
- 305 For all the saints who from their labours rest
- 343 Be thou my vision, O Lord of my heart
- 363 Glory to thee, O God
- 488 Lord God, we give you thanks for all your saints
- 532 Ye watchers and ye holy ones

48

Family

PREPARATION

Bible theme

The family (14TH SUNDAY AFTER PENTECOST)

The family is a very important image in the Jewish and Christian traditions for exploring God's relationship with men and women. The Old Testament reading is a famous poem on family life from the book of Proverbs. The Gospel reading gives Mark's version of Jesus' teaching on divorce. The New Testament reading from Ephesians combines advice on family relationships with teaching about the relationship between Christ and his church. We can begin to experience the significance of the bible's teaching about the family by exploring our own experiences of family.

Aims

- to build on our ideas about the family;
- to develop our understanding of the different ways in which the family may be expressed;
- to see the importance of the family in the Jewish and Christian traditions.

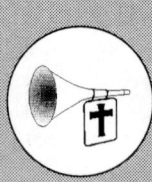

Hearing the scriptures

PROVERBS 31, 10-31

This poem on the 'good wife' is an acrostic (that is, each verse begins with a consecutive letter of the Hebrew alphabet). It is this structure which gives order to the poem rather than a consecutive flow of ideas. In the world in which the poet lived, the woman is praised for what she means to her husband, rather than for what she is in herself. While the role of women in society has changed considerably, the poem still contains some valuable images.

EPHESIANS 5, 25 TO 6, 4

In New Testament times the subordinate role of women in marriage was still unquestioned. The writer sees this subordinate relationship as a model for the relationship between Christ and his church. In the writer's world view, children are clearly instructed to be obedient to their parents.

Mark 10, 2-16

According to Mark's account, Jesus' teaching on divorce is clear and unqualified. It is supported by reference to God's plans in creation. However, when the same passage occurs in Matthew 19, 9, and a similar saying in Matthew 5, 32, it is qualified by the exception for 'unchastity'. The problem is to know whether Matthew has softened Jesus' teaching or whether Mark has made it harder.

EXPLORING WITH CHILDREN

Starting

Invite the vicar or minister to show you the church marriage register. Look carefully at the information given on each page. Ask who has been to a wedding and if they know when the registers were signed. Draw out ideas of:

- the bride and groom have different surnames;
- the names of their fathers are different;
- the bride and groom may now take the same surname and become a new family unit;
- the marriage register is a legal document;
- the marriage registers have to be signed by witnesses;
- the legality stresses the importance of this new family unit.

Making

Give the children the opportunity to make a display about the family. Here are some suggestions.

- Design a collage, showing different things families do together.
- Copy a wedding certificate.
- Design a collage of all the roles of mother, including repairing the car and going out to work.
- Ask the children to display pictures of their own extended families, including grandparents, uncles, aunts, cousins, and so on.
- Make a family tree.

Doing

- Look at family pictures from the last century and note the larger sizes of family.
- Look at family pictures from other parts of the world and note different family structures.
- Invite someone who lives in an 'extended family' of more than two generations to talk about it.

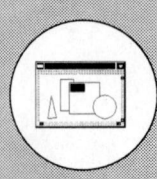

- Look at a family tree.
- Look at extracts from the marriage service in the new prayer book.
- Write poems on the 'good child', 'good mother', 'good father', and so on.

Display headings
- Today's theme is the family.
- There are many different forms of family.
- Marriage marks the beginning of a new family life.
- Our project today is about the family.

Using the bible
The poem on the good wife (PROVERBS 31, 10-31)
Read the Old Testament lesson from Proverbs and ask the children to listen very carefully. Then hold a quiz on the reading.

> When does the wife get up? (while it is still night).
> What does she do on rising? (prepare food).
> How does she use the field? (to plant).
> How does she use wool and flax? (to make clothes).
> What does she do for the poor? (give gifts).
> How do we know she is fit? (strong arms).
> What does she sell? (sewing).
> What does she teach? (kindness).
> When is she idle? (never).
> What does her husband say about her? (praises her).

Dance/drama
- Act out the signing of the registers in a marriage service.
- Pick a set of images from the Old Testament reading, for example spinning and sewing, and interpret in dance.

Games
Play 'Happy families' using cards with families of different nations.

EXPLORING WITH ADULTS

Introduction
Display pictures of different kinds of families. Ask the group to talk about the family today.

Experience
- What is your experience of families?
- How do you feel about family life today?
- How do you feel about your family?

Scripture
Read PROVERBS 31, 10-31
- What does the writer of Proverbs assume about family life?
- How do you interpret this teaching about the family for today?
- What does this teaching say about the relationships between men and women?

Integration
- What are the problems facing family life today?
- How is the church responding to family life today?
- How do you feel about the church's response to family life today?

Application
- How can the church support people who live in families?
- How can the church support people who do not live in families?
- How can your worship be sensitive to people from different backgrounds?

CELEBRATING TOGETHER

Welcoming children
Make space during the service for the display of the children's work on families to be viewed and discussed. If the children have prepared dance, this could follow immediately after the Old Testament lesson to interpret it. Then it would be appropriate to hear the children's poems on the 'good child', 'good mother', 'good father', and so on.

All age activity
Invite members of the congregation to bring photographs of their own family. Some may prefer to bring a copy of their family tree. After the Old Testament reading invite them to discuss what they have brought and to make a display in the church. The following ideas can be explored in buzz groups, discussion or teaching:

- our own family;
- our family roots;
- tracing the family tree;
- ideas of the family in the bible;
- how ideas of the family are changing.

Teaching point
The family is a very important image in the Jewish and Christian traditions for exploring God's relationship with men and women.

WORSHIP RESOURCES

Prayer

Lord God,
your Son Jesus Christ lived in a family at Nazareth:
Grant that in our families on earth
we may so learn to love and to live together
that we may rejoice as one family
in your heavenly home;
through Jesus Christ our Lord.

Readings

Old Testament - PROVERBS 31, 10-31
New Testament - EPHESIANS 5, 25 TO 6, 4
Gospel - MARK 10, 2-16

Hymns and songs

Come and Praise

- 16 When God made the garden of creation
- 51 Our father, who art in heaven
- 69 I belong to a family, the biggest on earth
- 141 Shalom, shalom, may peace be with you

Hymns Ancient and Modern New Standard

- 104 For the beauty of the earth
- 170 The church's one foundation
- 205 Now thank we all our God
- 407 O God in heaven, whose loving plan
- 482 Life is great! So sing about it
- 494 Lord of the home, your only Son
- 505 Our father, by whose name

49

Police

PREPARATION

Bible theme

Those in authority (15TH SUNDAY AFTER PENTECOST)

All three readings make the point that God is the ultimate source of all secular authority. It follows from this that the Christian has a responsibility to respect and obey secular authority. This point is made explicitly in the New Testament reading from Romans and illustrated in the Gospel reading when Jesus replies to the question about paying taxes to Caesar. The Old Testament reading makes the point that even secular rulers who have never known God still derive their power from God. We can begin to experience the significance of the bible's teaching about those in authority by exploring our own experiences of the police.

Aims

- to build on our ideas about the police;
- to develop our understanding of the need for law and order;
- to appreciate the Christian's responsibility to respect civil authority.

Hearing the scriptures

ISAIAH 45, 1-7

The context for this passage is the Jewish exile in Babylon. Cyrus was a foreign ruler who captured Babylon and made it possible for the exiles to return home. Isaiah believes that God has given Cyrus authority for this specific purpose. God says to Cyrus, 'I will strengthen you, though you have not known me.'

ROMANS 13, 1-7

Paul is a Jew by birth and his native country is under the rule of the occupying Roman army. Paul is a Christian by conversion and his saviour was crucified under Roman authority. Nevertheless, Paul still stresses that 'the civil authorities were appointed by God' and draws the implication that it is necessary to obey these authorities.

MATTHEW 22, 15-22

The Pharisees and Herodians ask Jesus a trick question: is it right to pay taxes to Caesar or not? If Jesus says 'yes', he will appear to support the army of occupation; if he says 'no', he will appear to promote political subversion. Jesus' reply acknowledges the need to differentiate between God's claims and the claims of the civil authorities.

EXPLORING WITH CHILDREN

Starting

Invite a policeman or policewoman to talk about their work, illustrated, for example, by the car, the flashing blue light, the radio contact with HQ, etc. (or look at publicity or career pamphlets which depict the work of the police). Draw out ideas of:

- the role played by the police;
- how the police promote road safety, traffic control, speed control, bicycle tests, etc.;
- how the police protect people and property;
- how the police keep the peace;
- how the police help people;
- how the police uphold the law;
- how the police get their authority from the community.

Making

Give the children the opportunity to make a display about the police. Here are some suggestions.

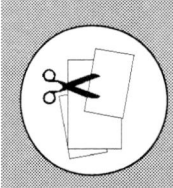

- Design a poster to produce a good image of the police.
- Design a collage of the different types of police work.
- Make rubbings of coins to illustrate the gospel reading, 'whose head is this?'.
- Display a collection of foreign and old coins, showing many different heads.
- Make papier mâché police helmets.
- Make a model police car.

Doing

- Watch an educational film about the police.
- Visit the local police station.
- Invite a police cadet to talk about the entry qualifications and training.
- Go for a walk or ride and see if you can spot signs of the police.
- Invite someone who has been helped by the police to tell about their experience.

Display headings
- Today's theme is those in authority.
- The police are there to help us.
- The police uphold the law.
- The police need our help.
- Our project today is about the police.

Using the bible
The story of Jesus answering the question about taxes (MATTHEW 22, 15-22)
Help the listeners to hear in this story how Jesus balances obedience to civil authorities with obedience to God.

> The Jewish people were ruled from Rome.
> The coins were Roman, stamped with Caesar's head.
> The Jewish people had to pay tax to the occupying authority.
> Jesus is asked a trick question.
> If Jesus says 'yes', some Jews will dislike him for supporting the occupying army.
> If Jesus says 'no', the Romans will regard him as a political threat.
> Jesus answers: obey the civil authorities, but do not disobey God.

Dance/drama
- Develop a mime about different aspects of police work.
- Act out today's gospel story.

Games
- Invite the police to organise a cycling safety course.

EXPLORING WITH ADULTS

Introduction
Watch a short video extract about the work of the police. Ask the group how they understand the authority of the police.

Experience
- What is your experience of the police?
- What is your experience of other people who carry authority?
- How do you feel about authority figures?

Scripture
Read MATTHEW 22, 15-22
- What does the story say about Jesus' attitude to authority?
- How do you interpret this story about authority for today?
- What does the story say about obedience to God's authority?

Integration
- How can Jesus' attitude to authority help Christians today?
- What does obedience to God's authority mean to you?
- To whom do you owe obedience?

Application
- How can the church show obedience to God's authority?
- How can you show obedience to God's authority?
- How can your worship affirm those in authority?

CELEBRATING TOGETHER

Welcoming children

Make space during the service for the display of the children's work on the police to be viewed and discussed. Invite a policeman or policewoman to take some part in the service, for example read a lesson, preach a sermon, give a talk, show some pictures. If a local or neighbouring police force includes a reader, local preacher or non-stipendiary priest this may be the person to invite. Use the children's prayers in the Intercessions.

All age activity

Invite members of the congregation to bring a cutting from a newspaper illustrating the work of the police. Invite them to discuss their cutting and to match up similar examples. Then create a display. The following ideas can be explored in buzz groups, discussion or teaching:

- our experiences of the police;
- media images of the police;
- our attitudes towards authority;
- Jesus' attitude towards authority.

Teaching point

The bible teaches us to respect civil authority because it claims that all authority is derived from God. Jesus reminds us that those in authority must themselves obey God's laws.

WORSHIP RESOURCES

Prayer

Lord God,
you are the source of all power and might:
Govern the hearts and minds of those in authority,
that peace and justice may flourish on earth,
and your church may ever serve you in godliness and joy;
through Jesus Christ our Lord.

Readings

Old Testament - Isaiah 45, 1-7
New Testament - Romans 13, 1-7
Gospel - Matthew 22, 15-22

Hymns and songs

Come and Praise

- 7 All creatures of our God and king
- 14 All the nations of the earth
- 20 Come, my brothers, praise the Lord, alleluia
- 146 We ask that we live and we labour

Hymns Ancient and Modern New Standard

- 107 The Lord is king! lift up thy voice
- 148 At the name of Jesus
- 296 Rejoice, O land, in God thy might
- 353 Eternal ruler of the ceaseless round
- 396 Lord of lords and king eternal
- 432 What does the Lord require
- 522 We turn to you, O God of every nation

50 Neighbours

PREPARATION

Bible theme
The neighbour (16TH SUNDAY AFTER PENTECOST)
In the gospels the Jewish law is summarised as two key principles: to love God and to love your neighbour. Today's theme focuses on the second of these principles. The Old Testament reading presents a range of moral instructions, leading to the concluding verse, 'You shall love your neighbour as a person like yourself.' These words are repeated in the Gospel reading and lead on to the question, 'Who is my neighbour?' In the New Testament reading Paul makes sure that this principle extends even to those who persecute us. We can begin to experience the significance of the bible's teaching about love for the neighbour by exploring our own experiences of neighbours.

Aims

- to build on our ideas about the people who live in our neighbourhood;
- to develop our understanding of God's care for individuals in our neighbourhood;
- to promote our fundamental respect for others.

Hearing the scriptures

LEVITICUS 19, 9-18
Leviticus chapters 17 to 26 present 'the law of holiness.' God's holiness requires holiness from the people of God, and this involves a fundamental respect for others. The neighbour explicitly includes 'the poor and the alien' (that is, those who have no land of their own), the labourer and the handicapped.

ROMANS 12, 9-21
In this part of his letter to the Romans, Paul offers practical advice on the Christian way of life. The Christian principle of love must extend even to 'those who persecute you.'

LUKE 10, 25-37

This reading presents the classic summary of the law, 'you shall love the Lord your God ... and your neighbour as yourself.' Here the words are spoken by a teacher of the law. In Matthew 22, 37-40 the words are spoken by Jesus himself. Luke goes on to tell the parable of the Good Samaritan in response to the further question, 'who is my neighbour?' In this parable the traveller is left for dead. It is for this reason that the priest and Levite pass by, because contact with a corpse would have made them ritually unclean and they would not have been able to fulfil their ministry in Jerusalem. The Samaritan who helps is a foreigner and an outcast. A number of commentators have noted that the parable does not exactly answer the question!

EXPLORING WITH CHILDREN

Starting

Look at a map or plan of your neighbourhood. Begin by inviting the children to name the streets and places of importance and interest. Find out where they live. Then develop a list of people they know who live or work in the neighbourhood. Draw out ideas of:

- the people who make a contribution to the neighbourhood through their job, for example the postman, the park keeper, etc.;
- the people who make a contribution to the neighbourhood through their voluntary work, for example the brownie and cub leaders, the meals on wheels service, etc.;
- the different ages of people in the neighbourhood, from babies to the very old;
- the different races in the neighbourhood;
- the different people we meet when we walk to church, go shopping, play in the park, go to school, etc.;
- how the neighbourhood is a community of people.

Making

Give the children the opportunity to make a display about their neighbourhood. Here are some suggestions.

- Make a model or map of your neighbourhood, noting in particular the community buildings, for example, churches, doctors' surgeries, dentists, sports centres, etc.
- Make a list of those who are employed in the community or who do voluntary work in the community.

- Make life-size models of some local people.
- Design a poster of the Good Samaritan.
- Compose a litany of praise for those who contribute to the life of your neighbourhood.
- Display photographs of the jobs people do in the neighbourhood.

Doing
- Take photographs of those who live or work in the neighbourhood.
- Invite a local person to talk about his or her work in the neighbourhood, for example, milkman, postman, shop keeper.
- Visit a centre of community in your neighbourhood, for example, community centre, health centre, sports centre, village hall, village post office.
- Hold a party for those in the neighbourhood who do not go out very much.
- Find out about the voluntary activities in your neighbourhood and the people who make these activities possible.
- Go for a walk in the neighbourhood and meet some local people.

Display headings
- Today's theme is the neighbour.
- Many different people live in my neighbourhood.
- Everyone who lives in my neighbourhood is valuable to God.
- Jesus tells us to love our neighbours.
- Jesus tells us to be like the Good Samaritan.
- Our project today is about neighbours.

Using the bible
The story of the Good Samaritan (LUKE 10, 25-37)
Help the listeners to hear in this story Jesus' invitation to take the needs of others seriously.

> Jesus tells a story about a traveller.
> The traveller was an ordinary Jew.
> It was a notoriously dangerous road.
> He is attacked and robbed.
> The traveller is left for dead.
> The priest and Levite passed by (they were not allowed to touch a dead body).
> The foreigner is the one who helps.
> Jesus says, 'Go and do likewise.'

Dance/drama
- Act out the parable of the Good Samaritan.
- Devise a dance about the attitudes of the priest, Levite and Samaritan towards the wounded man.

Games
- Play 'What's my Line?' Individual children mime some of the jobs represented in the local community and the others try to guess what this job is.

EXPLORING WITH ADULTS

Introduction
Display a copy of the local directory of shops and public services, or a street map of the neighbourhood. Ask the group the question, 'Who is your neighbour?'

Experience
- What is your experience of neighbours?
- Who lives in your neighbourhood?
- How do you relate to the people who live in your neighbourhood?

Scripture
Read LUKE 10, 25-37
- What does this parable say about neighbours?
- How do you interpret this parable of Jesus for today?
- What does this parable say about differences in race, class and religion?

Integration
- Who needs a good neighbour in your area?
- Who are the people most likely to offer help in your area?
- What is your Christian responsibility to your neighbour?

Application
- How can your church show respect for everyone in the neighbourhood?
- How can you show respect for everyone in the neighbourhood?
- How can neighbours be made welcome in your worship?

CELEBRATING TOGETHER

Welcoming children
Make space during the service for the display of the children's work on their neighbourhood and neighbours to be viewed and discussed. The children's 'What's my Line?' can be presented during the service and the litany of praise for the local community can be used during the prayers and thanksgivings.

All age activity
Ask members of the congregation to invite local people who are not generally part of the congregation to take a special part in this service. Perhaps a local band could provide the music and the local drama group can present a short play for the Ministry of the Word. The following ideas can be explored in buzz groups, discussion or teaching:

- how the local church is perceived in the neighbourhood;
- how the local church serves the neighbourhood;
- how the neighbourhood contributes to the local church;
- the Christian command to love our neighbours;
- the Good Samaritan.

Teaching point
In the gospels the whole of the Jewish law is summarised as two key principles: to love God and to love your neighbour as yourself.

WORSHIP RESOURCES

Prayer

Almighty God,
you have taught us through your Son
that love is the fulfilling of the law.
Grant that we may love you with our whole heart
and our neighbours as ourselves;
through Jesus Christ our Lord.

Readings

Old Testament - LEVITICUS 19, 9-18
New Testament - ROMANS 12, 9-21
Gospel - LUKE 10, 25-37

Hymns and songs

Come and Praise

- 16 When God made the garden of creation
- 65 When I needed a neighbour were you there, were you there?
- 70 Would you walk by on the other side
- 82 It's the springs up in mountains

Hymns Ancient and Modern New Standard

- 132 Son of God, eternal saviour
- 154 Gracious Spirit, Holy Ghost
- 239 Forth in thy name, O Lord, I go
- 374 Help us to help each other, Lord
- 381 Jesus, my Lord, how rich thy grace
- 430 We find thee, Lord, in others' need
- 457 For the fruits of his creation

51
Helping hands

PREPARATION

Bible theme

The proof of faith (17TH SUNDAY AFTER PENTECOST)

Church-going, prayer and spirituality are all very important parts of being a Christian; but it is equally important to put religion to work in daily life. Both the Old Testament reading and the New Testament reading point to the need for true religion to be reflected in social justice. In the Gospel reading Jesus gives a very practical example of true religion at work when he heals the ten lepers. We can begin to experience the significance of the bible's teaching on the proof of faith by exploring our experiences of helping hands.

Aims

- to build on our ideas about the service given to others by members of our church;
- to develop our understanding of the practical demands of our faith;
- to promote our personal response to the needs of others.

Hearing the scriptures

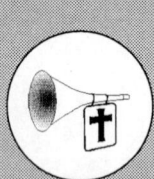

JEREMIAH 7, 1-11

Jeremiah is speaking to the people of Judah as they come through the temple gates during a festival procession. Jeremiah says that they are mistaken to place their trust in the temple ritual unless they also live out their religion in their daily lives: 'deal fairly with one another, do not oppress the alien, the orphan and the widow.'

JAMES 1, 16-27

The letter of James is a practical homily on Christian living. It argues that 'the kind of religion which is without stain or fault in the sight of God ... is ... to go to the help of orphans and widows,' that is, those who are themselves without power.

Luke 17, 11-19

There were two good reasons why Jesus should have ignored these ten men. First, they included at least one Samaritan among their number and Jews shunned Samaritans. Second, their leprosy made them ritually unclean and Jesus ran the risk of being made ritually unclean himself through contact with them. Jesus, however, demonstrates true religion by responding to their needs.

EXPLORING WITH CHILDREN

Starting

Talk about the voluntary organisations in the local community and the people in the church congregation who give time to these organisations. Draw out ideas of:

- voluntary work for the Red Cross;
- voluntary work for St John's Ambulance;
- people who help with meals on wheels;
- people who help with prison visiting;
- voluntary leaders for children's clubs;
- voluntary leaders for brownies, cubs, guides, scouts;
- the needs in the local community met by these groups;
- why people give their time to these groups;
- why churchgoers in particular become involved;
- the particular groups sponsored by the local church;
- the continuing need for more volunteers.

Making

Give the children the opportunity to make a display about helping hands. Here are some suggestions.

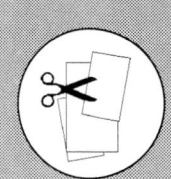

- Design a collage to illustrate the voluntary activities of members in the congregation.
- Draw round each other's hands: paint the hands, cut them out and paste them round a map of the town.
- Make a collage of the story of Jesus healing the ten lepers.
- Design a greeting card from the local church to accompany the meals on wheels service.
- Make a frieze of hands to stretch round the whole of the inside of the church.

Doing

- Invite a Christian councillor to talk about his or her work and why he or she does it.
- Invite members of the church who do voluntary work to talk about what they do.
- Find out how the local church is involved in helping in the community: perhaps it runs brownies or cubs, a day centre for the elderly, a drop in centre for the unemployed, a lunch or fellowship club, and so on.
- Invite the vicar to talk about how and why the church works in the community.
- Look at pictures of local voluntary organisations, for example the St John's Ambulance at a local sports event.
- Look at church magazines and notice boards to find out what different churches are doing in this area.
- Visit the local meals on wheels service and go round with some of their lunch time deliveries.

Display headings

- Today's theme is the proof of faith.
- Religion needs to be put to work in daily life.
- Members of our church help the local community in many ways.
- Our project today is about helping hands.

Using the bible

The story of Jesus and the ten lepers (LUKE 17, 11-19)

Help the listeners to hear in this story how Jesus shows true religion in practice by responding to the needs of the ten lepers.

> Lepers were outcasts of society.
> Lepers lived outside the town.
> Leprosy made them ritually unclean.
> Jesus would be made ritually unclean by contact with them.
> At least one of the lepers was a Samaritan.
> Jews like Jesus had little to do with Samaritans.
> Jesus shows his care by healing the lepers.
> Jesus shows true religion in practice.

Dance/drama

- Act out the story of Jesus healing the ten lepers.
- Devise a dance about 'helping hands'.

Games

- Play a co-operative game which requires the children to work together in groups with their hands, like building a house with Lego pieces.

EXPLORING WITH ADULTS

Introduction
Ask the group to draw up a list of the voluntary organisations in the local area. Then ask them to name members of your church who work with these groups.

Experience
- What voluntary groups offer a helping hand in your area?
- How do individuals offer a helping hand in your area?
- How do you offer a helping hand in your area?

Scripture
Read LUKE 17, 11-19
- What does this story say about Jesus' ministry?
- How do you interpret this story about Jesus' ministry for today?
- What does this story say about true religion?

Integration
- How is your church involved in giving a helping hand?
- What evidence can others see of your church's ministry?
- How do you express your faith in helping others?

Application
- How can your church express its faith in practice?
- How can you express your faith in practice?
- How can the Dismissal promote commitment to real action?

CELEBRATING TOGETHER

Welcoming children
Make space during the service for the display of the children's work on helping hands to be viewed and discussed. The hand clasp in the Peace can become an important symbol for the helping hands which the local church extends into the community. After the Peace, the dance on 'helping hands' can be offered.

All age activity
Invite members of the congregation to illustrate how the local church extends a helping hand to the wider local community. Bring photographs and newspaper cuttings showing church members involved in the community. The following ideas can be explored in buzz groups, discussion or teaching:

- our experiences of extending a helping hand;
- the helping hand extended by our local church;
- the needs for a helping hand in the wider community;
- how we as individuals can develop our helping hand.

Teaching point
Jeremiah in the Old Testament and James in the New Testament stress that true religion should be reflected in responding to the needs of others.

WORSHIP RESOURCES

Prayer

Lord of all power and might,
author and giver of all good things:
Graft in our hearts the love of your name,
increase in us true religion,
nourish us with all goodness,
and of your great mercy keep us in the same;
through Jesus Christ our Lord.

Readings

Old Testament - JEREMIAH 7, 1-11
New Testament - JAMES 1, 16-27
Gospel - LUKE 17, 11-19

Hymns and songs

Come and Praise

- 65 When I needed a neighbour were you there, were you there?
- 66 In Christ there is no east or west
- 70 Would you walk by on the other side?
- 88 I was lying in the roadway

Hymns Ancient and Modern New Standard

- 115 Dear Lord and father of mankind
- 239 Forth in thy name, O Lord, I go
- 240 Teach me, my God and king
- 367 God of grace and God of glory
- 403 Now let us from this table rise
- 510 Sent forth by God's blessing, our true faith confessing
- 515 There's a spirit in the air

52

Fair shares

PREPARATION

Bible theme

The offering of life (18TH SUNDAY AFTER PENTECOST)
We have an obligation to use responsibly the gifts and resources which God gives to us. This obligation involves both gratitude for God's gifts and sharing these gifts with others. Thus, in the Old Testament reading the Israelites are instructed to bring the first part of each crop to the temple both to thank God and to share with those who have no land of their own. In the Gospel reading Jesus emphasises the link between bringing the offering to the altar and getting our relationships right with those around us. In the New Testament reading Paul is exhorting the church in Corinth to share its resources with the poor church in Jerusalem. We can begin to experience the significance of the bible's teaching about the offering of life by exploring our own experiences of sharing.

Aims

- to build on our ideas about sharing;
- to develop our understanding of sharing gifts and resources;
- to see how the church is active in sharing resources with the Third World through agencies like Christian Aid.

Hearing the scriptures

DEUTERONOMY 26, 1-11
Each year at harvest time the Israelite people are instructed to bring a thank offering to the temple and to recollect their nation's history. Their harvest is possible solely because God led them to their rich and fertile land. Because God has been kind to them, they in turn have a responsibility to share their resources, even with the foreigners who live among them and those who have no land of their own.

2 CORINTHIANS 8, 1-9
Paul is exhorting the church in Corinth to copy the example of their fellow Christians in Macedonia and to support the collection for the poor Jewish Christians in Jerusalem.

MATTHEW 5, 17-26

In this passage from the sermon on the mount, Jesus teaches that it is necessary to go beyond the strict letter of the law. The law gives instructions about bringing gifts to the altar; Jesus says that it is important to mend broken relationships before bringing these gifts.

EXPLORING WITH CHILDREN

Starting

Let the children watch you cut a cake into pieces, but make sure that there are a couple of pieces less than the number of children present. Then share out the cake, asking the children not to eat their piece until they are sure that everyone has some. Draw out ideas of:

- how the children who have no cake feel;
- how the children who have cake feel, seeing that others have none;
- what went wrong with the cutting;
- how the problem can be sorted out;
- if all had slightly less, there would have been enough to go round.

Making

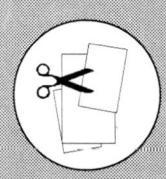

Give the children the opportunity to make a display about fair shares. Here are some suggestions.

- Design a poster for Christian Aid.
- Design a collage of the ways in which Christian Aid helps.
- Organise a hunger lunch, price it out and make invitation cards.
- Each knit a square for a Christian Aid blanket.
- Make a poster showing the Israelite harvest of first fruits.
- Make a display of Christian Aid work.

Doing

- Look at pictures from Christian Aid, showing poverty, starvation, refugees, etc.
- Invite someone who has worked with a relief agency to talk about the problem.
- Take an interest in a special Christian Aid project.
- Visit a craft centre which promotes fair trading in Third World crafts.
- Look at information from the Church Army about needs in this country.
- Invite your local Christian Aid organiser to talk about their work.

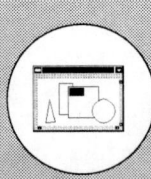

Display headings
- Today's theme is the offering of life.
- All our gifts and resources come from God.
- God asks us to share our gifts and resources.
- Christian Aid works to share our resources with those in need.
- Our project today is about fair shares.

Using the bible
The story of the Israelite harvest of first fruits (DEUTERONOMY 26, 1-11)
Help the listeners to hear in this story how the Israelite people share their harvest celebration with those who have no land of their own.

> The first part of each crop is special.
> It is placed in a basket.
> It is taken to the temple.
> It is given to the priest.
> It is offered as a reminder of God's help in the past.
> It is offered as a thank you to God.
> It is offered as part of a celebration feast.
> The celebration is shared with those who have no land of their own.

Dance/drama
- Devise a dance about the Israelite harvest of first fruits, cutting the corn or harvesting the grapes, placing an offering in the basket, bringing to the temple, placing before the priest, celebrating with the stranger.
- Develop a short play about the work of Christian Aid.

Games
- Use one of the 'sharing games' devised by Christian Aid or Oxfam.

EXPLORING WITH ADULTS

Introduction
Display material from Christian Aid or a similar organisation. Ask the group to look at the material and discuss how fairly the world's resources are shared.

Experience
- What is your experience of unfairness in sharing the world's resources?
- How do you feel about unfairness in sharing the world's resources?
- How does this unfairness affect your life?

Scripture
Read DEUTERONOMY 26, 1-11
- What does this story say about sharing resources?
- How do you interpret this story about the harvest for today?
- What does this story say about God's concern for the poor?

Integration
- How are Christians responding to the needs of the poor?
- How do you feel about this response?
- How do the needs of the poor affect your life?

Application
- How can your church promote fair shares in the world?
- How can you promote fair shares in the world?
- How can you express today's theme in the eucharist?

CELEBRATING TOGETHER

Welcoming children
Make space during the service for the display of the children's work on fair shares to be viewed and discussed. The dance about the Israelite harvest of first fruits can follow on immediately after the Old Testament reading.

All age activity
Invite members of the congregation to bring something which speaks to them about fair shares, for example, a clipping from a newspaper, a Christian Aid poster, or something they have bought in the interests of fair trading. After the Old Testament reading invite them to share and discuss what they have brought and to arrange a display. The following ideas can be explored in buzz groups, discussion or teaching:

- our experiences of fair shares;
- our experiences of unfair shares;
- how experiences of fairness and unfairness shape our attitudes;
- where today's world needs fair shares;
- the example of the Israelite harvest.

Follow the church service with a hunger lunch and a Tradecraft fair.

Teaching point
We show our gratitude to God for all his gifts by sharing our resources with others.

WORSHIP RESOURCES

Prayer

> Almighty God,
> you have made us for yourself,
> and our hearts are restless
> till they find their rest in you:
> Teach us to offer ourselves to your service,
> that here we may have your peace,
> and in the world to come may see you face to face;
> through Jesus Christ our Lord.

Readings

> Old Testament - DEUTERONOMY 26, 1-11
> New Testament - 2 CORINTHIANS 8, 1-9
> Gospel - MATTHEW 5, 17-26

Hymns and songs

Come and Praise

> 6 The earth is yours, O God
> 8 Let us with a gladsome mind
> 16 When God made the garden of creation
> 139 Now the harvest is all gathered

Hymns Ancient and Modern New Standard

> 132 Son of God, eternal saviour
> 249 Take my life, and let it be
> 267 Almighty father, Lord most high
> 393 Lord of all good, our gifts we bring to thee
> 507 Reap me the earth as a harvest to God
> 519 We are your people
> 529 Who are we who stand and sing?

53 Journeys

PREPARATION

Bible theme

The life of faith (19TH SUNDAY AFTER PENTECOST)

The life of faith is often spoken about as a journey. In the Old Testament reading Jacob is on a journey from Beersheba to Haran. It is during this journey that God speaks with Jacob through a dream. The New Testament reading from the letter to the Hebrews makes a long list of people of faith. The list begins with Abraham who set out on a journey. In the Gospel reading Jesus compares those who journey towards God's kingdom with those who run after the things that the world values. We can begin to experience the significance of the bible's teaching about the life of faith by exploring our own experiences of journeys.

Aims

- to build on our ideas of journeys;
- to develop our understanding of the Christian life as a journey;
- to help us to be aware that God is with us on our journey.

Hearing the scriptures

GENESIS 28, 10-22

Jacob's journey began as a way of escaping from the anger of his brother Esau, whom he had cheated out of his father's blessing and birthright. On the journey Jacob has a dream through which God's plans for him are communicated. It is this vision which now gives shape and purpose to Jacob's journey.

HEBREWS 11, 1-2 and 8-16

The author of the letter to the Hebrews illustrates the life of faith by quoting examples from the characters of the Old Testament. These are people who set out longing for a better country, and who are sustained in their journey by faith in God's promises. The list begins with Abraham.

MATTHEW 6, 24-34

In this passage from the sermon on the mount, Jesus compares those who journey towards God's country with those who run after the things that the world values. He exhorts his followers to have faith in God as the one who provides.

EXPLORING WITH CHILDREN

Starting

Bring a set of model cars, buses, trains and aeroplanes and so on (or invite the children to do so). Encourage the children to talk about their experience of travelling in these different ways and some of the journeys they have experienced. Draw out ideas of:

- making plans for the journey;
- getting ready for the journey;
- the new things seen on the way;
- the excitement of going to new places;
- feeling tired after a journey;
- arriving in unknown places;
- exploring new areas.

Making

Give the children the opportunity to make a display about journeys. Here are some suggestions.

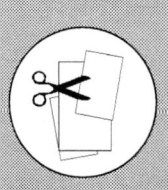

- Make models of cars, aeroplanes, etc.
- Set up a model train set.
- Make a poster showing Jacob at Bethel.
- Design a collage of brochures from travel agents.
- Design a collage about journeys or holidays.

Doing

- Look at holiday brochures or discuss holidays.
- Invite someone to talk about their holiday or a journey.
- Arrange to meet a travel agent.
- Visit a railway station or airport.
- Find out about a great explorer in the past.
- Hire a coach for a mystery tour.
- Other journeys in the bible, like Abraham's journey from Ur.

Display headings

- Today's theme is the life of faith.
- Journeys bring us to new places and show us new things.
- People of faith in the bible obey God's call to set out for new places.
- Jacob set out on a journey from Beersheba to Haran.
- Abraham set out from the city of Ur.
- We are called to journey with God.
- Our project today is about journeys.

Using the bible

The story of Jacob's journey (GENESIS 28, 10-22)

Help the listeners to hear in this story the great themes of the journey illustrated by Jacob's experiences.

> Jacob leaves Beersheba to escape his brother's anger.
> He sets out for Haran.
> Travel is very difficult in those days.
> Jacob rests in the open air.
> He chooses a stone for a pillow.
> He dreams about the ladder.
> God promises Jacob a future for himself and for his descendants.
> Jacob erects a stone to mark the place.
> Jacob calls the place 'Bethel' which means 'house of God'.

Dance/drama

- Devise a dance about Jacob's dream.
- Act out a scene in a travel agency, or a railway station, or an airport.

Games

- Play a board game which develops the idea of travel round the board, like 'snakes and ladders'.

EXPLORING WITH ADULTS

Introduction
Display some road atlases, travel brochures or route planners. Ask the group how they feel about undertaking a long journey.

Experience
- What are your experiences of journeys?
- How do you feel about these experiences?
- How do these experiences affect your life?

Scripture
Read GENESIS 28, 10-22
- What does this story say about Jacob's journey of life?
- How do you interpret this story about Jacob for today?
- What does this story say about God's encounter with Jacob?

Integration
- Why is the journey a symbol of the life of faith?
- In what ways is your life of faith like a journey?
- What has challenged you on your journey of faith?

Application
- How can your church help people on the journey of faith?
- How can you help people on the journey of faith?
- How can the eucharist best express the journey of faith?

CELEBRATING TOGETHER

Welcoming children

Make space during the service for the display of the children's work on journeys to be viewed and discussed. During the service organise a great procession inside and outside the church. See this procession as a journey of faith. If the children have prepared dance or drama on the theme of journeys, this can be shared immediately before the procession.

All age activity

Invite members of the congregation to bring with them something which reminds them of a journey they have undertaken, for example, photographs, tickets, travel brochures. After the Old Testament reading invite them to discuss and to display what they have chosen to bring. The following ideas can be explored in buzz groups, discussion or teaching:

- our experiences of undertaking journeys;
- what makes journeys enjoyable;
- what makes journeys tiring, frustrating, unenjoyable;
- journeys in the age of Jacob;
- how journeys speak of the life of faith.

Teaching point

Throughout the bible the people of God are called to undertake the journey of faith. God calls them to leave behind the old and to grasp the new beginning which is held out to them.

WORSHIP RESOURCES

Prayer

Almighty and everlasting God,
increase in us your gift of faith;
that, forsaking what lies behind
and reaching out to that which is before,
we may run the way of your commandments
and win the crown of everlasting joy;
through Jesus Christ our Lord.

Readings

Old Testament - GENESIS 28, 10-22
New Testament - HEBREWS 11, 1-2 and 8-16
Gospel - MATTHEW 6, 24-34

Hymns and songs

Come and Praise

    42 Travel on, travel on, there's a river that is flowing
    45 The journey of life
    47 One more step along the world I go
    49 We are climbing Jesus' ladder, ladder
  103 I am planting my feet in the footsteps

Hymns Ancient and Modern New Standard

  216 O God of Bethel, by whose hand
  223 Put thou thy trust in God
  231 O for a closer walk with God
  343 Be thou my vision, O Lord of my heart
  435 As Jacob with travel was weary one day
  515 There's a spirit in the air

54

Treasure trail

PREPARATION

Bible theme

Endurance (20TH SUNDAY AFTER PENTECOST)
All three readings encourage the Christian disciple to persevere when the going is tough. God's promised reward awaits those who keep going in faith. In the Old Testament reading Shadrach, Meshach and Abed-nego endure Nebuchadnezzar's furnace to witness to their faith. In the New Testament reading Paul pictures the whole world as enduring pain while waiting to enter on a new life. In the Gospel reading Jesus begins his long last journey to Jerusalem and to the cross. He endures the rejection of the Samaritans and refuses to punish them. He expects his disciples to follow in the same path. We can begin to experience the significance of the bible's teaching about endurance by exploring our own experiences of treasure trails.

Aims

- to build on our ideas of treasure trails;
- to develop our understanding of the Christian life as a treasure trail;
- to help us to be aware of the need for perseverance in the Christian life.

Hearing the scriptures

DANIEL 3, 13-26
Daniel was written to encourage the Jewish people at the time of their terrible persecution by Antiochus IV Epiphanes in 168 BC. The message is to follow the examples of earlier heroes of the faith. God will reward endurance today just as he rewarded endurance in the past.

ROMANS 8, 18-25
Paul understands the church to be living in an interim period between Christ's victory and the last judgement. The whole universe, he argues, is enduring the pains of childbirth until the new age arrives.

LUKE 9, 51-62

In Luke's gospel, directly after the transfiguration Jesus begins his journey to Jerusalem, knowing full well that he is journeying to his death. Not only does Jesus refuse to escape the hardships of this journey, he also exhorts his followers to accept the same discipline.

EXPLORING WITH CHILDREN

Starting

Prepare a treasure trail around the church, the church buildings and perhaps some of the neighbourhood, with a series of clues, each leading on to the next clue. Invite the children to work in small groups with one of the leaders in order to follow the treasure trail. The treasure could be something that all can share. Draw out ideas of:

- excitement at the beginning of the trail;
- hunting for clues;
- search, frustration, impatience;
- feelings of giving up;
- determination to continue;
- losing heart and regaining confidence;
- what makes them carry on;
- excitement of finding the treasure.

Making

Give the children the opportunity to make a display about treasure trails. Here are some suggestions.

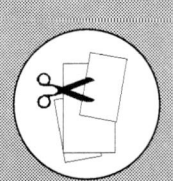

- Make a collage of the story of Shadrach, Meshach and Abed-nego.
- Draw a map showing a treasure trail.
- Make a series of faces showing different feelings at different stages of the treasure trail.
- Make a set of posters about people who have persisted until they have discovered something important or special.
- Make a display about great discoveries like finding King Henry's flagship, the Mary Rose.

Doing
- Follow clues in a detective story.
- Search for something that is lost.
- Invite someone to talk about searching for archaeological finds, especially local sites.
- Invite someone to talk about a car treasure trail.
- Plan a treasure trail in which members of the congregation can participate.
- Find out about great discoveries like drilling for oil.
- Find out about great discoveries like medical research.
- Find out about saints who persisted to martyrdom.

Display headings
- Today's theme is endurance.
- Following the trail needs perseverance.
- The treasure makes the trail worthwhile.
- Jesus asks his followers to persist to the end.
- Shadrach, Meshach and Abed-nego remain faithful to God.
- God rewards Shadrach, Meshach and Abed-nego for their faithfulness.
- Our project today is about the treasure trail.

Using the bible
The story of Shadrach, Meshach and Abed-nego (DANIEL 3, 13-26)
Help the listeners to hear in this story the great themes of endurance displayed by the three heroes.

> King Nebuchadnezzar gives the order that everyone shall worship his golden image.
> Shadrach, Meshach and Abed-nego remain faithful to their God.
> They refuse to worship the golden image.
> They know Nebuchadnezzar will punish them.
> They prefer to be faithful to God.
> Nebuchadnezzar has them thrown into a furnace as punishment.
> God sends his angel to rescue them.
> God helps those who remain faithful to him.

Dance/drama
- Devise a dance to demonstrate the story of Shadrach, Meshach and Abed-nego.

Games
- Adapt games like hunt the thimble.

EXPLORING WITH ADULTS

Introduction
Make a treasure trail around the room or building. Give the group clues. Ask them how it feels when the clues are hard and it is tempting to give up.

Experience
- What are your experiences of treasure trails?
- How do you feel about the effort that has to be made to find the treasure?
- Why do people go on treasure trails?

Scripture
Read DANIEL 3, 13-26
- What does this story say about the perseverance of Shadrach, Meshach and Abed-nego?
- How do you interpret this story about perseverance for today?
- What does this story say about the rewards of perseverance?

Integration
- When is perseverance needed in the Christian faith?
- When have you needed perseverance in your Christian faith?
- How has the need for perseverance affected your life?

Application
- How can your church help others to persevere in faith?
- How can you help others to persevere in faith?
- How can perseverance be expressed in the worship?

CELEBRATING TOGETHER

Welcoming children
Make space during the service for the display of the children's work on treasure trails to be viewed and discussed. If the children have prepared dance on the story of Shadrach, Meshach and Abed-nego, this can be shared immediately after the Old Testament reading.

All age activity
Invite the congregation to come prepared to take part in a treasure trail, to be arranged after the service. The following ideas can be explored in buzz groups, discussion or teaching:

- our experiences of treasure trails;
- our experiences of endurance;
- how good things are worth struggling for;
- the message of Shadrach, Meshach and Abed-nego for today's church.

Teaching point
The Christian disciple needs to persevere when the going is tough, just as people persevere on a treasure trail until they reach the promised goal.

WORSHIP RESOURCES

Prayer

Almighty God,
your Son has opened for us
a new and living way into your presence:
Give us pure hearts and steadfast wills
to worship you in spirit and in truth;
through Jesus Christ our Lord.

Readings

Old Testament - DANIEL 3, 13-26
New Testament - ROMANS 8, 18-25
Gospel - LUKE 9, 51-62

Hymns and songs

Come and Praise

- 29 From the darkness came light
- 31 Can you be sure that the rain will fall?
- 42 Travel on, travel on, there's a river that is flowing
- 45 The journey of life
- 106 It's a new day

Hymns Ancient and Modern New Standard

- 208 O happy band of pilgrims
- 210 Oft in danger, oft in woe
- 212 Who would true valour see
- 372 Have faith in God, my heart
- 378 Jesus, good above all other
- 436 Awake, our souls; away, our fears

55

Autumn days

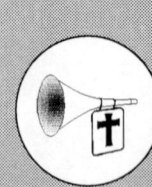

PREPARATION

Bible theme
The Christian hope (21st Sunday after Pentecost)
The Christian hope is guaranteed through God's promises. In the Old Testament reading the prophet Habakkuk proclaims God's promise that 'those who are righteous will live because they are faithful to God.' In the New Testament reading Paul proclaims the resurrection as fulfilment and guarantee of God's promises. In the Gospel reading Luke argues that the Christian disciple should not lose heart in waiting for God's promises to be realised. We can begin to experience the significance of the bible's teaching about the Christian hope by exploring our own experiences of autumn days.

Aims
- to build on our experiences of autumn;
- to help us see signs of spring and new life through the autumn signs of death;
- to help us trust God's promises.

Hearing the scriptures
HABAKKUK 2, 1-4
In chapter 1 Habakkuk cries out against God, asking how long must he witness violence, misery and wrongdoing without God intervening. Now in chapter 2, the prophet proclaims the hope that God will preserve the righteous who remain faithful.

ACTS 26, 1-8
Having been arrested in Jerusalem, Paul is now awaiting trial as a prisoner at Caesarea. In making his case before King Agrippa, Paul sees the resurrection both as fulfilment of God's promises and as hope for the future.

LUKE 18, 1-8

This parable teaches that God, who is the righteous judge, will see that justice is done to the chosen people, even though God may seem to delay to help them.

EXPLORING WITH CHILDREN

Starting

Go for a walk in the churchyard, garden, park or countryside. Collect signs of autumn, like seeds, berries, coloured leaves. Look at the tree branches where leaves have dropped. Draw out ideas of:

- the colours of the leaves;
- reasons for leaves changing colour;
- the buds of next year beneath the 'dead' leaves;
- the varieties of seeds, like those carried by the wind (for example, sycamore), carried by animals (for example, berries and burrs), nuts (for example, acorns and chestnuts) and garden seeds;
- animals preparing for hibernation;
- birds preparing for migration;
- signs of the end of the year and death;
- signs of new life, promise and hope for the spring.

Making

Give the children the opportunity to make a display about autumn days. Here are some suggestions.

- Plant some autumn bulbs, to display in church at Christmas or to give as Christmas presents.
- Use leaves for leaf printing.
- Press leaves to make a collage of autumn.
- Make a wormery in a glass tank, so that children can see how worms work in the autumn soil to prepare for the new growth of spring.
- Make wine from blackberries, to symbolise the new product from the autumn fruit.
- Make a display of autumn seeds and fruits to decorate the church.
- Make a large collection of conkers, or nuts, or leaves, so that there is one for each member of the congregation.

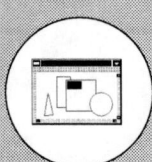

Doing

- Invite someone who has a tortoise to explain what happens to it in winter and why.
- Invite a gardener to talk about his or her autumn tasks.
- Find out how worms use dead leaves and 'recycle' them.
- Classify the different sorts of seeds found on the walk.
- Look at pictures of migrating birds.

Display headings

- Today's theme is the Christian hope.
- In autumn many trees and plants seem to die, but they are preparing for new life in spring.
- Autumn berries contain the seeds of new life.
- Autumn days give signs of hope.
- Our project today is about autumn days.

Using the bible

The story of the unjust judge and the widow (LUKE 18, 1-8)

Help the listeners to hear in this story God's guarantee to keep the promises made with the people of God.

> The widow is poor and powerless.
> She keeps asking the judge for justice.
> The judge ignores her requests many times.
> The widow keeps on asking.
> The judge gives her justice to keep her quiet.
> God is not unjust like that judge.
> God keeps the promise to do right by the people of God.

Dance/drama

- Devise a dance about the falling leaves of autumn and the trees preparing for a new spring.
- Act out a television interview with the unjust judge and the widow.

Games

- Hold a contest with autumn conkers.

EXPLORING WITH ADULTS

Introduction
Have a display of autumn leaves. Invite the group to take a leaf and to smell, look and feel it. Ask them how they feel about autumn days.

Experience
- What do you see happening to nature in autumn?
- How do you feel about the shortening autumn days?
- How is nature preparing for the return of new life?

Scripture
Read LUKE 18, 1-8
- What does this parable say about God's promises?
- How do you interpret the parable of the judge for today?
- What does this parable say about the source of Christian hope?

Integration
- What does Christian hope mean in today's world?
- What is your Christian hope?
- What is the source of your Christian hope?

Application
- How can the church proclaim hope in God's promises?
- How can you proclaim hope in God's promises?
- How can the theme of Christian hope be shared in the worship?

CELEBRATING TOGETHER

Welcoming children

Make space during the service for the display of the children's work on autumn days to be viewed and discussed. If the children have made a large collection of conkers, nuts or leaves, these can be distributed to the congregation at an appropriate point during the service, so that they can all hold and feel 'a sign of autumn.' The television interview can be shared as an explanation on the Gospel reading. The fermenting blackberry wine can be involved in the offertory procession alongside the wine for the eucharist.

All age activity

Invite members of the congregation to bring something which speaks to them of autumn days, for example, a leaf, a bare branch, a picture, etc. During the service invite them to share and discuss what they have brought and to arrange a display in the church. The following ideas can be explored in buzz groups, discussion or teaching:

- our experiences of autumn days;
- the feelings generated by autumn days;
- the signs of hope and promise communicated by autumn days;
- God's promises and the Christian hope.

Teaching point

Even when times seem bad, God gives to the people signs of hope and the promises stand firm.

WORSHIP RESOURCES

Prayer

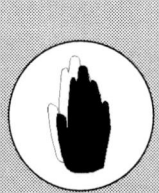

Eternal God,
whose Son Jesus Christ
ascended to the throne of heaven
that he might rule all things as Lord:
Keep the church in the unity of the Spirit
and in the bond of peace,
and bring the whole created order
to worship at his feet;
who lives and reigns with you and the Holy Spirit,
one God, now and for ever.

Readings

Old Testament - HABAKKUK 2, 1-4
New Testament - ACTS 26, 1-8
Gospel - LUKE 18, 1-8

Hymns and songs

Come and Praise

    1 Morning has broken
    4 Autumn days when the grass is jewelled
    9 Fill your hearts with joy and gladness
  31 Can you be sure that the rain will fall?
113 To everything, turn, turn, turn

Hymns Ancient and Modern New Standard

  99 O God, our help in ages past
108 Sometimes a light surprises
211 Through the night of doubt and sorrow
336 All my hope on God is founded
372 Have faith in God, my heart
428 Thine be the glory, risen, conquering Son

56 Crossroads

PREPARATION

Bible theme

The two ways (22ND SUNDAY AFTER PENTECOST)
Throughout the bible God presents men and women with the fundamental choice of choosing God's way or rejecting it. The choice is between good and evil, blessing and cursing, life and death. In the Old Testament reading Moses presents this choice to the people of Israel, 'the choice of a blessing and a curse.' In the New Testament reading the writer of the first letter of John exhorts his readers to choose between his true teaching and 'the people who are trying to lead you astray.' In the Gospel reading Luke examines the choice made by the dishonest manager. We can begin to experience the significance of the bible's teaching on the two ways by exploring our own experiences of crossroads.

Aims

- to build on our ideas of crossroads;
- to help us understand the choice which God offers to everyone;
- to help us want to choose God's way.

Hearing the scriptures

DEUTERONOMY 11, 18-28
In Deuteronomy chapters 5 to 11 Moses sets out what God requires of the people, beginning with a restatement of the ten commandments. Now Moses offers them the stark choice of listening to God's commandments or of rejecting them.

1 JOHN 2, 22-29
The first letter of John is setting out to warn the readers against a heresy or false teaching which denies that Jesus is the Christ. The readers are exhorted to reject this heresy and to keep to the true doctrine which they were taught in the beginning.

LUKE 16, 1-9

This is a parable of crisis. The dishonest manager is in a crisis situation and needs to make some quick and important choices. Jesus applauds the dishonest steward for acting so astutely. The people of God need to make up their minds on the choices that confront them just as astutely.

EXPLORING WITH CHILDREN

Starting

Make a large picture of a maze, or photocopy a smaller picture so each child can have a copy. Invite the children to find their way to the centre of the maze. Draw out ideas of:

- the start is easy;
- crossroads are where decisions have to be made;
- choices are hard;
- wrong choices lead to a dead end;
- wrong choices waste time;
- wrong choices frustrate;
- the pleasure of making the right choices;
- right choices lead to the centre.

Making

Give the children the opportunity to make a display about crossroads. Here are some suggestions.

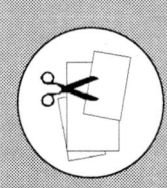

- Make some large crossroad signs to display in church.
- Design mazes to display in church.
- Make enough mazes for each member of the congregation to have one.
- Design a collage showing everyday choices (tea or coffee, marmalade or honey).
- Design a collage showing moral choices (to cheat at games, to steal sweets).

Doing

- Visit a real maze.
- Go out to a crossroads and explore what happens if you take different roads.
- Invite a policeman to talk about signs at crossroads.
- Make a list of choices we make every day:
    - to get up quickly or spend a few extra minutes in bed;
    - to drink milk or fruit juice for breakfast;
    - to choose toast or cereal;
    - to run or to walk to school;
    - what to wear.

- Talk about some of the more important choices:
    - to cheat at games if no-one is watching;
    - to help yourself to sweets in the shop;
    - to copy someone else's work;
    - to tell lies.

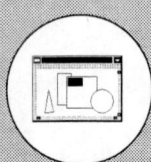

Display headings
- Today's theme is the two ways.
- At crossroads we have to make choices.
- We all have to make choices every day.
- God gives us all a choice.
- We can choose to follow Jesus or not.
- Our project today is about crossroads.

Using the bible
The story of the dishonest manager (LUKE 16, 1-9)
Help the listeners to hear in this story how the manager faces a major crossroads and how he deals with the choices before him.

> The manager is called up before his employer.
> He is accused of failing to manage the business properly.
> The manager has to decide what to do next.
> The manager thinks quickly.
> He calls in the people who owe his employer money.
> He reduces their debts on the condition that they settle quickly.
> The employer has a lot of his money back.
> The manager now has made a set of friends who owe him a favour.
> Jesus praises the dishonest manager for coming to terms with his situation.

Dance/drama
- Devise a dance about finding your way through a maze.
- Act out the story of the dishonest manager.

Games
Conceal a coin in one hand and invite the children to choose which hand. The first child to choose the correct hand then takes over as leader and the game proceeds.

EXPLORING WITH ADULTS

Introduction
Prepare a tray of refreshments for the group. Invite them to make a series of choices: tea or coffee, with or without milk, biscuits or cake. Ask them to describe other everyday choices.

Experience
What major crossroads have you faced in your life?
What choices were open to you?
How did you make your choice?

Scripture
Read LUKE 16, 1-9
- What does the parable of the steward say about choices?
- How do you interpret the parable of the steward for today?
- Why does Jesus praise the steward?

Integration
- What choices does God offer people?
- What choices does God offer you?
- How do these choices affect your life?

Application
- How can your church help people to face the choices God offers?
- How can you help people to face the choices God offers?
- How can the eucharist present people with the choices God offers?

CELEBRATING TOGETHER

Welcoming children

Make space during the service for the display of the children's work on crossroads to be viewed and discussed. If the children have made copies of a maze for each member of the congregation, distribute them before the service; during the Ministry of the Word invite the congregation to trace a way through their maze. The maze can be reinterpreted through the children's dance. The drama can be presented in place of or following the Gospel reading.

All age activity

Invite members of the congregation to bring something which speaks to them of crossroads, for example, a photograph of where roads meet or of a signpost. After the Old Testament reading invite them to discuss what they have chosen to bring and to make a display in church. The following ideas can be explored in buzz groups, discussion or teaching:

- our experiences of crossroads;
- the major crossroads we face in life;
- how we deal with crossroads;
- the choice between the two ways offered by God.

Teaching point

Throughout the bible God presents men and women with the fundamental choice of choosing God's way or rejecting it. Our choice is the major crossroad in life.

WORSHIP RESOURCES

Prayer

Almighty God
you gave your Son Jesus Christ
to break the power of evil:
Free us from all darkness and temptation,
and bring us to eternal light and joy;
through the power of him
who lives and reigns with you and the Holy Spirit,
one God, now and ever.

Readings

Old Testament - DEUTERONOMY 11, 18-28
New Testament - 1 JOHN 2, 22-29
Gospel - LUKE 16, 1-9

Hymns and songs

Come and Praise

    45 The journey of life
    47 One more step along the world I go
    49 We are climbing Jesus' ladder, ladder
    91 You can build a wall around you

Hymns Ancient and Modern New Standard

    128 Thou art the way: by thee alone
    212 Who would true valour see
    217 Be thou my guardian and my guide
    235 O Jesus, I have promised
    343 Be thou my vision, O Lord of my heart
    395 Lord of all power, I give you my will
    490 Lord, I have made thy word my choice

57 Light

PREPARATION

Bible theme

Citizens of heaven (LAST SUNDAY AFTER PENTECOST)

The readings for the last Sunday in the church's lectionary year focus attention on God's promises and on God's call for the people of God to share with the saints of heaven. In the Old Testament reading Jeremiah exhorts the exiles in Babylon to live life in the present, confident in God's promises for the future. In the New Testament reading, Paul sees the Christian life as a race, leading to the prize which God promises. In the Gospel reading Jesus prays for those to whom God promises eternal life. These promises for the future involve the Christian disciples' citizenship of heaven and fellowship with the saints. We can begin to experience the significance of the bible's teaching about the citizens of heaven by exploring our own experiences of light.

Aims

- to build on our ideas of light;
- to develop our understanding of the saints as lights for God's people;
- to help us recognise our fellowship with the saints in heaven.

Hearing the scriptures

JEREMIAH 29, 1 and 4-14

The Israelite people are in exile in Babylon. Their prophets are stirring up hope of escape. Jeremiah's message is that they must accept their exile and put down roots in their alien land. The hope which will sustain them through this exile is knowledge that God will eventually bring them back to their own native land.

PHILIPPIANS 3, 7-21

Paul likens the Christian life to a race. The whole time he is straining ahead for what is to come: 'For us, our homeland is in heaven, and from heaven comes the saviour we are waiting for, the Lord Jesus Christ.'

JOHN 17, 1-10

In John's gospel this prayer comes in the context of the Last Supper. Jesus celebrates the unity which he shares with the Father and the unity which his followers share with him. We, too, are invited to share in his eternal life with the citizens of heaven.

EXPLORING WITH CHILDREN

Starting

Give each child a pen and sheet of paper. Ask them to draw or write names of as many different lights as possible. Draw out ideas of:

- what light is;
- where light comes from;
- street lights;
- car lights;
- lights at home, at school and at church;
- lighthouses;
- traffic lights;
- lights on instrument panels;
- torches.

Making

Give the children the opportunity to make a display about light. Here are some suggestions.

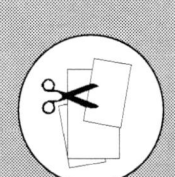

- Make real candles.
- Make candle holders for small candles, like those used at baptism services.
- Make a display of imitation candles, using cardboard tubes and tissue paper for flames.
- Use tissue paper to make a 'stained glass window' and place a light behind it.
- Design a collage showing all different types of lights.
- Design a collage of saints.
- Make a model lighthouse.
- Make a model car with working lights.
- Arrange spotlights in church for special lighting effects.

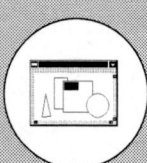

Doing

- Look at pictures of lights.
- Darken the room and light a candle in one corner.
- Shut your eyes and imagine it is dark.
- Find out about some of the saints who have been lights to the church.
- Switch on a string of Christmas fairy lights and talk about how they transform the room.
- Talk about the use of candles in church.
- Talk about the light of the sun.

Display headings

- Today's theme is citizens of heaven.
- Light gives life.
- Light warns.
- Light informs.
- Light guides.
- The saints are lights for God's people.
- Our project today is about light.

Using the bible

Give bibles to the children and invite them to find and copy out some passages about light, for example:

Psalm 27, 1	The Lord is my light.
Psalm 119, 105	God's word is a lamp.
Genesis 1, 3	Let there be light.
Matthew 5, 14-16	Jesus tells parables of light.
John 8, 12	Jesus says, 'I am the light'.
Ephesians 5, 8	Now you are light.
1 Thessalonians 5, 5	You are children of light.
1 Peter 2, 9	God called you into light.

Dance/drama

- Devise a dance about sunrise transforming the dark and sleepy world.
- Act out the story of sailors in a storm being guided by the lighthouse.

Games

Children take it in turns to be blindfolded. Somewhere in the room a torch is hidden under a bowl. The other children guide the blindfolded children by making a louder sound when they are progressing in the right direction and a softer sound when they are moving in the wrong direction.

EXPLORING WITH ADULTS

Introduction
Darken the room as much as possible and light a candle. In silence look at the candle burning. Ask the group to describe their feelings.

Experience
- What experiences do you have of light?
- How do you feel about these experiences?
- How do these experiences affect your life?

Scripture
Read JOHN 17,1-10
- What does this teaching say about the citizens of heaven?
- How do you interpret this teaching of Jesus for today?
- How are we to share with the citizens of heaven?

Integration
- Who is a guiding light to you?
- How are the saints lights to the church?
- How do the saints throw light on your life?

Application
- How can the church share in the light of the saints?
- How can you share in the light of the saints?
- How can your worship use light to celebrate the citizens of heaven?

CELEBRATING TOGETHER

Welcoming children
Make space during the service for the display of the children's work on light to be viewed and discussed. As the congregation arrives give each individual a candle. Use candles and candle holders made by the children. After the last section of the prayer for the church and for the world pass the light around the church from candle to candle to demonstrate our solidarity with the citizens of heaven. While the congregation hold their lighted candles, the children can present their dance on sunrise coming to a darkened world and bringing it to life.

All age activity
Invite members of the congregation to bring a favourite poem, passage from a book, prayer or picture about light. At the beginning of the service invite them to discuss what they have brought and to display or present these items. The following ideas can be explored in buzz groups, discussion or teaching:

- our experiences of light;
- how light transforms our environment;
- how the saints are lights to the church;
- how the saints inspire us as individuals.

Teaching point
The saints are lights to the church. We are called to share with them as citizens of heaven.

WORSHIP RESOURCES

Prayer

Merciful God,
you have prepared for those who love you
such good things as pass our understanding:
Pour into our hearts such love towards you,
that we, loving you above all things,
may obtain your promises,
which exceed all that we can desire;
through Jesus Christ our Lord.

Readings

Old Testament - JEREMIAH 29, 1 and 4-14
New Testament - PHILIPPIANS 3, 7-21
Gospel - JOHN 17, 1-10

Hymns and songs

Come and Praise

- 29 From the darkness came light
- 44 He who would valiant be
- 55 Colours of day dawn into the mind
- 98 You shall go out with joy

Hymns Ancient and Modern New Standard

- 185 Light's abode, celestial Salem
- 305 For all the saints who from their labours rest
- 306 How bright these glorious spirits shine!
- 363 Glory to thee, O God
- 488 Lord God, we give you thanks for all your saints
- 508 Rejoice in God's saints, today and all days
- 532 Ye watchers and ye holy ones